EXPLORING
ENGLISH

1

Teacher's Resource Manual

Tim Harris, illustrated by Allan Rowe
Jean Zukowski/Faust

Longman

Exploring English 1: Teacher's Resource Manual

Addison-Wesley Longman, 10 Bank Street, White Plains, NY 10606

Editorial Director: Joanne Dresner
Acquisitions Editor: Anne Boynton-Trigg
Production Editor: Liza Pleva
Text design: Curt Belshe
Text design adaptation: PC&F
Cover design: Curt Belshe

ISBN 0-201-83316-6

1 2 3 4 5 6 7 8 9 10-CRS-99 98 97 96 95

Contents

Preface

Welcome to *Exploring English*! You will find here, in the first book of a six-book series, a context-rich introduction to English language.

Brilliant with color in a broad variety of presentations, based on the development of a number of interesting character-caricatures, and predicated on task-based pair work exercises and individual understanding in written work, *Exploring English* is an organic progression of grammatical concepts and vocabulary, shared developmental experiences in language, and opportunity for expansion and growth.

For both learning and teaching, *Exploring English* integrates all aspects of a progressive, context-based, communicative approach to language:

Listening is practiced through teacher presentation of Conversations and Readings; through use of the cassette tapes; by following the instructions the teacher gives for the practice exercises; through the Pair Work exercises; and through the spin-off activities.

Speaking is practiced through repetition of Conversations, by imitating the taped segments, by doing the Pair Work exercises, by responding to in-class invitations to communication such as the Free Response activities, and by answering the questions in the exercises.

Reading is practiced as the student follows the taped presentations, reads along with the teacher, does individual preparation for Pair Work, strives to understand the directions, and relates to and recognizes the concepts that are depicted in the illustrations.

Writing is practiced from the beginning in the Written Exercises that are part of the carefully planned progression and interweaving of skills in the text. Students can also be encouraged to copy sections of the text and to combine elements in the text to expand on their naturally growing ability in English. They can also be encouraged to write out the exercises, filling in the blanks with newly learned and carefully cued items.

The text offers a great deal for a teacher to work with. The illustrations will often remind students of experiences of their own. Encourage your students to talk about these experiences in English as they explore their own worlds through the medium of the English language.

Good teaching involves the students in the real use of the language; hence, *Exploring English* is full of naturally generated opportunities for natural verbal interaction on topics of interest to students because the topics are relevant to their lives and necessary for them to learn. Students will eagerly do oral practice of the kinds that are found in the text because the topics relate to them in a clear context.

ABOUT THE STUDENT'S BOOK

The Student's Book (*Exploring English 1*) has eight units and a Preview of *Exploring English 2*. Chapters 4 and 8 are Review Chapters. Within each unit there are several sections, although the units are not so formalized as to be totally predictable.

Typically, a chapter opens with illustrated Conversations. Each of these Conversations is presented on cassette tape as well as in the text. By using the audiotape, the teacher can provide an alternative presentation of the material in a different voice. The tape can also be viewed as advantageous from another perspective: the material is presented through a mono-channel medium—listening only—a practice which gradually lessens student dependence on the teacher and increases tolerance for reduced input cues. Every foreign language learner, for instance, knows how much harder it is to understand the new language over the telephone because the phone represents mono-channel input.

Each Conversation is likely to serve as a springboard for a Pair Work exercise in which the students practice the newly presented elements.

New vocabulary is taught in New Vocabulary sections and throughout all aspects of the chapters. Additional new vocabulary is taught within Conversations and even within exercises. The new words and concepts are presented in contexts—in ways that illustrate the concepts and give students useful sentences. The teacher can act out some words, point to some words as they are pictured in the illustrations, and use realia to teach and reinforce the new concepts. Practice exercises are provided to reinforce the pronunciation and recognition of these words. It is important to note that new words are introduced gradually; the heaviest concentration of new words in each chapter is generally found in the What's Happening Here? section, a reading with one or more illustrations that have been planned to demonstrate the meanings of new concepts.

Grammar Treatment

In *Exploring English,* all new grammar is presented as a natural extension of the preceding elements. The teacher will find no clinical grammar explanations as all new grammatical elements are presented in carefully controlled contexts so that the input is likely to be totally comprehensible. In addition, each grammatical form is both reinforced and respiraled in clearly illustrated formats such as cartoon stories, dialogue stories, and regular prose stories.

New structures are presented in heavily contextualized and illustrated formats. A light and easily understood sense of humor pervades all aspects of the presentation, making it thoroughly enjoyable and thereby indirectly reducing the stress of learning a new language.

Preview

The end of the book is a section called "Preview." It includes some of the grammatical items that will be introduced in Book 2. These grammar elements are concepts that the students may need or want even while they are in the first book, so they are presented here. When students request information on how to say something that is included in the preview section, you can refer them to it, show them how the form works, and give them some practice with the form.

The Characters of the Book

The characters who populate the pages of the text are based on classic personality types. Through the use of such colorful characters, cultural types, ideals, and expectations are not only taught but applied. For example, much of the meaning of vocabulary-generating situations involving these characters can be indirectly inferred: the artist is typical of artists, relaxed in dress and yet passionate about his art. The banker is a staid and proper fellow, carrying all of the cultural expectations of a person to whom others entrust their life savings. The pilot is a woman of adventurous spirit, the doctor a woman of high principles and generous caring. The absent-minded professor is an interesting man with esoteric interests and predictable habits. The children are typical of young people everywhere, interested in friends, sports, and having fun. The taxi driver and the mechanic, the restaurant owner and the waiter, the young married couple and the couple of many years of married life, the secretary and the schoolteacher—all fall into culturally identifiable roles.

The interactions and the tensions between the characters also mirror real life. Their conversations provide ready models for students to understand and use in role-play and real-life situations. Thus the use of colorful characters and classic personality types in common life situations enhances the learning by presenting familiar descriptions of behavior and attitudes. In the text, therefore, a full and broad range of functions and notions are included as well as cultural expectations: many artists are passionate about their work, many bankers are conservative, many taxi drivers are congenial people, and many pilots are risk-takers. Thus these characters work for the language learner, embodying the norms and expectations of English-speaking society. The cultural perceptions of a waiter as having dreams of advancing to a better job, a mechanic as a person who loves to tinker with any machine, and a teacher as both patient and impatient—all add to the students' awareness of the full range of possible cultural interpretations and manifestations of human experience in the U.S. environment.

ABOUT THE TEACHER'S RESOURCE MANUAL

The *Teacher's Resource Manual* is designed for use by all teachers, but it particularly aims to meet the needs of those with less experience. In order to facilitate teaching, every page from the Student Book is reproduced in this manual opposite a page of teaching notes. These teaching notes consist of the following:

Page Summary: a quick reference list of what the student page contains.
Functions: the language uses taught and/or practiced on the student page.
New Elements: the vocabulary and expressions that are new to the student.
Grammar: the grammatical elements introduced or respiraled.
Preliminary Oral Work: suggestions for oral presentation of new material before students open their books.
Ideas for Instruction: suggestions for introducing the material, facilitating the learning, exploiting the illustrations, and using the tapes, plus ideas for using realia, prereading activities, and games.
Pronunciation Tips: suggestions to foster native-like intonation and stress.
Answers (to the exercises).

The *Teacher's Resource Manual* also includes a section with answers to all of the exercises in *Workbook 1* and a comprehensive vocabulary list for *Exploring English 1*.

Suggestions For Using Pronunciation Tips

The audio cassette tapes provide models for good pronunciation. If the students have trouble with certain sounds, play the tapes and have the students repeat the sentences after the voice on the tape. Pronunciation can be a lesson focus for five to ten minutes at any time that the students seem to need it. In the *Teacher's Resource Manual*, for example, there are clues for intonation and stress patterns. If the intonation patterns of your students' first language interfere with natural sounding English, you might want to introduce pronunciation at the beginning of the lesson. The audio cassettes will be useful because the natural intonation can be found there and the same pattern can be repeated as many times as you need to for your students to hear the music and cadence of English.

In English, there are three common levels of stress and a less common fourth level that shows shock or surprise. The basic pattern is to start in the middle intonation level, to rise to the third level when emphasizing an element (such as the accented syllable of a noun or verb) and then to return to the middle level until the last emphasized word, to rise to the third level on that word, and then to fall to the base level. This pattern occurs naturally in all affirmative sentences and *Wh-* questions:

Who **are** you?\
My **name** is **Al**-bert.\

If there is only one emphasized element in a sentence, that element appears in **boldface** type. If there is more than one, the one with the greater or greatest emphasis is also **underlined.**

If a person is calling to another person, counting, recounting, or asking a yes/no question, a rising intonation is natural:

one/, two/, three/, and four\ (Note that the falling intonation on the word "four" shows that the counting is finished.)

Do you **want** some **pizz**a?/ (Note that the questioning can be shown with the rising intonation only: "Some **pizz**a?" with rising tone means, "Do you want some pizza?")

HOW TO TEACH EACH PART OF A LESSON

The different parts of a lesson can be taught in a variety of ways. The suggestions that are given here are general; more specific ideas are provided in the pages that follow.

Conversations and Cartoon Stories

The Conversations can be introduced by having the students examine the pictures for clues first, then brainstorm words and ideas that they anticipate, and then read or listen to the Conversation on audio cassette tape. The class can be divided into groups to read the parts of individual characters along with the teacher or the tape, individual students can play the parts using the very words of the text.

The Conversations and Cartoon Stories in *Exploring English* are dramatizations that can be used naturally as models for role-playing. Students can adapt many of the dialogues to their own situations by substituting vocabulary items that they already know (or ask for help in learning). Be ready to help the students with words that they feel they need. Words learned in this way are almost always remembered the most easily because the need for the concept is real to the students.

Pair Work

When students are directed to "Have similar conversations," they are being asked to role-play. Only the students themselves know what language elements they have to use, so, by making up their own conversations, they are building on their own language bases. It is important to encourage students to share their role-plays and also to provide the new words they want as they experiment with new concepts and applications.

Students can greatly increase the amount of language input and output by working with a partner. You might decide to set up a rotation of partners so that students work with different partners each day or each week. You can accomplish this goal by making two teams of approximately equal number of people. Make two disks of card stock, one a little larger than the other, large enough to write the names of the students on one team around the outside rim. Draw lines to divide the disk into equal pie sections. If one team has one more person, write that team on the larger disk. Write the names of the second team on the outside edge of the smaller disk. And match the partners for each day or each week by rotating the smaller disk the amount of one person's name. If one team has an extra person, change who works in a triad each week.

Pair work should always have a clear objective. The amount of control on the students' production will be a fairly good indicator of how effective the practice in pairs will be. It is a good idea to require that pairs who have been working together show what language variations they have produced.

Structure and New Vocabulary

The direction "Listen and repeat" signals an opportunity to build students' aural skills. They need to learn to discriminate sounds and words from similar ones in English. They also need to listen to the teacher's model or the model on the tape to build the bridge between the printed and the spoken word.

The best way to introduce these exercises is to concentrate on the focus of the lesson by having the students listen to the model several times and then chant the model several times. In chorus or individually, the repetition makes familiar what was not familiar at all.

Practice

The oral Practice exercises provide a clear, close focus on the grammatical element that is being taught. Some of the oral practice exercises require a change; the teacher presents the example or examples to the class and then asks the students to do the exercise.

Some of these exercises require a transformation of the sentence, perhaps replacing proper names with appropriate personal pronouns.

Some of the exercises ask the students to manipulate the sentences to practice different forms:

That is your pencil. → **That pencil is yours.**

Other exercises are presented to help students learn to expand ideas:

Peter likes ketchup. (a bottle of ketchup) →
He wants a bottle of ketchup.

Another format for practice asks the student to make an addition to the information in the first sentence. The student should read the first sentence and then make up a second sentence with the information that is provided:

Make sentences using **one** *and the* **other.**
I have two new shirts. (blue/green)
I have two new shirts. One is blue and the other is green.

Make negative sentences.
Tino and Barbara are eating sandwiches. (pizza)
They aren't eating pizza.

Make sentences using **have** + **any** *or* **one**.
Peter needs some gasoline.
He doesn't have any.

The Golos need a car.
They don't have one.

Exercises to stimulate question-asking may simply direct the students to do so:

Change the sentences to questions.
They're bankers.
Are they bankers?

Or a substitution word may be given to use in forming the question:

> *Make questions as indicated.*
> They don't have a desk. (a table)
> **Do they have a table?**
>
> *Make questions with **who**, **what**, or **where**.*
> Albert went *to the beach.*
> **Where did he go?**

Readings

Before you read the story or play the tape, spend a few moments with the students going over the illustration. What concepts do they expect to find in the reading as suggested in the picture or pictures? Brainstorming ideas will establish an anticipatory set for the class; they will find it easier to process the content and concepts of the reading passage if they are mentally prepared by calling to consciousness the ideas in their first language and being ready with at least some of the English labels for things. Remember, your students collectively may know a great deal of English language. The time you spend helping them to realize that they know words, that some words may be cognates or borrowings, and that there are relationships among the concepts will be well spent in making the lesson easier for them to comprehend. For example, on page 41, there is a drawing of a kitchen scene with flowers in a vase on a table, pots hanging from hooks on the wall, and cups and glasses on shelves. If you ask the students what is in the picture and write the names of the things they see on the board, you won't have to do any more "teaching" of these words because they have already been provided by the students themselves.

Then read the story. You can read it yourself, play the tape, or do both. In any case, the students should hear the story several times, reading along silently or out loud as they follow the words in the textbook. If there are words or phrases that seem difficult for the students, stop and repeat the sentence several times. If necessary, use the backward build-up technique to keep the intonation and rhythm of the sentence true:

> Tell him the meeting is at ten o'clock.
> ten o'clock.
> at ten o'clock.
> the meeting is at ten o'clock.
> Tell him the meeting is at ten o'clock.

Ask the students to write down the words that they don't know. Teach them the new items by acting them out or showing pictures. It is also acceptable to translate words occasionally or to consult a bilingual dictionary if other methods do not work efficiently.

Ask students different kinds of questions about the reading. Encourage them to use their own words in giving answers rather than searching in the text for the sentence that answers the question. As much as possible, include different kinds of questions: detail questions, main idea questions (for example, ask for key words or for a title for a reading), inferences (for example, how do you think [a character] feels about this situation? Or do you think [a character such as Mr. Bascomb] is a good banker?), definitions, and sequence questions. Also, ask your students personal questions that relate to the topic of the story in order to draw them into the story. If a story deals with shopping, ask your students about their own shopping, thus making the lesson a point of departure for class discussion.

It is important to stimulate real responses to the characters, to get the students to think about them as real personality types. The people in the textbook and the people in the class may be considered the English-speaking community for the learner. Through thoughtful questioning, you as the teacher can use the readings to simulate language use in society. When they laugh about Mr. Wilson's miserable time at the dentist's office (Cartoon Story, page 56), they understand what is appropriate behavior in a similar real situation and how inappropriate Miss Tracey's words and actions are.

What's Happening Here?

The What's Happening Here? section is an integrated skills presentation. The picture stimulus, which has potential for brainstorming and creating a story before the students read or hear the story that is provided in the text, is followed by an audiotaped story to listen to and then to read. This format is used to introduce new vocabulary and grammatical elements. There are many ways to teach the What's Happening Here? sequence of skills, which are included in the Teacher's Resource Manual. A general suggestion is to follow this sequence:

1. Have the students examine the illustration.
2. On the board, write the elements in the illustration that they can name or label.
3. Play the tape as the students look at the illustration.
4. Play the tape a second time and have the students point to the elements in the picture that are being mentioned on the tape.
5. Play the tape and have the students try to repeat with the tape.
6. Turn to the story and have the students read along with the tape.
7. Have individual students read the story and then attempt to answer the questions.

Grammar Summaries

At the end of Chapters 1, 2, 3, 4, 5, 6, and 7 you will find Grammar Summaries. (Chapters 4 and 8 are review chapters.) These one-page presentations of the grammatical items in the chapter can be used in several ways:

The students can be referred to the grammar summaries throughout the lesson for an unencumbered presentation of the basic forms. Because of the differences in students' learning styles, you are likely to find that some students will frequently look to the grammar summary pages and others will hardly notice that they are there.

If your students are having difficulty with a grammatical structure, you can refer to the box on the Grammar Summary page which contains the problematic form. Show them how a slot-and-filler approach can work by writing the boxed sentences across the top of the board (not one under the other). Then—just like in the boxes on the Grammar Summary page—draw vertical lines between the sentence constituents; the subject should be separated from the verb phrase, the object noun phrase from the adverbials, etc. Show the students how to expand by adding or substituting other information: how a pronoun can substitute for the subject phrase, how elements within the verb phrase can change, and how different object nouns can be used in place of the original one. For some students, it might be useful to point out that one column is the subject, another the verb phrase, and so on. You can write under each heading all kinds of variations, brainstorming with the students or requiring a pair of students to come up with new sentences using this structure.

On page 54, for example, you will find the grammar summary for Chapter 3. The negative imperative is shown:

| Don't | close the door! |
| Don't | close the window! |

Using other verbs and objects in the slots, the students can expand their active language:

Don't	look at me!
	give them an apple.
	close the book!
	give her the watch.

IMPORTANCE OF A PRELIMINARY ORAL PHASE: PRESENTATION AND WRITTEN REINFORCEMENT

Presentation

It's important that students hear examples of the sentences they are going to practice before they are asked to produce them. We refer to this step as the preliminary oral phase. The most effective preliminary oral phase requires care in the sequencing of the affirmative, interrogative, and negative forms of each structure presented. The following is a demonstration of the procedure, giving an abbreviated lesson teaching the simple past.

1. Introduce the structure with affirmative sentences. (A good way of teaching the simple past is by describing what you did this morning as you mime the various activities.)

Teacher: This morning I got up at seven o'clock. I went to the bathroom and I took a shower. After I took a shower, I got dressed. Then I went to the kitchen and had breakfast. I had coffee and eggs for breakfast. After breakfast, I read the newspaper.

Get students to make affirmative sentences by asking them information questions. (You can ask *or* questions, which are easier because they include the answer.)

Teacher: _____, when did you get up this morning?
Student: I got up at seven-thirty.

Teacher: Did you take a bath or a shower?
Student: I took a shower.

2. Give students practice in making information questions.

Teacher: Listen. When did you get up this morning? Everyone.
Students: When did you get up this morning?

Have students ask each other information questions using what, where, when, how, etc.

Teacher: _____, ask _____: When did you get up this morning?
Student: _____, when did you get up this morning?

3. Give examples of the negative form.

Teacher: I got up at seven o'clock. I didn't get up at six o'clock. I took a shower. I didn't take a bath. I had coffee and eggs for breakfast. I didn't have coke and French fries. I didn't have pizza. I didn't have ice cream.

Ask students Yes/No questions that will elicit negative responses. (At this point, have students respond with complete sentences; the short answer comes later.)

Teacher: Listen. Did you have pizza for breakfast? Everyone.
Students: Did you have pizza for breakfast?

Have students ask each other Yes/No questions.

Teacher: _____, ask _____ if he had pizza for breakfast?
Student 1: _____, did you have pizza for breakfast?
Student 2: No, I didn't have pizza for breakfast.

4. Give examples of the short answer form.

Teacher: Did I have eggs for breakfast? Yes, I did. Did I have French fries for breakfast? No, I didn't.

Ask students questions that will elicit the short answer form.

Teacher: _____, did you take a shower this morning?
Student: Yes, I did.

Teacher: Did you watch TV this morning?
Student: No, I didn't.

Notice that all of the sentences in the demonstration above use *you* and *I*. When introducing new tenses, it's best to start with *you* and *I* before moving on to the third-person singular, since the third-person form requires an ending change that complicates initial presentation. Once students are comfortable with the structure, the third-person form can be introduced with success.

With other, simpler structures (there is/there are, some/any, etc.) the presentation can be shorter, but always maintaining the sequencing of forms: affirmative, interrogative, negative, etc. It's always a good idea to limit the vocabulary in the preliminary oral work to familiar words and expressions and words whose meanings can be demonstrated through physical actions. Hand gestures are useful in telling students to listen, to repeat, to make complete sentences, etc.

Written Reinforcement

Your students can improve their understanding and retention of the structures they are practicing orally by writing them on the blackboard—preferably after they have had a few minutes of preliminary oral work as in the demonstration above. For example, in the same lesson on the simple past, Maria could ask another student, Pedro: "What did you eat yesterday for breakfast?" She should then write her question on the chalkboard. After Pedro answers, "I ate eggs," he should write this on the chalkboard. The students should continue writing their questions and answers until there are at least six to eight sentences in the simple past on the blackboard. Number these sentences and have the class correct any mistakes in grammar and spelling. Avoid correcting the mistakes yourself; students learn more when they are actively involved in the correction process. At times you may need to guide your students, but usually they see the mistakes and are eager to correct them themselves. After all the corrections have been made, have the students read the sentences on the blackboard, first in chorus and then individually.

DEVELOPING YOUR METHODOLOGY

To use this text effectively, the teacher is encouraged to use a variety of techniques. The *Teacher's Resource Manual* includes ideas to use for implementing and complementing each page of lesson material. A productive pedagogical perspective is to recognize the respiraling nature of the human language learner and the matching growth pattern in the text. What students can hear and understand, they can easily learn to say. What they can say and understand, they can also learn to read. What they can read, they can write. And then the circle begins again: What they can write, they can easily read and they can also learn to produce orally. For one student, the written word may seem easier to process for a while, and for another, the listening and speaking skills may advance more quickly; however, there will be a catch-up and evening out of skills if all are taught in a manageable, integrated way. Thus, ultimately, the most effective approach is a general multiskill development focus.

Good teaching of the informed eclectic kind uses the best of many methods from the years of language teaching experience. The teacher models unfamiliar sounds and intonation patterns in sentences; the students listen and then imitate the teacher. The teacher shows how to do something and then the students try it out in role-play. New elements are presented through as many channels as possible:

The visual channel is used in the pictures and the print in the book, in written words and sentences on the board.

The auditory channel is used as the students listen to the teacher reading, to the tape presentations, and to their fellow students.

The kinesthetic channel is used as the students manipulate items of realia, write on the board or in their journals, and participate in games and role-plays.

CORRECTING ERRORS

Errors can be considered "mis-takes." The student might well know how to say something correctly but his or her competence in the language may not always match the performance. Therefore, be judicious and gentle in correcting students' language. You might want to draw their attention to the most important problems, those that interfere with communication. For example, if a student's mispronunciation of the short vowel in *ship* makes the word sound like *sheep* and the context is clearly nautical, there will probably not be any difficulty with understanding the message. However, if the context is not clear, then the teacher may ask the student to listen to a model of the two words, listen to be able to hear the difference, and then have the student attempt a more accurate pronunciation.

In oral work, make corrections by giving a student a chance to redo his or her own work. For example, you might ask the student, "Is that the right way to make a question with a *Yes* or *No* answer?" Or, if you think the student is still learning how to form the desired utterance, and the student makes a small mistake, you can just work a correct repetition of the form or structure into your next utterance. Look at this example:

Student: **Who that is?**
Teacher: **Who is that? I don't know. Let's ask . . .**

Note that it is generally not a good idea to ask one student to correct another: if a student doesn't know the answer to a question, the student might well be embarrassed. You can provide students with coping strategies in an early lesson: "I don't know. Why don't you ask . . . ?" A student who learns early to tag another student for an answer always feels in control of his or her language learning situation. Such a student is less likely to feel frustrated and anxious.

HOW TO PLAN A COURSE SYLLABUS

It is important for a teacher to know how much time to spend on each part of a lesson and how to fit the text materials into a time frame. If your class meets for an hour a day, five days a week, through a sixteen-week semester, it is easy to gauge the amount of time: eight lessons in sixteen weeks means one chapter every two weeks. If your class meets frequently for longer periods of time, you must adjust the material and the time to each other: you might be able to complete a chapter in a week, for example, if you meet for 2–3 hours a day every day.

The more your students practice with vocabulary and grammatical elements, the more natural their use of the language elements will be. For the reinforcement of some elements, you may find it useful to return to a completed chapter and have the students read passages aloud, answer questions, expand on the topic, or combine elements. A useful exercise for students who are quick to learn is to have them revise (rewrite) the stories of earlier chapters incorporating elements from later chapters into more sophisticated sentences.

By recognizing that a textbook like *Exploring English* can be expanded and that the material is flexible, you can make the text fit your teaching situation and your schedules.

SUGGESTIONS FOR SETTING UP THE CLASSROOM

The object of a good language lesson is to keep the students engaged and involved. Some general suggestions, included here, will help you to make your classroom a dynamic and energy-filled learning environment.

The Arrangement of Desks

Ideal for a language classroom is an arrangement of desks that makes pair work and group work natural. Movable tables and chairs work well if they are arranged in a horseshoe or circular pattern or in slanted rows like a chevron with the point of the chevron farthest from the teacher and the board. Another possible arrangement is to make clusters of desks: individual student desks can be arranged in sets of four, facing one another but allowing for a clear view of the board in the front of the room.

Classroom Paraphernalia and Decorations

In the *Teacher's Resource Manual,* there are many suggestions of ways to enrich the experience of *Exploring English.* For example, besides chalk or dry-erase white boards, ideal classrooms contain bulletin boards for posting student work and realia of relevant types (pictures, forms, labels, etc.); wall space for charts and maps; a large calendar; shelves for books and magazines; boxes to store supplies of paper, pencils, colored markers, tape, and scissors; and boxes for manipulable learning aids such as picture files, English language greeting cards and travel brochures, color samples, examples of texture, colored chalk, plastic fruit and vegetables, Cuisenaire rods and blocks, play money, sample forms of all kinds like checks and receipts, and a mock clock to use to teach telling time. The idea is to use these items in ways that help create a rich English language environment within the classroom.

If a teacher works with students to keep developing the displays of English language in use (through, for example, a bulletin board display for a holiday done in English and including symbols of the holiday and greeting cards), the students will have access to more than just the language—they will begin to participate in the culture of their new language.

Chalkboard (or Whiteboard) Use

Even before your students open the textbook, you might want to have them become familiar with writing on the board. You can begin by writing your name and then having the students write theirs. Familiarity and comfort with writing on the board do not always come easily to students, and shy students need to be introduced to the concept in an anxiety-free way. As you get them to write more and more on the board, they will find that it offers advantages: one has more time to think and other students help with the idea to be expressed.

Chapter 1

TOPICS
People
Occupations

GRAMMAR
"To be"
Indefinite and definite articles
This/that/these/those
Where + prepositional phrases

FUNCTIONS
Introducing yourself
Greeting people
Taking leave
Asking about and identifying objects
Indicating location

CONVERSATION 1

 Listen and practice.

PETER: Hello. What's your name?

MARIA: My name's Maria.

PETER: My name's Peter.

MARIA: Nice to meet you, Peter.

PAIR WORK 1 • *Have similar conversations.*

STUDENT A: Hello. What's your name?

STUDENT B: My name's _____.

STUDENT A: My name's _____.

STUDENT B: Nice to meet you, _____.

CONVERSATION 2

 Listen and practice.

BARBARA: Good morning.

TINO: Good morning. How are you?

BARBARA: I'm fine. And you?

TINO: Fine, thank you.

PAIR WORK 2 • *Have similar conversations.*

PAGE SUMMARY

CONVERSATION 1 and **PAIR WORK 1:** Simple introductions
CONVERSATION 2 and **PAIR WORK 2:** Exchanging greetings

▶ FUNCTIONS

Introductions and greetings

▶ NEW ELEMENTS

Hel**lo.**	**page**
Good **morn**ing.	**have**
What's your **name**?	**prac**tice
My name's _____.	**pair**
How **are** you?	**chap**ter
I'm **fine.** And **you**?	**work**
Fine, thank you.	con**ver**sation

▶ GRAMMAR

Parts of the verb *to be*	**'m** for am
's for is	**are**

▶ PRELIMINARY ORAL WORK

Teacher:	My name is _____. (Point to yourself.) What's your name? (Point to a student.)
Student:	My name is _____.
Teacher:	Your name is _____, etc. (Point to a student.) My name is _____. What's my name?
Students:	Your name is _____.
Teacher:	What's your name? Listen. What's your name? Everyone!
Students:	What's your name?
Teacher:	(Point to a student.)
Student:	What's your name?
Teacher:	Ask _____. (Point to student.)
Student 1:	What's your name?
Student 2:	My name is _____.
Teacher:	How are you? Listen. How are you? Everyone!
Students:	How are you?
Teacher:	(Point to a student.)
Student:	How are you?
Teacher:	Fine, thank you, and you?
Student:	Fine.
Teacher:	Ask _____, "How are you?" (Point.)
Student 1:	How are you, _____?
Student 2:	Fine, thank you, and you?
Student 1:	Fine.

▶ IDEAS FOR INSTRUCTION

Conversations 1 and 2

If a tape recorder is not available, read the lines of the conversation to the class yourself. If it is nat-ural for you, use a deeper voice for Peter's lines and a higher voice for Maria's lines. Alternatively, choose a student to be one of the characters. Repeat the conversation with this student taking one part and you the other.

Or, you can divide the class into two sections, a Peter section and a Maria section. Have the class repeat the lines of Peter and Maria after you. For your students, these lines may represent the first English they have ever spoken. Repetition after a teacher model is a safe kind of practice. Encourage your students to repeat sentences but avoid repetition as the only tactic in your classroom.

Pair Work 1 and 2

Assign each student a partner. "Count off" A, B, and then put groups of two (one A and one B) together.

Then students should practice the Pair Work with their partners, which are straightforward. Some interest can be added by making cards with the names of half of the students on them. Each student whose name is not on a card draws the name of a classmate and then practices the Pair Work with that person.

▶ PRONUNCIATION TIPS

It is important to introduce the right intonation, the right stress, and natural juncture. In this text, the emphasis or emphases in a sample sentence will be noted through the use of bold type.

For example, in the list of New Elements, the part of the word that is in bold is given the highest stress. The word is "Hel-**lo**," with the high point of the intonation on the *lo*. The first time the question "What's your name?" is asked, the emphasis is on *name:* "What's your **name**?"

In Conversation 2, Barbara asks, "And **you**?" This question shows that there is a new emphasis on the contrasted element, *you*. If the whole question is echoed by the second person in the conversation, the contrasting element will be *your,* and so the emphasis in the sentence will change: "What's **your** name?" This rule of shift in emphasis to give a high stress to the element in contrast is universally followed in English.

The same is true with the question, "How **are** you?" The repeated question, after the first person has identified him/herself, gets a different emphasis: "**How** are **you**?"

PAGE SUMMARY

CONVERSATION 1 and **GROUP WORK:** Introducing others
CONVERSATION 2 and **PAIR WORK:** Leave taking

▶ **FUNCTIONS**

Introductions, greetings, and leave taking

▶ **NEW ELEMENTS**

Hi, _____.	**group**
This is _____.	**group** work
Nice to **meet** you, too.	
Good-bye.	
Bye.	
See you **lat**er.	

▶ **GRAMMAR**

This is _____.
There is _____. / There's _____.
_____, too.

▶ **IDEAS FOR INSTRUCTION**

Conversations 1 and **2**

First listen to the tape or read the lines of the conversation. Repeat each line several times. The speech balloons show the order of the greetings and introduction sentences.

Group Work

Have the students practice the conversations with one another. Encourage them to role-play rather than memorize a dialogue.

Next, form a circle with the students and do a chain-introduction exercise. For example, the teacher starts with his/her card: "I am ___A___. **This** is ___B___. And, ___B___, **this** is ___C___." Then B responds with, "Nice to **meet** you, ___name___." Next B turns to the two people next to him/her and says, "I am ___B___. **This** is ___C___. And, ___C___, **this** is ___D___. C and D respond with "Nice to **meet** you, _____" and "Nice to meet **you, too**." Continue around the circle.

Intercultural Awareness

If it seems appropriate, add an American style handshake to the introduction. Explain that people in business generally shake hands; young people in informal situations usually do not. The handshake that is most common on the North American continent is a firm touch, but not a hard grip. Generally two "shakes" is enough, and people do not continue holding hands after the handshaking.

Pair Work

Practice the Pair Work exercise at the bottom of the page by starting with the last person in the circle. He or she turns to the next person and says, "Good-**bye**, ___Z___." Z says in return, "**Bye.** See you **later**."

▶ **PRONUNCIATION TIPS**

Be sure to show the difference between the two lines, "Nice to **meet** you, ___name___." and "Nice to meet **you, too**."

"Count off" A, B, C, with the students to form groups of three to practice the new introduction forms.

▶ **ANSWERS**

The blanks need to be filled only with a name.

Listen and practice.

GROUP WORK • *Have similar conversations.*

STUDENT A: _____, this is _____.

STUDENT B: Nice to meet you, _____.

STUDENT C: Nice to meet you, too.

 Listen and practice.

PAIR WORK • *Have similar conversations.*

STUDENT A: Good-bye, _____.

STUDENT B: Bye. See you later.

Listen and repeat.

This is John Bascomb.

He's a banker.

This is Maria Miranda.

She's a doctor.

This is Peter Smith.

He's a businessman.

This is Anne Jones.

She's a secretary.

PAGE SUMMARY

NEW VOCABULARY: Occupations

STRUCTURE: Subject pronouns *he/she;* indefinite article with occupations

---

►FUNCTIONS

Talking about people and their occupations

►NEW ELEMENTS

banker	re**peat**
business**man**	**sec**tion
doctor	occu**pa**tion
secretary	vo**cab**ulary

►GRAMMAR

He's a _____.

She's a _____.

►PRELIMINARY ORAL WORK

Indefinite Article with Occupations

Teacher: I'm a teacher. (Point to yourself.) You're a student. (Point to individual students.) She's a doctor. (Point to the picture of the doctor.) Everyone!

Students: She's a doctor.

Question form:

Teacher: What's her job? Listen. What's her job? Everyone!

Students: What's his job?

Point to the pictures on this page to get students to ask questions.

►IDEAS FOR INSTRUCTION

New Vocabulary

Four of the characters in the book are introduced on this page. Use the pictures with the tape to reinforce the new elements or read each sentence with careful intonation.

This is John **Bas**comb. He's a **ban**ker.
This is Maria Mir**an**da. She's a **doc**tor.
This is Peter **Smith.** He's a **bus**iness**man.**
This is Anne **Jones.** She's a **sec**retary.

Expansion Activities

1. Elicit the names of other occupations. If you have a picture file, find pictures of all kinds of work situations. Be sure to include the occupations of all the students in the class. Remember that students can use *student* as an occupation if they want to.

2. For additional reinforcement, have students write their names and occupations on pieces of paper. Put the pieces of paper in a hat, let them draw names, and then introduce the classmate whose name is drawn to the class as a whole.

This is **Hel**en. She's a **house**wife.
This is **Dan**iel. He's a **car-wash**er
This is **Mar**tin. He's a **stu**dent.

►PRONUNCIATION TIPS

Practice the intonation with the accent on the accented syllable(s) of the occupation label.

banker
business**man**
doctor
secretary

Then, practice with the emphasis of the intonation on the accented syllable of the last name:

This is John **Bas**comb.
This is Maria Mir**and**a.
This is Peter **Smith.**
This is Anne **Jones.**

PAGE SUMMARY
NEW VOCABULARY: Occupations *(continued)*
STRUCTURE: *Be,* negative; *a/an*

▶**FUNCTIONS**
Talking about people and their occupations

▶**NEW ELEMENTS**
artist
me**chan**ic
movie **star**
pilot

▶**GRAMMAR**
Negative statement with *be*
She **isn't** a _____.
He **isn't** a _____.
a/an—a pilot/an artist

▶**PRELIMINARY ORAL WORK**
Negative form:

Teacher:	Is he a doctor? (Point to the picture of Otis.) No, he isn't a doctor. Listen. No, he isn't a doctor. He's an artist. Everyone!
Students:	No, he isn't a doctor. He's an artist.

▶**IDEAS FOR INSTRUCTION**

New Vocabulary
Four more characters are introduced. Read each line of the page, being careful with the emphasis on the name. Point out, by exaggerating somewhat, that the negative *isn't* also gets a strong stress. Ask the students to imitate you. When they have caught on, make your emphasis patterns natural. If you speak the students' first language, you might explain what you are doing with the emphasis.

Expansion Activities
1. Practice all the names thus far in the book. They provide a good review of the most common sounds of English: John **Bas**comb, Maria Mi**ran**da, Peter **Smith,** Anne **Jones,** Nancy **Paine,** Otis **Jack**son, Ula **Hack**ey, and Nick Vi**tak**is.

2. Consider practicing with the students' names, giving them an American pronunciation. The goal of learning English is to be able to participate in English language interchanges. Therefore, it is important for English-speakers to be able to hear the names of the students—which is possible only if a student's name is pronounced "Englishly."

3. Make a circle. It is best to have no more than 15 people in a circle, so divide the class into two or more groups if you have a larger class. Each student should know the names of the students standing on either side of him/her. The first student turns to his/her left, and introduces the student on the left by saying, "This is __**name**__. This **isn't** __the **name** of the person on the right__." Then she/he turns to the person on the right and does the same thing: "This is __**name**__. This **isn't** __**name** of the person on the left__."

▶**PRONUNCIATION TIPS**
This is Nancy **Paine.**
She **isn't** a **doc**tor.
She's a **pi**lot.

This is Otis **Jack**son.
He **isn't** a **bus**iness**man.**
He's an **art**ist.

This is Ula **Hack**ey.
She **isn't** a **sec**re**tary.**
She's a **mov**ie **star.**

This is Nick Vi**tak**is.
He **isn't** a **bank**er.
He's a me**chan**ic.

This is Nancy Paine.

She isn't a doctor.

She's a pilot.

This is Otis Jackson.

He isn't a businessman.

He's an artist.

This is Ula Hackey.

She isn't a secretary.

She's a movie star.

This is Nick Vitakis.

He isn't a banker.

He's a mechanic.

Listen and practice.

FRED: Who's that?

BARNEY: Her name is Nancy Paine.

FRED: Is she a mechanic?

BARNEY: No, she isn't. She's a pilot.

FRED: What's his name?

BARNEY: Otis Jackson.

FRED: Is he a pilot, too?

BARNEY: No, he isn't. He's an artist.

CONVERSATION: Talking about a third person (*she* and *he*)

▶FUNCTIONS
Asking questions about other people

▶NEW ELEMENTS
who
that

▶GRAMMAR
Question word: *who*
Yes/No question with *is*
    Is she/he _____?
Short answer with a contraction in the negative
    No, he **isn't.**
his/her + noun
    Her name/his name

▶PRELIMINARY ORAL WORK
Teacher goes around the class saying "His name is . . ." while pointing to the male students.

Teacher:	His name is _____. (Point to a male student, supplying his name.) Listen. His name is _____. Everyone!
Students:	His name is _____.
Teacher:	What's his name, _____? (Ask a student.)
Students:	His name is _____.

Do the same pattern for *her*.
Point to the picture of Nancy Paine.

Teacher:	Is she a doctor? Listen. No, she isn't. Everyone!
Students:	No, she isn't.
Teacher:	Is she a mechanic? (Point to a student.)
Student:	No, she isn't.
Teacher:	What's her job? Everyone!
Students:	She's a pilot.

▶IDEAS FOR INSTRUCTION

Conversation
Listen to the tape with the students or read the lines of the conversation. Ask for two volunteers from among the students or assign two students the roles of Fred and Barney. Read each line and have "Fred" and "Barney" repeat them after you.

Expansion Activities
1. If the students need reinforcement, a teacher might use his/her own picture file to identify a mechanic, a pilot, a movie star, an artist, a doctor, a banker, and a student. Name each one and then ask questions while showing the pictures to the class.

2. If possible, find pictures of the occupations of the students in the class. If a student's occupation is one she/he doesn't want to talk about or if the student does not have an occupation, the student's occupation should be defined as *student*. Use the pictures to ask the questions:

    Is **he** a **stud**ent?/
    Is **she** a **teach**er?/ etc.

▶PRONUNCIATION TIPS
To practice good pronunciation, emphasize the rising (/) intonation of the Yes/No question.

    Is she a me**chan**ic?/
    Is he a **pil**ot, **too**?/

PAGE SUMMARY

NEW VOCABULARY: Identifying common objects

▶ **FUNCTIONS**

Asking about the names of items
Identifying objects

▶ **NEW ELEMENTS**

book	bottle
chair	clock
coat	glass
hat	newspaper
watch	new

▶ **GRAMMAR**

What's **this**?
It's a _____.
Is this a _____?
Yes, it **is.** or **No,** it **isn't.**

▶ **PRELIMINARY ORAL WORK**

Teacher: It's a glass. (Hold up a glass.)
Listen. It's a glass. Everyone!
Students: It's a glass.
Teacher: What's this? (Hold up a book.)
Students: It's a book.
Teacher: (Point to a student.)
Student: It's a book.

Question form:

Teacher: What's this? Listen. What's this?
Everyone!
Students: What's this?
Teacher: _____, ask _____, "What's this?"
(Hand a pen to first student.)
Student 1: What's this? (Hold up a pen.)
Student 2: It's a pen.

Negative form:

Teacher: Is this pen? (Hold up a book.) No, it
isn't. Listen. No, it isn't. Everyone!
Students: No, it isn't.

▶ **IDEAS FOR INSTRUCTION**

New Vocabulary

The most important question for language use is
"What's this/that?" with a falling (\\) intonation.
With this question, the language learner can elicit
new words from native speakers.

Use the tape to introduce the lesson so
that the students hear the names of the objects
pronounced in different voices. Then repeat each
item with *a* or *an* in front of it. Say, "This is a
_____" or "This is an _____." Use all the
objects in the list (see **Expansion Activities** for
more ideas).

Expansion Activities

1. Collect the items in the list of new elements for
hands-on practice. Make labels for the common
nouns in the classroom: BOOK, CLOCK, CHAIR,
COAT, DOOR, DESK, WINDOW, WALL. Also bring to
class a GLASS, BOTTLE, HAT, NEWSPAPER, and
WATCH. (Students may have some of these things
with them, but if you bring your own, you'll be sure
to have them for the practice.) You will need to
have these special items to cover all of the variations in plural forms later on, so bring them to
class now to familiarize your students with them.

2. Encourage the students to identify the items in
their possession. If you think the class needs
practice with this form, take a bag of other
common objects (realia) to class. Let each student
pull one item out of the bag and ask another
student what it is.

3. A variation is to take a mysterious tool to class
(such as an unusual can opener or another
specialized kitchen utensil) and ask what it is.

4. Another variation is to put the items that have
already been taught in a separate bag and let the
students feel inside to guess what they are.

▶ **PRONUNCIATION TIPS**

Practice the intonation of the question "What's
this?" with the students. When there is a
contraction, the *this/that* is emphasized:

What's **this**? What's **that**?

If the full form of *is* is used, the emphasis should be
on *is*.

What **is** it? What **is** this?

▶ **ANSWERS**

3. It's a **bot**tle.
4. It's a **hat.**
8. It's a **glass.**
9. **No,** it **isn't.** It's a **watch.**
10. **No,** it **isn't.** It's a **coat.**

Listen and practice.

1. What's this?   It's a book.

2. What's this?   It's a chair.

3. What's this?   _____ bottle.

4. What's this?   _____ hat.

5. Is this a clock?   Yes, it is.

6. Is this a table?   Yes, it is.

7. Is this a book?   No, it isn't.
   What is it?   It's a newspaper.

8. Is this a bottle?   No, it isn't.
   What is it?   _____ glass.

9. Is this a clock?   _____.
   What is it?   _____ watch.

10. Is this a hat?   _____.
    What is it?   _____ coat.

Listen and practice.

1. What's this?
   It's a rabbit.

2. What's this?
   It's a chicken.

3. What's _____?
   It's a pear.

4. What's that?   It's a bird.

5. What's that?   It's a dog.

6. What's _____?   _____ an apple.

7. Is that a cat?   Yes, it is.

8. Is this a dog?
   No, it isn't.

   It's a _____.

9. Is _____ an apple?
   No, it isn't.

   It's a _____.

10. Is _____ an apple?   Yes, it is.

PAGE SUMMARY

STRUCTURE: *This* and *That;* identifying nearby and distant objects (singular)

▶**FUNCTIONS**

Asking about and identifying singular objects

▶**NEW ELEMENTS**

an **app**le   **struc**ture
a **bird**
a **cat**
a **chick**en
a **dog**
a **rab**bit

▶**GRAMMAR**

this versus *that*
What's **that**?
Is **this/that** a/an _____?

▶**PRELIMINARY ORAL WORK**

This/That

Teacher:	This is a book. (Hold up a book.)
	That's a chair. (Point to a chair.)
	What's this? (Hand a book to a student.)
Student:	It's a book.
Teacher:	What's that? (Point to the clock.)
Student:	It's a clock.

Get students to ask each other questions using *this* and *that.*

Teacher:	_____, ask _____, "What's this?" (Hand object to student.)
Student 1:	_____, what's this? (Hold up a book.)
Student 2:	It's a book.
Teacher:	_____, ask _____, "What's that?" (Point to a clock.)
Student 3:	_____, what's that? (Point to the clock.)
Student 4:	It's a clock.

▶**IDEAS FOR INSTRUCTION**

Structure

Show the students the difference between *this* and *that* by taking two identical objects into your hands, placing one on a table several steps from you and holding the other in your hand. Say, "**This** is a **book**" as you hold it up. Then say, "**That** is a **book, too**" as you point to the other book. Then pick up a student's pencil and say, "**This** is a **pen**cil." Point to a pen on a student's desk and say, "And **that's** a **pen**."

Expansion Activities

1. Practice the rhythm and intonation with the article + noun: an **app**le, a **chick**en, etc. Use some of the realia items that you collected for page 7, and let the students identify the objects for the other students.

2. A variation is to write the name of each object in your realia collection on a card, shuffle the cards, and distribute them to the students. The "magician" in the class asks one student for the name of the object on the card, and then points to one object and asks a student in the class, "Is this a <u> (the object name on the student's card) </u> ?"

▶**PRONUNCIATION TIPS**

Note the importance of enunciating clearly the *n* of *an* before a noun that begins with a vowel sound. If this element of English grammar is to be taught inductively, each noun must be accompanied by *a* or *an* as it is taught.

▶**ANSWERS**

3. What's <u>this</u>?
6. What's <u>that</u>?
 <u>It's</u> an apple.
8. <u>It's</u> a <u>rabbit</u>.
9. Is <u>this</u> an apple? No, it isn't. It's a <u>pear</u>.
10. Is <u>that</u> an apple?

PAGE SUMMARY
STRUCTURE: *These* and *Those;* identifying nearby and distant objects (plural)

▶ FUNCTIONS
Asking about and identifying plural objects

▶ NEW ELEMENTS

Plural with /s/	Plural with /z/	
cats	**app**les	**these**
rabbits	**birds**	**those**
	cards	
	chickens	
	dogs	
	flowers	
	pears	

▶ GRAMMAR
these versus *those*
> What are **these**? What are **those**?

Two variants of the plural morpheme
> /ts/ as in cats and rabbits
> /voiced consonant + z/ as in apples, cards, chickens, dogs, flowers, and pears

Contracted form of *are* as in They're
> **Yes,** they **are.**
> **No,** they **aren't.**

▶ PRELIMINARY ORAL WORK

These/Those

Teacher:	This is a book. (Hold up one.) These are books. (Hold up several.) What are these? Listen. What are these? Everyone!
Students:	What are these?
Teacher:	They're books. Listen. They're books. Everyone!
Students:	They're books.
Teacher:	What are these? (Hold up papers.)
Students:	They're papers.

Get students to ask each other questions using *these.*

Teacher:	_____, ask _____, "What are these?" (Hand pens to a student.)
Student 1:	_____, what are these? (Holds up pens.)
Student 2:	They're pens.

Negative form:

Teacher:	Are these pens? (Hold up pencils.) No, they aren't. Listen. No, they aren't. Everyone!
Students:	No, they aren't.

Introduce *those:*

Teacher:	That's a window. (Point to one.) Those are windows. (Point to several.) What are those? (Point to bananas on the table.)
Students:	They're bananas.

Get students to ask each other questions using *those.*

▶ IDEAS FOR INSTRUCTION
Structure
Use the tape so that students hear a different voice. Use realia or picture file excerpts to create an inviting learning environment.

▶ PRONUNCIATION TIPS
Encourage the students to imitate the voice on the tape. Be sure that the intonation and stress are correct. You can pass out rubber bands (elastic bands) to students; have them put their index fingers through the band and hold it taut, but not stretched, in front of themselves. Then, ask them to show how much "emphasis" each word gets in the "What's this?" question or any other utterance by expanding the rubber band relative to the amount of stress or emphasis. (The idea for rubber bands comes from Lori Brown.) Such an activity tends to take their minds off the newness and artificiality of learning new pronunciation patterns. It also incorporates a visual and a kinesthetic channel of learning into what is essentially an auditory learning task.

A variation is to have the students tap out the rhythm with their pencils on their desktops.

▶ ANSWERS
3. What are <u>these</u>?
6. What are <u>those</u>? They're dogs.
9. Are those <u>cats</u>? No, they aren't. They're <u>birds</u>.
10. Are <u>these</u> apples? No, they aren't. They're <u>flowers</u>.

Listen and practice.

1. What are these?
   They're flowers.

2. What are these?
   They're cards.

3. What are _____?
   They're rabbits.

4. What are those?   They're chickens.

5. What are those?   They're cats.

6. What are _____?   _____ dogs.

7. Are these rabbits? Yes, they are.

8. Are those pears?   Yes, they are.

9. Are _____ cats?
   No, they aren't.
   They're _____.

10. Are _____ apples?
    No, they aren't.
    They're _____.

Listen and repeat.

The cat is <u>under</u> the table.

   The ball is <u>in front of</u> the cat.

The vase is <u>on</u> the table.

   The flower is <u>in</u> the vase.

The envelope is <u>on</u> the table.

   The envelope is <u>next to</u> the vase.

The bookcase is <u>behind</u> the table.

   The books are <u>in</u> the bookcase.

PAIR WORK • *Ask and answer questions. Choose the correct preposition.*

Student A: **Where's the cat now?**
Student B: **It's on the table.**

1. Where's the dog?
   It's (on/under) the table.

2. Where's the vase?
   It's (on/under) the floor.

3. Where's the flower?
   It's (in/next to) the vase.

4. Where's the envelope?
   It's (in front of/behind) the cat.

5. Where's the ball?
   It's (in front of/behind) the dog.

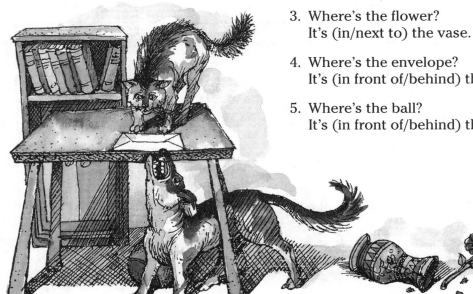

▶**FUNCTIONS**
Indicating location

▶**NEW ELEMENTS**

Prepositions	Nouns
be**hind**	the **ball**
in **front** of	the **bookcase**
in	the **en**velope
next to	the **floor**
on	the **table**
under	the **vase**

answer (v)
question
choose
co**rrect**
prepos**i**tion
ask

▶**GRAMMAR**
Where's the _____?
The _____ is + prepositional phrase
   (preposition + article + noun).
The _____ are + prepositional phrase.
It's _____ + prepositional phrase.

Prepositional phrases: behind, in front of, in, next to, on, and under

▶**PRELIMINARY ORAL WORK**

Questions with "Where" + Prepositions

Teacher:	What's this? (Hold up a book.)
Students:	It's a book.
Teacher:	Right. It's a book. And it's on the table. Listen. It's on the table. Everyone!
Students:	It's on the table.
Teacher:	Where's the book?
Students:	It's on the table.

Introduce other prepositional phrases: It's under the chair, in front of the desk, behind the table, in the box, etc.

Question form:

Teacher:	Where's the book? Listen. Where's the book? Everyone!
Students:	Where's the book?
Teacher:	(Name a student.)
Student:	Where's the book?

Get students to ask each other questions using *where*.

▶**IDEAS FOR INSTRUCTION**

Structure
Six prepositions of location are presented on this page. The students should study the relative placements of the objects in the pictures.

Pair Work
Manipulables are an essential part of teaching the prepositions of location. Bring a toy cat, a ball, a vase, a flower, a book, and an envelope to class. Show the students the location of each item on your table or desk. Invite the students to move the objects around: for example, put the envelope on top of the vase, and then ask, "Where's the envelope?"

Expansion Activity
Bring a small sturdy box with half of its top taped open to class. If it is a plain box (or if you paint it a plain color), you can write some key words on the box: Write IN and INSIDE on the inside of the box, UNDER and BENEATH on the bottom of the box. On the half top, write ON and ON TOP OF. You can label a front and back to facilitate teaching IN FRONT OF, IN BACK OF, and BEHIND. Use the box to show relative positions with an easily seen object, like a colorful stuffed cat. (The idea for a preposition box comes from Wm. Browder Swetnam.)

▶**ANSWERS**
1. It's <u>under</u> the table.
2. It's <u>on</u> the floor.
3. It's <u>next to</u> the vase.
4. It's <u>in front of</u> the cat.
5. It's <u>behind</u> the dog.

PAGE SUMMARY
WRITTEN EXERCISE and **PAIR WORK**: Prepositions of location

▶FUNCTIONS
Indicating location

▶NEW ELEMENTS
None

▶GRAMMAR
Prepositions of location: in, on, under, next to, behind, in front of.

▶PRELIMINARY ORAL WORK

Prepositions of Location with Plural Nouns

Teacher: What are these? (Hold up books.)
Students: They're books.
Teacher: Right. They're books. (Put them on a chair.) Where are they?
Students: They're on the chair.

Question form:
Teacher: Where are the books? Listen. Where are the books? Everyone!
Students: Where are the books?

Get students to ask each other the location of plural objects.

▶IDEAS FOR INSTRUCTION

Expansion Activity
Play "Twenty Questions"—you think of an object in the room and the students have to figure out what the object is by asking questions. However, the students can only ask you questions which can be answered by a yes or a no. They should ask you questions using the prepositions introduced on this page.

▶PRONUNCIATION TIPS
Remind the students that the preposition does not usually take strong stress unless it is in contrast.

Normal: The **coat**'s on the **chair.**
Contrast: No, it's not. It's **un**der the **tab**le.

▶ANSWERS

Written Exercise
1. The rabbit is __in__ the hat.
2. The chicken is __under__ the table.
3. The apples are __on__ the table.
4. The flowers are __in__ the vase.
5. The bottle is __next to__ the vase.
6. Suzi is __behind__ the clock.
7. The dog is __in front of__ the clock.
8. The clock is __next to__ the bookcase.
9. The books are __in__ the bookcase.
10. The cat is __under__ the newspaper.
11. The ball is __in front of__ the cat.
12. The coat is __on__ the chair.

Pair Work
1. A: Where are the books?
   B: They're in the bookcase.
2. A: Where is Suzi?
   B: She's behind the clock.
3. A: Where is the coat?
   B: It's on the chair.
4. A: Where is the ball?
   B: It's in front of the cat.
5. A: Where is the chicken?
   B: It's under the table.
6. A: Where are the flowers?
   B: They're in the vase.
7. A: Where is the bottle?
   B: It's next to the vase. *or* It's on the table.
8. A: Where is Simon?
   B: He's behind the door.
9. A: Where is the rabbit?
   B: It's in the hat.

WRITTEN EXERCISE • *Complete the sentences using these prepositions:* ***in, on, under, next to, behind,*** *and* ***in front of.***

Simon is ___*behind*___ the door.

1. The rabbit is _____ the hat.
2. The chicken is _____ the table.
3. The apples are _____ the table.
4. The flowers are _____ the vase.
5. The bottle is _____ the vase.
6. Suzi is _____ the clock.

7. The dog is _____ the clock.
8. The clock is _____ the bookcase.
9. The books are _____ the bookcase.
10. The cat is _____ the newspaper.
11. The ball is _____ the cat.
12. The coat is _____ the chair.

PAIR WORK • *Ask and answer questions.*

	apples		dog
	Student A: **Where are the apples?**		Student A: **Where is the dog?**
	Student B: **They're on the table.**		Student B: **It's in front of the clock.**

1. books
2. Suzi
3. coat

4. ball
5. chicken
6. flowers

7. bottle
8. Simon
9. rabbit

Listen and repeat.

1.

Ula Hackey is at the movies.

2.

Otis is at the museum.

3.

Mr. Bascomb is at the bank.

4.

Nick is at the garage.

5.

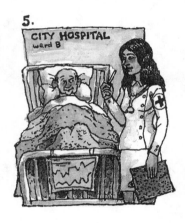

Maria is at the hospital.

6.

Peter is at the office.

7.

Nancy is at the airport.

8.

Anne is at the post office.

9.

Barney is at the gas station.

PAGE SUMMARY

NEW VOCABULARY: Places; locations requiring *the* before noun

▶**FUNCTIONS**
Identifying location

▶**NEW ELEMENTS**

at   the **airport**
         the **bank**
         the gar**age**
         the **gas sta**tion
         the **hos**pital
         the **mov**ies
         the mu**se**um
         the **off**ice
         the **post off**ice

place (n)

▶**GRAMMAR**
Point out that each of these places (the airport or the post office, for example) is a place that everyone knows—not just any airport or any post office. You can do this identifying as a particular airport by asking, "Where's the airport?" (It's on Airport Road, for example.) "Where's the post office?" (It's on Main Street.)

▶**IDEAS FOR INSTRUCTION**

New Vocabulary
Use the tape so that the students can hear another voice and intonation.

Expansion Activities
1. Write the names of the characters and the places on different cards:

Ula Hackey—the movies
Otis Jackson—the art museum
John Bascomb—the bank
Nick Vitakis—the garage
Maria Miranda—the hospital

Peter Smith—the office
Anne Jones—the post office
Nancy Paine—the airport
Barney—the gas station
Fred—the snack bar

Distribute the cards, and ask the students to match them up according to the pictures in the book.

2. Create a jazz chant (such as those suggested by Carolyn Graham in *Jazz Chants* [Oxford University Press]) with the cards and places.
   Follow these steps to do a jazz chant: First establish a clear 1-2-3-4 beat. Then ask, with normal intonation and stress, "Where's Ula?" This utterance will take two of the four beats. On the next 1 beat of the four-beat sequence, the student or students who have the card with the movie theater on it answer, "**She's** at the **mov**ies." This utterance will likewise take beats 1 and 2. Everyone should rest on beats three and four. Then ask the next question.

3. A variation is to have all of the students answer in chorus for each of the names.

▶**PRONUNCIATION TIPS**
Use the rubber band manipulable to emphasize the pronunciation and intonation of these phrases:

at the **air**port
at the **bank**
at the gar**age**
at the **gas sta**tion
at the **hos**pital
at the **mov**ies
at the mu**se**um
at the **off**ice
at the **post off**ice

PAGE SUMMARY

PRACTICE and **PAIR WORK:** Substituting *he* and *she* for subject nouns
WRITTEN EXERCISE: Practicing *a* vs. *an*

▶ **FUNCTIONS**

Locating people
Identifying objects

▶ **NEW ELEMENTS**

a **ta**xi **driv**er	a **car**	**prac**tice (n)
a **teach**er	an **egg**	**conson**ant
	an **envel**ope	re**place** (v)
	a **library**	com**plete** (v)
	an **or**ange	**note**
	a **tree**	be**fore**
		look at
		change
		sentence
		written
		exer**cise**

▶ **GRAMMAR**

Practice
Is she/he + prepositional phrase of location?
Substituting *she* and *he* for subject nouns.

Pair Work
Yes, she/he **is.** *or* **No,** he/she **isn't.**
Substituting *she* and *he* for subject names.

Written Exercise
An in place of *a* in front of a noun that begins with a vowel sound (respiraling of concept that is first introduced on page 6: Otis is an artist).

▶ **IDEAS FOR INSTRUCTION**

Written Exercise
You can use realia or pictures of an egg (preferably wooden, plastic, or at least hard-boiled!), a glass, a tree, an apple, a car, an envelope, an orange, a bottle, a newspaper, and an airport. You can use the pictures in the book as well to point out the objects for practice with *a/an*. The exercise will have more meaning, however, if you hold up a bottle and ask, "What's this?" and the students reply, "It's a bottle." You can also distribute the pictures or realia items to the class members and have them ask one another the questions.

Expansion Activity
Review all of the occupations, adding the distinction between *a/an* and *the*. For example, "**Bar**ney is a **ta**xi **driv**er. He's the **ta**xi **driv**er in the **book.**"

▶ **ANSWERS**

Practice
3. He's at the bank.
4. He's at the garage.
5. She's at the hospital.
6. He's at the office.
7. She's at the airport.
8. She's at the post office.
9. He's at the gas station.

Pair Work
3. No, he isn't. He's at the bank.
4. Yes, he is.
5. No, she isn't. She's at the hospital.
6. Yes, he is.
7. No, she isn't. She's at the airport.
8. No, she isn't. She's at the post office.
9. Yes, he is.

Written Exercise
1. It's _a_ tree.
2. It's _an_ apple.
3. It's _a_ car.
4. It's _a_ bottle.
5. It's _an_ orange.
6. It's _an_ envelope.
7. It's _a_ library.
8. It's _a_ newspaper.
9. It's _an_ airport.

PRACTICE • *Look at the pictures on page 12. Replace with* **he** *or* **she.**

1. Ula is at the movies.
   She's at the movies.
2. Otis is at the museum.
   He's at the museum.
3. Mr. Bascomb is at the bank.
4. Nick is at the garage.

5. Maria is at the hospital.
6. Peter is at the office.
7. Nancy is at the airport.
8. Anne is at the post office.
9. Barney is at the gas station.

PAIR WORK • *Look at the pictures on page 12. Ask and answer questions.*

1. A. **Is Ula at the movies?**
   B. **Yes, she is.**
2. A. **Is Otis at the post office?**
   B. **No, he isn't. He's at the museum.**
3. Is Mr. Bascomb at the hospital?
4. Is Nick at the garage?

5. Is Maria at the airport?
6. Is Peter at the office?
7. Is Nancy at the movies?
8. Is Anne at the bank?
9. Is Barney at the gas station?

WRITTEN EXERCISE • *Complete with* **a** *or* **an.**

It's ___*a*___ glass.   It's ___*an*___ egg.

1. It's _____ tree.
2. It's _____ apple.
3. It's _____ car.

4. It's _____ bottle.
5. It's _____ orange.
6. It's _____ envelope.

7. It's _____ library.
8. It's _____ newspaper.
9. It's _____ airport.

a car   a library   a tree

an apple   an orange   an egg

Note: **a** before consonant   **an** before a, e, i, o, u

WRITTEN EXERCISE • *Look at the picture and complete the sentences. Use **at, in, on, under, next to, in front of,** and **behind**.*

> Where's the bus stop? It's _____ *at* _____ the corner.

1. Where's Barbara? She's _____ the bus stop.

2. Where's the truck? It's _____ the bus.

3. Where's the post office? It's _____ the garage.

4. Where's the tree? It's _____ the garage.

5. Where's the car? It's _____ the garage.

6. Where's Nick? He's _____ the car.

PAIR WORK • *Ask and answer questions about the picture.*

> Student A: Is the bus stop at the corner?
> Student B: **Yes, It is.**
>
> Student A: Is Barbara in the post office?
> Student B: **No, she isn't. She's at the bus stop.**

1. Is the truck behind the bus?
2. Is the post office next to the garage?
3. Is the tree behind the post office?
4. Is the car in front of the garage?
5. Is Nick in the car?

PAGE SUMMARY

WRITTEN EXERCISE: Review of prepositional phrases as adverbs of location
PAIR WORK: Review of Yes/No questions about location

▶**FUNCTIONS**

Review of location phrases

▶**NEW ELEMENTS**

the **bus**   review
the **bus stop**
the **corner**
the **truck**

▶**GRAMMAR**

Review

▶**IDEAS FOR INSTRUCTION**

This page begins the Review Section for Chapter 1.

Pair Work

Note the difference between "Barbara is *in* the post office" and "Barbara is *at* the bus stop." A person can be in a building or at a building. But outside the building, the person is *at* the place (Barbara is at the corner at the bus stop).

▶**ANSWERS**

Written Exercise

1. Where's Barbara? She's __at__ the bus stop.
2. Where's the truck? It's __in front of__ the bus.
3. Where's the post office? It's __next to__ the garage.
4. Where's the tree? It' __behind__ the garage.
5. Where's the car? It's __in front of__ the garage.
6. Where's Nick? He's __under__ the car.

Pair Work

1. A. Is the truck behind the bus?
   B. No, it isn't. It's in front of the bus.
2. A. Is the post office next to the garage?
   B. Yes, it is.
3. A. Is the tree behind the post office?
   B. No, it isn't. It's behind the garage.
4. A. Is the car in front of the garage?
   B. Yes, it is.
5. A. Is Nick in the car?
   B. No, he isn't. He's under the car.

PAGE SUMMARY
WRITTEN EXERCISE: Review of *this/that* and *these/those*

▶**FUNCTIONS**
Asking about and identifying objects

▶**GRAMMAR**
Review

▶**NEW ELEMENTS**
None

▶**ANSWERS**

2. What's __that__? It's __a glass__ .
3. What's __this__ ? It's __a bottle__ .
4. What's __that__ ? It's __a chair__ .
5. What are __those__ ? They're __apples__ .
6. What are __these__ ? They're __cards__ .
7. What are __these__ ? They're __chickens__ .
8. What are __those__ ? They're __dogs__ .

WRITTEN EXERCISE • *Complete the sentences.*

1. What's ___*this*___ ? It's ___*a hat*___.

2. What's _____ ? It's _____.

3. What's _____ ? It's _____.

4. What's _____ ? It's _____.

5. What are _____ ? They're _____.

6. What are _____ ? They're _____.

7. What are _____ ? They're _____.

8. What are _____ ? They're _____.

PAIR WORK • *Ask and answer questions.*

1. Tony Romero/singer

2. Susan Steel/police officer

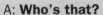

3. Donald Poole/teacher

A: **Who's that?**	A: **Who's that?**
B: **His name is Tony Romero.**	B: **Her name is Susan Steel.**
A: **What's his job?**	A: **What's her job?**
B: **He's a singer.**	B: **She's a police officer.**

4. Maria Miranda/doctor

5. Nick Vitakis/mechanic

6. Nancy Paine/pilot

7. Otis Jackson/artist

8. Florence Golo/teacher

9. John Bascomb/banker

10. Anne Jones/secretary

11. Peter Smith/businessman

12. Bonita Cantata/singer

PAGE SUMMARY
PAIR WORK: Review of talking about people and occupations

▶FUNCTIONS
Identifying people and their occupations

▶NEW ELEMENTS
Tony Ro**mer**o	a **sing**er
Susan **Steel**	a **police off**icer
Donald **Poole**	his **job**
Florence **Go**lo	her **job**
Bo**ni**ta Can**ta**ta	

▶GRAMMAR
Three logical extensions of the information learned thus far are included as new elements:

"Who's that?" (parallel to "What's that?")

"What's his/her job?"

"His/her name is _____."

▶IDEAS FOR INSTRUCTION

Pair Work
Discuss the 12 items, pronouncing each name and each occupation. Then read the two examples with students. Have two students act out the parts of A and B to demonstrate how to do the pair work.

▶PRONUNCIATION TIPS
What's his **job**?

What's her **job**?

▶ANSWERS

3. A: Who's that?
   B: His name is Donald Poole.
   A: What's his job?
   B: He's a teacher.
4. A: Who's that?
   B: Her name is Maria Miranda.
   A: What's her job?
   B: She's a doctor.
5. A: Who's that?
   B: His name is Nick Vitakis.
   A: What's his job?
   B: He's a mechanic.
6. A: Who's that?
   B: Her name is Nancy Paine.
   A: What's her job?
   B: She's a pilot.
7. A: Who's that?
   B: His name is Otis Jackson.
   A: What's his job?
   B: He's an artist.

8. A: Who's that?
   B: Her name is Florence Golo.
   A: What's her job?
   B: She's a teacher.
9. A: Who's that?
   B: His name is John Bascomb.
   A: What's his job?
   B: He's a banker.
10. A: Who's that?
    B: Her name is Anne Jones.
    A: What's her job?
    B: She's a secretary.
11. A: Who's that?
    B: His name is Peter Smith.
    A: What's his job?
    B: He's a businessman.
12. A: Who's that?
    B: Her name is Bonita Cantata.
    A: What's her job?
    B: She's a singer.

TO BE Affirmative

He She It	's (is)	in the office.

Negative

He She It	isn't (is not) 's not	in the office.

Interrogative

Is	he she it	in the office?

Short Answers

Yes,	he she it	is.		No,	he she it	isn't.

Question with WHAT

What	's (is)	this? that?
	are	these? those?

SINGULAR AND PLURAL NOUNS

It	's (is)	a pear. an apple.
They	're (are)	cards. flowers.

Question with WHERE

Where	's (is)	Mr. Bascomb?
	's (is)	the newspaper?
	are	the books?

PREPOSITIONS

He	's (is)	at in	the bank. his office.
It	's (is)	on under next to	the table.
They	're (are)	behind in front of	

Question with WHO

Who	's (is)	that?	Otis Jackson.

Chapter

TOPICS
Colors
Clothes
Numbers 1–20
Time

GRAMMAR
"To be" (continued)
Adjectives
Singular and plural nouns

FUNCTIONS
Asking where others are from
Describing people
Giving compliments
Asking for and telling the time

CHAPTER 2

PAGE SUMMARY
NEW VOCABULARY: *I'm* and *you're* with adjectives

▶**FUNCTIONS**
Describing states of being

▶**NEW ELEMENTS**
I'm for *I am*
You're for *You are*
hot—cold
hungry
thirsty
in**telli**gent
beautiful
rich
married

▶**GRAMMAR**
I'm + predicate adjective
You're + predicate adjective

▶**PRELIMINARY ORAL WORK**
Direct students to look at the pictures on page 19.
Say the adjectives as you point to each picture.

Teacher:	(Point to self.) I'm hot. Everyone.
Students:	I'm hot.
Teacher:	(Hug self and shiver.) I'm cold. Everyone.
Students:	I'm cold.

Continue, using all the adjectives.

Teacher:	(Point to student.) You're intelligent. Everyone.
Students:	You're intelligent.
Teacher:	_____, tell _____ she's intelligent.
Student:	_____, you're intelligent.

▶**IDEAS FOR INSTRUCTION**

New Vocabulary
Use the tape so that the students can hear other voices saying the target sentences. Ask the students to repeat the sentences after the taped voice.

Expansion Activity
For this exercise you will need as many cards as you have students, a gold or silver foil strip to be a wedding ring, and a fake necklace to show "rich." Write the words: hot, cold, hungry, thirsty, intelligent, beautiful, rich, and married on separate cards. There will be duplicate cards if you have more than eight students. Distribute the cards to your students.

Make circles of eight or fewer students and ask the students to say first what they are: "I'm rich." The student should show the other students in the circle the card.

Then go around the circle again, with Student A reading what is on Student B's card, and saying, "You're intelligent." Continue around the circle.

Next, redistribute the cards so each student has a new card. Each student must stand up and "act out" the word that is on the card she or he receives. The class guesses, "You're _____," and, when the class guesses correctly, the student who has done the acting out says, "Yes, I'm _____."

▶**PRONUNCIATION TIPS**
I'm **hot.**
I'm **cold.**
I'm **hung**ry.
I'm **thirs**ty.
You're in**telli**gent.
You're **beau**tiful.
You're **rich.**
You're **mar**ried.

Listen and repeat.

Listen and practice.

WAITER: Excuse me. Are you a tourist?

TOURIST: Yes, I am.

WAITER: Are you English?

TOURIST: No, I'm not.

WAITER: What nationality are you?

TOURIST: I'm American.

PAIR WORK • *Ask and answer questions.*

> A: Are you an artist?
> B: **Yes, I am.** OR **No, I'm not.**

1. Are you Italian?
2. Are you a student?
3. Are you rich?
4. Are you married?
5. Are you a tourist?
6. Are you hot?
7. Are you thirsty?
8. Are you happy?
9. Are you sad?
10. Are you cold?

happy   sad

PAGE SUMMARY

CONVERSATION and **PAIR WORK:** Asking and responding to questions about states of being, nationality, and occupations

▶ FUNCTIONS
Identifying nationality

▶ NEW ELEMENTS

Ex**cuse** me.	**Eng**lish
tourist	**Ital**ian
waiter	**hap**py
nation**a**lity	**sad**

▶ GRAMMAR
Yes/No questions with *be* and *you*

▶ PRELIMINARY ORAL WORK

The Verb "to be" with *I* and *you*

Teacher:	I'm a teacher. (Point to yourself.) You're a student, you're a student, etc. What am I? (Point to yourself.)
Students:	You're a teacher.
Teacher:	That's right. I'm a teacher. What are you? (Point to a student.)
Student 1:	I'm a student.
Teacher:	What are you? (Point to student 2.)
Student 2:	I'm a student.
Teacher:	That's right. Now look. You're in class (point to students) and I'm in class (point to yourself). We're in class. (Point to students and to yourself.) Listen. We're in class. Everyone!
Students:	We're in class.
Teacher:	Where are we?
Students:	We're in class.

Negative form:

Teacher:	Am I a banker? (Point to yourself and shake your head.) No, I'm not. Listen. No, I'm not. Everyone!
Students:	No, I'm not.
Teacher:	_____, are you a teacher? (Ask questions that will elicit negative responses.)
Student 3:	No, I'm not.
Teacher:	_____, are you a pilot? (Answer for her.) No, you aren't. Listen. No, you aren't. Everyone!
Students:	No, you aren't.

▶ IDEAS FOR INSTRUCTION

Conversation
Use the tape to introduce the dialogue.

Expansion Activity
For this game, use the cards from the previous page (rich, intelligent, married, beautiful, thirsty, hungry, hot, and cold). You will need more cards, too—ten of them in a color if possible. Write a white card for "happy" and another for "sad." On each of the white cards, write Italian, American, English, and any other national groups that are represented in your class. On five colored cards, make a +; write a – on the other five.

Split the class into two teams. Put the two stacks of cards on the table in the middle of the room. A person from Team A chooses a white card, and a person from Team B takes a colored card. A asks B, "Are you _____ (whatever is on the card)?" B answers according to + (yes) or – (no) on the colored card. "**Yes**, I **am**" or "**No**, I'm **not**." If both students ask and answer appropriately, then each team gets a point.

▶ PRONUNCIATION TIPS
Be sure students understand that the verb gets the emphasis in the affirmative sentence and that *not* gets the emphasis in the negative sentence.

Yes, I **am**. /**No**, I'm **not**.

Note that with Yes/No questions, the voice goes up at the end of the question. Note also that one word can be a question with that intonation: Tourist?/ (meaning, is she or he a tourist?)

Practice the polysyllabic words by asking the students to repeat after you:

A-**mer**-ican	Can-**ad**-ian
I-**tal**-ian	**na**-tion-**al**-ity

Introduce the two new words.

waiter   **tour**ist

The endings on these two words (*-er* and *-ist*) will prove productive later, so it is good to be sure that the students understand the pronunciation early in their language learning experience.

▶ ANSWERS

Pair Work
Answers will vary.

PAGE SUMMARY

CONVERSATIONS: Asking and responding to questions about place of origin and occupation

▶**FUNCTIONS**

Asking personal information about others

▶**NEW ELEMENTS**

the United <u>States</u>

<u>Hollywood</u>

▶**GRAMMAR**

Yes/No questions with *be, you,*
  and *they*
are and *aren't*
We're for *we are*
They're for *they are*
Yes, we are.
No, we aren't.
Yes, they are.
No, they aren't.
Where are you from?
Who are you?

▶**PRELIMINARY ORAL WORK**

Teacher:	_____ and _____ are students. (pause) They're students. Listen. They're students. Everyone!
Students:	They're students.
Teacher:	What are they?
Students:	They're students.
Teacher:	Are _____ and _____ bankers? (pause) No, they aren't. Listen. No, they aren't. Everyone!
Students:	No, they aren't.
Teacher:	Are they doctors?
Students:	No, they aren't. (They're students.)
Teacher:	Are they in the library?
Students:	No, they aren't. (They're in class.)

Question form:

Teacher:	Are they movie stars? Listen. Are they movie stars? Everyone!
Students:	Are they movie stars?
Teacher:	_____, ask _____, "Are they movie stars?" (Point to two students.)
Student 1:	_____, are they movie stars? (Point to the two students.)
Student 2:	No, they aren't. (They're students.)

Teach the question form with *we* and *you*.

▶**IDEAS FOR INSTRUCTION**

Conversations

Listen to the tape. Ask the students to mime the tape voices. (As the tape voice is reading the dialogue, the students "pretend" to be saying the words by moving their lips.) After they have done the dialogue enough to be comfortable with it, choose a Pedro, a Steve, a Steve's girlfriend (who says nothing), and a Juanita to "act out" the dialogue with the tape in front of the class. Be sure that you choose students who like to act. The last time through the dialogue, have the students do the dialogue without the tape.

Make a list of the places that students are from, and write the names of the country or state on the board. Also include <u>here</u> as an option. One student at a time comes to the board, points at a place name and asks a fellow student, " <u>(name)</u> , are you from _____?" The student answers in one of three ways:

Yes, I am. I'm from <u>(name of town or city)</u> .
No, I'm not. I'm from <u>(name of country or state)</u> .
No, I'm not. I'm from here.

Expansion Activity

Write cards with the names for the nationalities on pages 20 and 21: Italian, American, Canadian, English, and so on. Divide the class into groups of four. Ask students to prepare dialogues to act out for their classmates based on these cards.

▶**PRONUNCIATION TIPS**

Yes, we **<u>are</u>.**
No, we **<u>aren't</u>.**
Yes, they **<u>are</u>.**
No, they **<u>aren't</u>.**
Where are you **<u>from</u>?**
Who **are** you?

Remember to emphasize that Wh- questions have normal intonation patterns.

Listen and practice.

PEDRO: Are you from the United States?

STEVE: Yes, we are. We're from Hollywood.

PEDRO: Are you movie stars?

STEVE: No, we aren't movie stars. We're students.

JUANITA: Who are they?

PEDRO: They're Americans. They're from Hollywood.

JUANITA: Are they movie stars?

PEDRO: No, they aren't. They're students.

PRACTICE

*1. Replace with **you, we,** or **they**.*

Barney and I are friends.
We're friends.

1. Anne and Nancy are Americans.
2. You and Nancy are from New York.
3. Anne and Peter are from Los Angeles.
4. Anne and I are friends.
5. You and Nancy are friends.
6. You and I are students.
7. Those girls are students.

2. Change the sentences to questions.

They're bankers.
Are they bankers?

1. They're at a meeting.
2. They're at the City Bank.
3. They're on Franklin Avenue.
4. We're on Main Street.
5. We're at the post office.
6. You're doctors.
7. You're from the hospital.

3. Change the sentences to the negative.

You're movie stars.
You aren't movie stars.

1. You're tourists.
2. You're from England.
3. You're rich.
4. We're happy.
5. We're teachers.
6. They're pilots.
7. They're Americans.

PAGE SUMMARY

PRACTICE 1: Substituting *you, we, they* for subject nouns
PRACTICE 2: Making questions by inverting pronouns and *to be* verbs
PRACTICE 3: Making negative sentences

▶FUNCTIONS

Asking where others are from
Describing people

▶NEW ELEMENTS

meeting
Los **Ang**eles
New **York**
re**place** (v)

▶GRAMMAR

Review of contractions *we're, you're, they're*
Review of prepositional phrases:

from a city (from New York)
at a place (at a meeting)
at a building (at City Bank)
on a street (on Franklin Avenue)

▶IDEAS FOR INSTRUCTION

Practice

Students should listen as the teacher models the example for each exercise. Then the teacher calls on students to recite the answers to the seven numbered items in each exercise.

▶PRONUNCIATION TIPS

They're **Ameri**cans.
They're at a **meet**ing.
They're on **Frank**lin **Ave**nue.

▶ANSWERS

Practice 1

1. They're Americans.
2. You're from New York.
3. They're from Los Angeles.
4. We're friends.
5. You're friends.
6. We're students.
7. They're students.

Practice 2

1. Are they at a meeting?
2. Are they at the City Bank?
3. Are they on Franklin Avenue?
4. Are we on Main Street?
5. Are we at the post office?
6. Are you doctors?
7. Are you from the hospital?

Practice 3

1. You aren't tourists.
2. You aren't from England.
3. You aren't rich.
4. We aren't happy.
5. We aren't teachers.
6. They aren't pilots.
7. They aren't Americans.

PAGE SUMMARY
READINGS 1, 2, and 3: Describing people

▶**FUNCTIONS**
Asking questions about people

▶**NEW ELEMENTS**

wait**er**	**Russ**ian	**sto**ry
short	A**ri**zona	**read**ing
handsome	Cali**forn**ia	
tall	**Mos**cow	
blond	in **fact**	
dancer	**or**	
bal**let danc**er	**but**	
singer		
country **sing**er		
very **good**		
very **bad**		

▶**GRAMMAR**
Use of *very* to intensify an adjective
Use of *in fact* as a transition form
Alternatives with *or*

▶**IDEAS FOR INSTRUCTION**

Prereading Activity
Point to each picture as you convey the meaning of new words. For example:

Teacher: This is Tino. He's **tall**. (Mime tall, reaching up high.) This is Barbara. She's not tall. She's short.

Continue until students are familiar with the new words. Ask questions about what you said. Do the same type of presentation for each of the three readings.

Readings 1–3
Use the tape to introduce the readings, one at a time. Ask the students to keep their books closed the first three times you play the tape. Then read the story yourself, and ask the questions.

Expansion Activity
As homework or in-class pair work, ask students to write sentences about themselves. Model the activity by writing one about yourself and someone else on the board. " (your name) is a teacher. She/He's _____. (a student's name) is a student. She/He's _____."

▶**PRONUNCIATION TIPS**
They're bal**let danc**ers.
And they're very **good.**
They're **coun**try **sing**ers.
And they're very **bad.**

▶**ANSWERS**

Reading 1
1. No, he isn't. He's a waiter.
2. No, he isn't. He's tall.
3. Yes, he is.
4. No, he isn't.
5. Yes, she is.
6. No, she isn't. She's short.
7. Yes, she is.
8. Yes, she is.
9. Yes, they are.
10. No, they're not. They're from California.

Reading 2
1. They're ballet dancers.
2. They're from Moscow.
3. Yes, they are.

Reading 3
1. They're singers.
2. They're from Nashville.
3. No, they're not.

Listen to the stories and answer the questions.

1 Tino is a waiter. He's tall and handsome. He isn't rich, but he's happy. Barbara is a secretary. She's short and blond. And she's beautiful. Barbara and Tino are good friends. They're from California.

1. Is Tino a businessman?
2. Is he short?
3. Is he handsome?
4. Is he rich?
5. Is Barbara a secretary?
6. Is she tall?
7. Is she blond?
8. Is she beautiful?
9. Are Barbara and Tino good friends?
10. Are they from New York?

2 Natalya and Boris are Russian ballet dancers. They're from Moscow. They're very good dancers.

1. Are Natalya and Boris ballet dancers or movie stars?
2. Where are they from?
3. Are they good dancers?

3 Sammy and Tammy are country singers. They're from Nashville. They aren't very good singers. In fact, they're very bad.

1. Are Sammy and Tammy singers or dancers?
2. Where are they from?
3. Are they good singers?

Listen and repeat.

This woman is fat.

That man is thin.

This bicycle is cheap.

That bicycle is expensive.

These women are young.

Those men are old.

These boys are dirty.

Those girls are clean.

WRITTEN EXERCISE • *Complete the sentences using "to be" and these adjectives: **bad, clean, beautiful, hot, cheap, fat, rich, married, short.***

1. Barbara *is beautiful*.

2. Mr. and Mrs. Bascomb _____.

3. Mr. Twaddle _____.

4. Mrs. Brown _____.

5. Albert _____.

6. Tino _____.

7. The pots _____.

8. The guitar _____.

9. The apples _____.

PAIR WORK • *Ask and answer questions.*

1. A: Is Barbara beautiful?
   B: **Yes, she is.**
2. A: Are Mr. and Mrs. Bascomb poor?
   B: **No, they aren't. They're rich.**
3. Is Mr. Twaddle tall?
4. Is Mrs. Brown married?
5. Is Albert thin?
6. Is Tino cold?
7. Are the pots clean?
8. Is the guitar expensive?
9. Are the apples good?

Listen and repeat.

red   orange   yellow   green   blue   white   black   gray   brown

shirt   pants   dress   blouse   sweater   shoes

PRACTICE 1

What colors are the clothes above?

The shirt is red. The pants are blue.

PRACTICE 2

What color are your clothes?

My shirt is green. My shoes are black.

CONVERSATION

 Listen and practice.

TINO: That's a beautiful dress, Barbara.

BARBARA: Thank you, Tino.

TINO: Red is a good color for you.

BARBARA: Yes. It's my favorite color.

PAIR WORK • *Have similar conversations. Use new vocabulary such as **shirt, dress,** and **sweater**.*

A: That's a beautiful shirt, ＿＿＿＿＿＿＿＿＿.

B: Thank you, ＿＿＿＿＿＿＿＿＿.

A: ＿＿＿＿＿＿＿＿＿ is a good color for you.

B: Yes. It's my favorite color.

PAGE SUMMARY

NEW VOCABULARY and **PRACTICE 1** and **2:** Colors and clothes
CONVERSATION and **PAIR WORK:** Complimenting others

▶ **FUNCTIONS**
Talking about colors and clothes

▶ **NEW ELEMENTS**

red	**or**ange
yellow	**green**
blue	**white**
black	**gray**
brown	a**bove**
shirt	**pants** (used like a plural)
dress	**blouse**
sweater	**shoes** (plural)
clothes	**color**
Thank you.	**fav**orite

▶ **GRAMMAR**
What color is/are _____?

determiner	+ adjective +	noun
a	good	color
my	favorite	color
a	beautiful	shirt

▶ **IDEAS FOR INSTRUCTION**

Conversation and **Pair Work**
Play the tape, which contains the new words and the conversation. Ask students to role-play, using the colors and names of clothing that they are wearing. Model this by going up to a student and saying, "That's a beautiful <u>(whatever the student is wearing)</u>, <u>(student's name)</u>." When the student says, "Thank you," say something about the color: "<u>(name of color)</u> is a good color for you."

Expansion Activity
Bring catalogs or pictures from a picture file to discuss ideas about clothes.

Play a game of concentration using cards that have pictures of items of clothing of any one color (not patterns, plaids, dots, or stripes): a red coat, a green sweater, a blue dress, a yellow hat. Choose up to the nine colors that are taught in this lesson. For each picture make a card of a different color or shape (so that it can be identified as a color card) with the name of the color printed on it: red, green, blue, yellow. . . . Turn the picture cards and the matching color-name cards upside down and mix them up so that all of the cards are face down and no one knows which card is which. Students should be able to tell from the backs of the cards which ones are picture cards and which ones have the color names printed on them.

A student from Team A picks up one clothing card and one color-name card. They are identified (the student says, for example, "A green sweater," and "Red.") The cards are put down in the same places. A student from Team B does the same thing. Students try to remember where the cards are—they want to match the green sweater with the color-name card that says "green," for example. When a match is made, the team gets a point and those two cards are removed from play. The game can be expanded by having two or more items of the same color, but for each picture card, there must be a color card.

▶ **PRONUNCIATION TIPS**
Practice the intonation patterns of the adjective + noun structure.

> It's my **favorite** _**col**or_.
> **Red** is a **good** _**col**or_ for **you.** (Red's)
> That's a **beautiful** _**dress**_, **Barb**ara.

▶ **ANSWERS**

Practice 1
   The dress is green.
   The blouse is yellow.
   The sweater is orange.
   The shoes are brown.

Practice 2
Answers will vary.

Pair Work
Names are needed for the first two blanks. The third blank can be filled with any color name.

PAGE SUMMARY

NEW VOCABULARY: Numbers one to twenty

▶**FUNCTIONS**
Counting

▶**NEW ELEMENTS**

one	eleven
two	twelve
three	thirteen
four	fourteen
five	fifteen
six	sixteen
seven	seventeen
eight	eighteen
nine	nineteen
ten	twenty

▶**GRAMMAR**
None

▶**IDEAS FOR INSTRUCTION**

New Vocabulary
Listen to the tape and have the students repeat after it.

▶**PRONUNCIATION TIPS**
Practice the stresses on the numbers. It is important for students to recognize that the *-teen* part of the numbers gets a secondary stress and that the *-ty* on twenty does not. This stress can be heard more clearly in a noun phrase:

There are **thirteen basketball play**ers.
There are **thirty football play**ers.

Listen and repeat.

one two three four five six seven eight nine ten

eleven twelve thirteen fourteen fifteen sixteen seventeen eighteen nineteen twenty

Listen and practice.

What time is it?
It's one o'clock.

What time is it?
It's eight o'clock.

What time is it?
It's three o'clock.

PAIR WORK • *Ask and answer questions.*

1. 　2. 　3.

A: **What time is it?**
B: **It's six o'clock.**

4. 　5. 　6.

7. 　8. 　9.

PAGE SUMMARY

TIME and **PAIR WORK:** Using numbers for telling time, exactly on the hour

---

▶FUNCTIONS

Telling time
Asking for time and answering
  with the hour

▶NEW ELEMENTS

What time is it?
It's _____ o'**clock.**

▶GRAMMAR

What + time (*what* is used as an interrogative adjective)

▶IDEAS FOR INSTRUCTION

Time

The tape can be used to give the time patterns. Alternatively, say "It's _____ o'clock," and require that the students point to the clock face with that time on it. If the students are in groups, they will check one another.

▶PRONUNCIATION TIPS

Remind students that the intonation in a
Wh- question asking the time is just like a normal sentence: "What **time** is it?" The voice falls at the end of the sentence.

Point out that the strong stress goes on the *clock,* but that the number gets secondary stress:

It's **one** o'**clock.**
It's **two** o'**clock.**
It's **three** o'**clock.**
It's **four** o'**clock.**
It's **five** o'**clock.**
It's **six** o'**clock.**
It's **seven** o'**clock.**
It's **eight** o'**clock.**
It's **nine** o'**clock.**
It's **ten** o'**clock.**
It's **eleven** o'**clock.**
It's **twelve** o'**clock.**

▶ANSWERS

2. It's nine o'clock.
3. It's four o'clock.
4. It's seven o'clock.
5. It's twelve o'clock.
6. It's five o'clock.
7. It's eleven o'clock.
8. It's two o'clock.
9. It's ten o'clock.

PAGE SUMMARY
CONVERSATION: Talking about people and places

▶**FUNCTIONS**
Asking about other people

▶**NEW ELEMENTS**
Mr. Watkins
Albert
Lucia **Mendes**
Mexican
Brazilian
Rio de Janeiro
Bra**sí**lia

▶**GRAMMAR**
What as an interrogative adjective (What city . . . ? What's . . . ?)
Who as an interrogative pronoun (Who's . . . ?)
Two adjectives before a noun (a beautiful modern city)
That as a pronoun (Is that the capital of Brazil?)
With (to be with someone)

[Please remember: Students do not need to know the grammatical names of the elements they are learning. These explanations are given only for the teacher!]

▶**IDEAS FOR INSTRUCTION**
This page begins the Review Section for Chapter 2.

Conversation
The students should listen to each part of the conversation on the tape several times; then, a pair of students can role-play the two characters, Albert and Mr. Watkins.

Expansion Activity
Put up a map and point out the countries and the capitals of the countries on the map.

▶**PRONUNCIATION TIPS**
If you and/or your students have been pronouncing names and places authentically, consider practicing with American English pronunciation.

That's **Lucia Men**des.
Is she from **Mexico**?
No, she isn't **Mex**ican.
Is she Bra**zil**ian?
Yes, she's from **Ri**o de Janeiro.
She **isn't** from Bra**sí**lia.

Remember that the intonation on a Yes/No question is rising.

Listen and practice.

ALBERT: Who's that girl over there?

MR. WATKINS: Her name's Lúcia Mendes.

ALBERT: She's very pretty. Is she a student?

MR. WATKINS: Yes. She's a history student.

ALBERT: Is Lúcia Mexican?

MR. WATKINS: No, she isn't. She's Brazilian.

ALBERT: What city is she from?

MR. WATKINS: She's from Rio de Janeiro.

ALBERT: Is that the capital of Brazil?

MR. WATKINS: No. Brasília is the capital.

ALBERT: What's Brasília like?

MR. WATKINS: It's a beautiful modern city.

DIALOGUE QUESTIONS

1. Who's Albert with?
2. Is Mr. Watkins an intelligent man?
3. Who's the girl by the window?
4. Is she very pretty?
5. Is she American?
6. What nationality is she?
7. What city is she from?
8. Is Rio de Janeiro the capital of Brazil?
9. What is the capital of Brazil?
10. What's Brasília like?
11. What's the capital of your country?
12. What's your capital like?

PAIR WORK • *Ask and answer questions about the students in your class.*

A: Who's that student over there?

B: His/her name is _____.

A: Is he/she Mexican? /Chinese? /French?

B: _____.

A: What city is he/she from?

B: _____.

WRITTEN EXERCISE • *Put a or an before each word.*

1. *a* postcard
2. *an* umbrella
3. _____ wastebasket
4. _____ eye

5. _____ letter
6. _____ dictionary
7. _____ airplane
8. _____ magazine

PAGE SUMMARY

DIALOGUE QUESTIONS: Follow-up to the conversation on page 29
PAIR WORK: Discussing city and country of origin
WRITTEN EXERCISE: Review of *a* and *an*

▶FUNCTIONS

Answering two kinds of questions:
  Yes/No questions and questions with *what*

▶NEW ELEMENTS

Chinese	a wastebasket
French	a postcard
an umbrella	an airplane
a dictionary	a magazine
dialogue	class
a letter	

▶GRAMMAR

Review

▶IDEAS FOR INSTRUCTION

Dialogue Questions

These questions generate from the dialogue on the previous page. Accept answers that are not full sentences and short answers wherever appropriate. Note that some of these questions require students to make inferences.

▶PRONUNCIATION TIPS

Practice the pronunciation with your students.

Is she **Chinese**?   Are they **French**?

A: What **is** it?
B: A **postcard**.

Encourage students to listen for initial vowel and consonant sounds.

This is an um**brel**la.   It's a **wastebas**ket.
That's an **airplane.**   This is a **dict**ionary.
There's a **mag**azine.

▶ANSWERS

Dialogue Questions
1. Mr. Watkins. (straight from text)
2. Yes, he is. (He knows all the answers! This one requires an inference.)
3. Lucia Mendes.
4. Yes, she is. (according to Albert and Mr. Watkins)
5. No, she isn't.
6. She's Brazilian.
7. (She's from) Rio de Janeiro.
8. No, it isn't.
9. Brasília is the capital of Brazil.
10. It's a beautiful modern city.
11. (answers will vary)
12. (answers will vary)

Pair Work
Answers will vary.

Written Exercise
3. __a__ wastebasket
4. __an__ eye
5. __a__ letter
6. __a__ dictionary
7. __an__ airplane
8. __a__ magazine

PAGE SUMMARY

WRITTEN EXERCISE and **GROUP WORK:** Inferring appropriate questions from answers

▶**FUNCTIONS**

Asking questions

▶**NEW ELEMENTS**

How **much** . . . ?   **an**swer (n)
dollars   **oth**er
Saudi A**rab**ia
Mari**anne**
my **girlfriend**
a com**put**er

▶**GRAMMAR**

How much is that dress? (inquiring about cost)

▶**IDEAS FOR INSTRUCTION**

Expansion Activity

This exercise is like the game "Jeopardy." After the students have attempted to ask the questions that the answers indicate, write the answers and similar answers on large cards. Split the class into two teams. Put all of the answer cards (and also other parallel questions—see the list below) in a stack on a table. One at a time, alternating between the teams, a student comes to the table, uncovers one answer, asks the question, and either gets a point for a correct answer or doesn't earn a point. If the first person to attempt to answer the question fails, the other team gets a chance to ask the question that the answer card indicates.

Other answers to generate questions:

An um**brel**la.
My name's **Ang**ela.
That's my **dog.**
It's **twelve** o'**clock.**
On the **bookcase.**
I'm a **stud**ent.
Ten **dol**lars.
I'm from **Mexico.**

▶**PRONUNCIATION TIPS**

Note the pronunciation help given above.

▶**ANSWERS**

Written Exercise

2. What are you? or What's your job?
3. Where are you from?
4. What's your name?
5. How are you?
6. Who's that? or Who's she/that woman?
7. What's that?
8. Where's your dog?
9. What time is it?

OPPOSITES

 Listen and repeat.

tall≠short	strong≠weak	hot≠cold	rich≠poor
fat≠thin	clean≠dirty	black≠white	beautiful≠ugly
old≠young	big≠small	happy≠sad	cheap≠expensive

PRACTICE • *Describe the people and objects in the pictures. Use the adjectives in the box.*

1. Tino   Johnnie

Tino is strong.
Johnnie is weak.

2. Barbara   Bernice

Barbara is beautiful.
Bernice is ugly.

3. apple   pear

The apple is big.
The pear is small.

4. Mr. Bascomb   Eddie

5. umbrella   hat

6. Mrs. Morley   Linda

7. guitar   violin

8. Mr. Poole   Mrs. Poole

9. Suzi   Nobu

10. coffee   lemonade

11. Jenny   Marty

12. Lotta   Bill

PAGE SUMMARY
OPPOSITES and **PRACTICE:** Matching pictures with adjectives

▶**FUNCTIONS**
Describing people and things

▶**NEW ELEMENTS**
The adjectives have all been presented before this point in the text. New words include:

Mrs. **Mor**ley	des**cribe**
Linda	**peo**ple
Johnnie	**ob**ject
Eddie	**op**posite
vi**ol**in	**cof**fee
lemon**ade**	**ug**ly
weak	**strong**
big	**small**

▶**GRAMMAR**
Review

▶**IDEAS FOR INSTRUCTION**
Practice
Ask questions about the pictures first:

Who's rich?	Who's short?
Who's old?	Who's ugly?
What's expensive?	What's small?

Who's fat?	Who's young?
Who's clean?	Who's beautiful?
What's cheap?	Who's weak?
Who's strong?	What's black?
What's big?	Who's dirty?
What's white?	Who's tall?
Who's thin?	What's hot?
What's cold?	Who's sad?
Who's poor?	Who's happy?

Then, ask students to pair the opposite words. Divide the class into two teams. Call out one of a pair of opposite words and ask Team A and then Team B to give the opposite. Each team gets a point for a correct answer.

Then have the class do the Practice.

▶**ANSWERS**
Practice
4. Mr. Bascomb is <u>rich</u>.
   Eddie is <u>poor</u>.
5. The umbrella is <u>black</u>.
   The hat is <u>white</u>.
6. Mrs. Morley is <u>old</u>.
   Linda is <u>young</u>.
7. The guitar is <u>cheap</u>.
   The violin is <u>expensive</u>.
8. Mr. Poole is <u>tall</u>.
   Mrs. Poole is <u>short</u>.
9. Suzi is <u>happy</u>.
   Nobu is <u>sad</u>.
10. The coffee is <u>hot</u>.
    The lemonade is <u>cold</u>.
11. Jenny is <u>clean</u>.
    Marty is <u>dirty</u>.
12. Lotta is <u>fat</u>.
    Bill is <u>thin</u>.

PAGE SUMMARY
STRESS and **INTONATION PRACTICE:** Review of common patterns

▶**FUNCTIONS**
Asking and answering questions

▶**NEW ELEMENTS**
stress   intona̲tion

▶**GRAMMAR**
Review

▶**IDEAS FOR INSTRUCTION**

Stress
Use the tape to emphasize the stress patterns in the words.

Intonation
Ask the students to repeat the intonation after the voice on the tape.

Stress and Intonation
Point out that the dot above the syllable is the high point. The arrow up means rising intonation; the arrow down means that the voice falls.

Expansion Activities
1. On the board, write the names of some occupations like these:

doctor	movie star	singer
student	teacher	pilot
banker	mechanic	secretary
tourist	artist	dancer

Then make another list of the nationalities that the class knows:

Canadian	Italian	_____
English	Mexican	_____
American	Russian	
Brazilian	French	

Then ask about all of the people in the class.
Model: Is Barney a taxi driver or a doctor?

2. In order to practice asking for clarification and expressing certainty, have the following conversations.

    A: Carlos is from Mexico.
    B: From Mexico? Are you sure?
    A: Yes. I'm positive.

    A: That man is a movie star.
    B: A movie star? Are you sure?
    A: Yes. Absolutely.

Ask students to have similar conversations as Pair Work. Put the following statements on the board. Have students repeat the underlined words and use one of the following expressions to answer: Yes. I'm positive. OR Yes. Absolutely.

1. That woman is a pilot.
2. Her name is Nancy Paine.
3. She's from New York.
4. It's five o'clock.
5. Nick's at the garage.
6. The garage is on Main Street.

▶**PRONUNCIATION TIPS**
Or is used to show alternatives. It is important to note that there is a change in the intonation pattern of a question with an *or* alternative.

Is Tony a singer?/ (rising intonation)
Is Tony a dancer?/ (rising intonation)
Is Tony a singer/ or a dancer?\ (first rising, then falling)

STRESS

doctor	expensive	behind
student	intelligent	garage
hospital	American	police
favorite	museum	hotel
telephone	umbrella	today
dangerous	mechanic	tonight

INTONATION

Where's Anne?　　Are you hungry?　　Is Tony a singer or a dancer?

She's at work.　　Yes, I am.　　He's a singer.

STRESS AND INTONATION

Excuse me. Are you a tourist?　　Is John a doctor?

Yes, I am.　　No, he isn't. He's a banker.

Are you English?　　What city is he from?

No, I'm not.　　He's from Wickam City.

What nationality are you?

I'm American.

Is your name Barney or Fred?

My name is Barney.

TO BE Affirmative

He She It	's (is)	
I	'm (am)	in the library.
You We They	're (are)	

Negative

He She It	isn't (is not) 's not	
I	'm not (am not)	in the library.
You We They	aren't (are not) 're not	

Interrogative

Is	he she it	
Am	I	in the library?
Are	you we they	

Short Answers

	he she it	is.		he she it	isn't.
Yes,	I	am.	No,	I	'm not.
	you we they	are.		you we they	aren't.

ADJECTIVES AND WORD ORDER

The city The buildings	is are	beautiful. modern.	It's They're	a beautiful city. modern buildings.

PREPOSITIONS

Albert is Lúcia is She's	with from by	Mr. Watkins. Rio de Janeiro. the window.

PLURALS

bus	buses	city	cities
watch	watches	library	libraries
glass	glasses	secretary	secretaries

Irregular

man	men
woman	women
child	children

Chapter

TOPICS
Numbers and time (continued)
Furniture
Emergencies
Locations

GRAMMAR
Imperative
Object pronouns

FUNCTIONS
Giving and understanding commands
Asking for and telling the time
Reporting an emergency
Inquiring about location
Asking about prices

Listen and repeat.

Close your book.

Stand up.

Go to the blackboard.

Write your name.

Sit down.

Be quiet.

CHAPTER 3

PAGE SUMMARY
STRUCTURE: Imperatives

► FUNCTIONS
Giving commands

► NEW ELEMENTS

be	close	eat	imperative
go	laugh	quiet	
stand	write	sit	

► GRAMMAR
The imperative form in English is the simple root form of the verb. The person to whom the directions are given is *you*. (I want **you** to close your book. = Close your book.)

► PRELIMINARY ORAL WORK

Imperative
Give commands by making gestures. Get students to act as models.

> Teacher: _____, stand up.
>   Sit down.

Give several commands: Stand up. Go to the blackboard. Write your name. Take your seat. Open your book. etc.

► IDEAS FOR INSTRUCTION

Structure
Use the tape to introduce the lesson. As you and the students listen to the tape, you do what the tape instructs. The first time through, the students will probably want to follow along with the words in the text, but encourage them to follow the directions for actions with you on the second playing. On the third playing, ask that they do the actions and repeat with the tape.

When they seem comfortable with following the directions, turn the tape off and mix up the commands.

Expansion Activities
1. Explain that *please* is used to give orders more politely. *Please* gets a secondary stress.

> **Please** close your **books.**
> **Please stand up.**

2. A version of the games "Simon Says" or "Captain, may I?" can be played with this lesson. First, brainstorm a list of commands with your students and write their answers on the board:

Stand up.	Sit down.
Open your book.	Go to the blackboard.
Write your name on the board.	
Write your teacher's name on the blackboard.	
(etc.)	

Then make two teams and ask the members of each team to stand in a line. Give a command to the first person in Team A. The person must ask, "May I please?" after hearing the command and before doing it. If a person forgets to ask permission, that person must leave the game (sit down). Alternate between teams A and B. The team with more people still standing at the end of the game wins.

3. Form a circle with all members of the class. The teacher starts the game. He or she turns to the student on the right and gives a command. The student has two options: perform the action or ask another person to do so. The next student, the one to the student's right, must follow the order. The next student comes up with another command and turns to the student on the right, who has the same two options.

► PRONUNCIATION TIPS
Close your **book.**
Stand up.
Go to the **blackboard.**
Write your **name.**
Sit down.
Be quiet.

PAGE SUMMARY

STRUCTURE: Imperatives *(continued)*; making commands or requests in the negative

▶**FUNCTIONS**

Giving negative commands

▶**NEW ELEMENTS**

don't	**op**en
write	room
leave	eat
laugh	talk
window	class
leave	

▶**GRAMMAR**

The negative imperative = Don't + base form.

▶**PRELIMINARY ORAL WORK**

Give negative commands:

Teacher: Listen.
            Don't talk.
            Don't write.
            Don't open your book.

▶**IDEAS FOR INSTRUCTION**

Structure

Use the tape to provide other voice models.

Expansion Activity

Brainstorm a list of action verb phrases with the class: stand up, sit down, open the window/door, talk, eat something, leave, laugh, close your book, open your book. Write them on the board. Make a stack of ten cards—five with + and five with –. Turn these cards upside down. One student at a time (alternating from two teams, if your students like competition) goes to pick up a + or – card. The teacher (or a student referee) points to one of the phrases on the board. The student must make the sentence according to the + or – (affirmative or negative) and the phrase that is indicated.

▶**PRONUNCIATION TIPS**

Don't **talk.**
Don't **write** on the **tab**le.
Don't **op**en the **wind**ow.
Don't **eat** in **class.**
Don't **leave** the **room.**
Don't **laugh.**

Don't talk.

Don't write on the table.

Don't open the window.

Don't eat in class.

Don't leave the room.

Don't laugh.

Listen and repeat.

Hello, Johnnie. Come with <u>me</u>.

Oh, this bottle! Please open <u>it</u>.

There's Barbara and Tino.
Let's talk with <u>them</u>.

Peter is a very good dancer. Look at <u>him</u>.

Come and sit with <u>us</u>, Peter.

There's Alice. Go and talk with <u>her</u>.

PAGE SUMMARY

STRUCTURE: Substituting singular and plural nouns with object pronouns

▶**FUNCTIONS**
Giving commands

▶**NEW ELEMENTS**
come   object **pro**nouns
him
them
us

▶**GRAMMAR**
The pronoun replaces the noun to prevent repetition.

▶**PRELIMINARY ORAL WORK**

Introduce Object Pronouns

Teacher: Look at _____. (Point to a male student.) Look at him!
Look at _____. (Point to a female student.) Look at her.
Look at _____. (Point to both students.) Look at them.
Look at _____ and me. (Point to a student and yourself.) Look at us.
Look at the clock. (Point to the clock.) Look at it.

▶**IDEAS FOR INSTRUCTION**

Structure
First just listen to the tape with the students; then as they listen, they should repeat. Write the sentences on the board, circling the nouns and pronouns. Draw arrows between the object pronouns and the nouns that they replace. With the first sentence, the context makes clear that the woman is speaking to the man. Draw an arrow to the woman. When you write the second sentence on the board, you can show that the sentence still makes sense with "the bottle": "Oh, this bottle! Please open the bottle." It is important for students to recognize that the noun must be used at the beginning of the sentence; the pronoun cannot occur before the person knows what the real noun is.

Use the third and fourth sentences (on the board) to check whether students understand what the object pronouns stand for.

"There's Barbara and Tino. Let's talk with Barbara and Tino (them)."

"Peter is a very good dancer. Look at Peter (him)."

First underline the object pronouns, and then ask the students to draw the arrows. For the last two, ask the students to draw arrows to the drawings of the people to whom the pronouns refer.

Expansion Activity
Draw this chart on the board.

singular	plural
me	us
you	you
him, her, it	them

When students have shown that they understand the connection between the object and the object pronoun, refer them to the chart on the next page.

PAGE SUMMARY

PRACTICE and **WRITTEN EXERCISE:** Substituting object pronouns for nouns using chart as review

---

▶FUNCTIONS
Giving commands

▶NEW ELEMENTS
her	**com**mands
in**cred**ible	**make**
look at	**write**
really (adv)	

▶GRAMMAR
The pronoun must match the word it replaces in number (singular or plural) and gender (masculine or feminine). Because pronouns change according to whether they are subjects or objects, the correct inflected form must be used.

▶IDEAS FOR INSTRUCTION

Expansion Activity
After the students have filled in the blanks, ask them to take out a clean sheet of paper and make a dictation out of selected items from the two exercises. You read the sentence with the noun, and they write the sentence with the pronoun forms in place of the noun.

▶PRONUNCIATION TIPS
Note that the strong stress moves when a pronoun is used, and only one stress is used in the sentence:

Look at **Pet**er.	**Look** at the **clock.**
Look at him.	**Look** at it.

Practice the loss of the one stress with the students by repeating the sentences and having them imitate.

▶ANSWERS

Practice
1. He is very happy.
2. She is beautiful.
3. It is big.
4. They are really tall.
5. We are good dancers.
6. She is a bad dancer.
7. He is sad.
8. They are very pretty.

Written Exercise
1. Close ___it___.
2. Open ___them___.
3. Talk with ___her___.
4. Come with ___us___.
5. Dance with ___him___.
6. Look at ___them___.
7. Ask ___her___.
8. Repeat ___it___.

OBJECT PRONOUNS

Look at <u>Peter</u>.	Look at <u>him</u>.
Look at <u>Maria</u>.	Look at <u>her</u>.
Look at <u>Barbara and Tino</u>.	Look at <u>them</u>.
Look at <u>Johnnie and me</u>.	Look at <u>us</u>.
Look at <u>the clock</u>.	Look at <u>it</u>.

PRACTICE • *Make commands.*

Gladys is really strong. **Look at <u>her</u>.**	That cat is incredible. **Look at <u>it</u>.**

1. <u>Tino</u> is very happy.
2. <u>Barbara</u> is beautiful.
3. <u>That dog</u> is big.
4. <u>Those girls</u> are really tall.
5. <u>Peter and I</u> are good dancers.
6. <u>Alice</u> is a bad dancer.
7. <u>Johnnie</u> is sad.
8. <u>Those flowers</u> are very pretty.

WRITTEN EXERCISE • *Write sentences with object pronouns.*

Sit with <u>Johnnie and me</u>. *Sit with us*

1. Close <u>the door</u>. _____

2. Open <u>the windows</u>. _____

3. Talk with <u>Alice</u>. _____

4. Come with <u>Barbara and me</u>. _____

5. Dance with <u>Peter</u>. _____

6. Look at <u>those girls</u>. _____

7. Ask <u>Maria</u>. _____

8. Repeat <u>the question</u>. _____

Listen and repeat.

PRACTICE • *Give commands to other students in your class using these verbs:*

show	give	point (to)
put	bring	open
take	look at	close

Show me your watch.   **Give this pen to Nobu.**   **Point to the clock.**

PAGE SUMMARY
CARTOON STORY: Following orders
PRACTICE: Giving commands

▶ **FUNCTIONS**
Giving directions, doing things for others (indirect objects)

▶ **NEW ELEMENTS**

bring	call	candles	cartoon
dinner	dishes	father	give
light (v)	matches	me (as IO)	now
pen	point to	put	ready
shelf	show	story	take to + IO

▶ **GRAMMAR**
The book introduces indirect objects inductively; you do not need to offer a grammar explanation. However, some students may want one. If so, point out that the two ways that an indirect object (the receiver of the direct object, the person for whom or to whom it is done) is used are shown here:

a. Show me your watch.
   The object is watch; the watch is shown to me. Therefore, me is the indirect object.
b. Give this pen to Nobu.
   The pen is what is given. Therefore, pen is the direct object. The person to whom it is given is Nobu. Nobu is the indirect object.

▶ **PRELIMINARY ORAL WORK**
Indirect Object

Teacher:	Here you are. (Hand a pen to a student.) _____, give me the pen.
Student:	Here you are. (Hand the pen back to the teacher.)
Teacher:	Thank you. (Whisper "you're welcome" and motion for the student to repeat.)
Student:	You're welcome.

Get students to give each other commands:

Teacher:	_____, ask _____ to give you the book. (Point to student's book.)

Student 1:	_____, give me the book. (Points to book.)
Student 2:	Here you are. (Hands book to first student.)
Student 1:	Thank you. (Takes book from second student.)
Student 2:	You're welcome.

Bring in other verbs and pronouns: Take her, him, them the newspaper. Bring, show, give us the dictionary, etc.

▶ **IDEAS FOR INSTRUCTION**
Cartoon Story
While you play the tape, ask students to listen and read along. If you can, bring some realia to the classroom so that the students can act out the cartoon story: plastic dishes, candles and candle holders, an apron, and some matches.

Expansion Activity
Ask the students to role-play the story as it is in the cartoon; then, assign them to groups of three or four and let them create their own cartoon stories.

Help students in this task by displaying other items that they might use in their stories: a vase, plastic flowers, toy animals, books, a cloth for the table, etc. Put some sample sentences on the board.

▶ **PRONUNCIATION TIPS**
Note that the first balloon of the cartoon story contains a noun of direct address. Point out that a person's name (the person being spoken to) gets a rising intonation.

Bring me the **dish**es, **Jim**my./

▶ **ANSWERS**
Practice
Examples:

Show me your watch.
Put the dishes on the table.
Take these candles from me.
Give me your matches.
Bring that book to me.

Look at this picture.
Point to the table.
Open a window.
Close the door.

PAGE SUMMARY

PAIR WORK 1 and **2**: Asking questions about location

►FUNCTION
Locating things

►NEW ELEMENTS
oranges (as fruit)   **wall**

►GRAMMAR
Review of *on* as a preposition of location

►IDEAS FOR INSTRUCTION

Pair Work 1 and 2
On was presented in Chapter 1, but review this preposition by putting several familiar objects on your desk:

"This is my pencil."   (Hold it up for all to see.)

"It's **on** the desk."   (Put it on the desk.)

Be sure that the students know all of the words pertaining to the items in the picture. You can check by pointing to the items in the book. To facilitate this process, you could make a transparency of the picture and point out the items on the overhead projector.

You could also check for students' security with the vocabulary by reading off a list of items and asking the students to draw pictures of the items that you call out: pencil, glasses, oranges, vase, books, pots, cups, cards, etc.

Expansion Activity
Play "I Spy." Assemble a dozen or so items (realia) that are familiar to the students. The students should review the names of the objects as you hold them up. Then, while you place each item in a location *on something else* around the room, have one student write the names of the objects on the board. When all of the items are placed, students take turns. Student A goes to the board and points to one object's name. This student calls on a member of the other team to tell where the item is:

"Matches: The matches are on the bookcase."

If student B answers correctly, then she/he goes to the board and asks another student a question, etc. If a student misses an answer, the person at the board stays there and points to another object name.

Variation: Give the students a list of places (on the floor, on the wall, on the teacher's desk, on the bookcase, etc.) and ask them to name something that is *on* that place.

►PRONUNCIATION TIPS
Note that the preposition does not get a strong or a secondary stress unless the location contrasts of *pen* become important, as in this example:

The pen isn't **on** the desk; it's **under** the desk.

►ANSWERS

Pair Work 1
1. Where are the cups?
   They're on the shelf.
2. Where are the pots?
   They're on the wall.
3. Where are the books?
   They're on the chair.
4. Where are the flowers?
   They're in the vase.
5. Where are the magazines?
   They're on the floor.
6. Where are the candles?
   They're on the table.
7. Where are the glasses?
   They're on the shelf.
8. Where are the oranges?
   They're on the table.
9. Where are the dishes?
   They're on the shelf.

Pair Work 2
1. Are the glasses on the shelf?
   Yes, they are.
2. Are the candles on the shelf?
   No, they aren't. They're on the table.
3. Are the magazines on the chair?
   No, they aren't. They're on the floor.
4. Are the books on the chair?
   Yes, they are.
5. Are the dishes on the shelf?
   Yes, they are.
6. Are the cups on the table?
   No, they aren't. They're on the shelf.
7. Are the pots on the floor?
   No, they aren't. They're on the wall.
8. Are the cards on the floor?
   Yes, they are.

PAIR WORK 1 • *Ask and answer questions.*

> cards
> A: **Where are the cards?**
> B: **They're on the floor.**
>
> pots
> A: **Where are the pots?**
> B: **They're on the wall.**

1. cups
2. pots
3. books
4. flowers
5. magazines
6. candles
7. glasses
8. oranges
9. dishes

PAIR WORK 2 • *Ask and answer questions.*

> oranges/table?
> A: **Are the oranges on the table?**
> B: **Yes, they are.**
>
> dishes/table?
> A: **Are the dishes on the table?**
> B: **No, they aren't. They're on the shelf.**

1. glasses/shelf?
2. candles/shelf?
3. magazines/chair?
4. books/chair?
5. dishes/shelf?
6. cups/table?
7. pots/floor?
8. cards/floor?

CONVERSATION

 Listen and practice.

MR. BASCOMB: Good morning, Barbara.

BARBARA: Good morning, Mr. Bascomb. Here's a message from Mr. Grand.

MR. BASCOMB: Ah, yes. Please call him. Tell him the meeting is at ten o'clock.

BARBARA: Yes, sir. Is this an important meeting?

MR. BASCOMB: Very important. Mr. Grand is a big man in this city.

BARBARA: So are you, Mr. Bascomb.

MR. BASCOMB: Thanks, Barbara.

PAGE SUMMARY
CONVERSATION: Taking and relaying messages

▶**FUNCTIONS**

Giving information about time and place

▶**NEW ELEMENTS**

Here's . . .
im**port**ant
a **mess**age
tell
So you **are.**

▶**GRAMMAR**

Tell + indirect object (that) + sentence.
"Tell   him   (that)   the meeting is at
                                ten o'clock."

This form, which is an embedded sentence, need
not be difficult if the students understand it as a
chunk of meaning and do not attempt to figure out
the grammar.

▶**IDEAS FOR INSTRUCTION**

Conversation

Use the tape to familiarize students with the conversation. Ask students to role-play the conversation after they have listened to it a number of times.

▶**PRONUNCIATION TIPS**

These sentences might be unusual in their stress and intonation patterns.

Here's a **mess**age from **Mr. Grand**.
Very im**port**ant.
So are **you**, **Mr. Bas**comb./ (Note that the
  speaker's voice rises with *Mr. Bascomb*.)

PAGE SUMMARY

PAIR WORK: Taking and relaying messages; using object pronouns

▶ **FUNCTIONS**

Giving information about time and place

▶ **NEW ELEMENTS**

sir (title of respect, for men)
ma'am (title of respect, for women)

▶ **GRAMMAR**

Review

▶ **IDEAS FOR INSTRUCTION**

Pair Work

Assign a numbered item to each pair of students. Ask them to recite the message that they compose from the information in the book. Ask each pair of students to recite their dialogues.

▶ **PRONUNCIATION TIPS**

A: **Good morn**ing.
B: **Good morn**ing, _____/. Here's a **mess**age from _____.
A: **Ah**\, **yes**\. Please **call** _(object pronoun)_. Tell _____ the **meet**ing is at _(time)_.

▶ **ANSWERS**

Pair Work

(Students may use other characters' names or their own names in the greetings.)

1. A: Good morning, Barbara.
   B: Good morning, Mr. Bascomb. Here's a message from Otis and Gloria.
   A: Ah, yes. Please call them. Tell them the meeting is at one o'clock.
   B: Yes, sir.
2. A: Good morning, Albert.
   B: Good morning, Mrs. Golo. Here's a message from Maria.
   A: Ah, yes. Please call her. Tell her the meeting is at five o'clock.
   B: Yes, ma'am.
3. A: Good morning, Barbara.
   B: Good morning, Mrs. Bascomb. Here's a message from Johnnie.
   A: Ah, yes. Please call him. Tell him the meeting is at twelve o'clock.
   B: Yes, ma'am.
4. A: Good morning, Barney.
   B: Good morning, Mr. Moto. Here's a message from Anne.
   A: Ah, yes. Please call her. Tell her the meeting is at eight o'clock.
   B: Yes, sir.
5. A: Good morning, Anne.
   B: Good morning, Mr. Bascomb. Here's a message from Tino and Barbara.
   A: Ah, yes. Please call them. Tell them the meeting is at three o'clock.
   B: Yes, sir.

6. A: Good morning, Barbara.
   B: Good morning, Mr. Bascomb. Here's a message from Nick.
   A: Ah, yes. Please call him. Tell him the meeting is at six o'clock.
   B: Yes, sir.
7. A: Good morning, Nancy.
   B: Good morning, Mr. Moto. Here's a message from Fred and Barney.
   A: Ah, yes. Please call them. Tell them the meeting is at nine o'clock.
   B: Yes, sir.
8. A: Good morning, Fred.
   B: Good morning, Mrs. Golo. Here's a message from Mr. Moto.
   A: Ah, yes. Please call him. Tell him the meeting is at four o'clock.
   B: Yes, ma'am.
9. A: Good morning, Barbara.
   B: Good morning, Mr. Bascomb. Here's a message from Mrs. Golo.
   A: Ah, yes. Please call her. Tell her the meeting is at eleven o'clock.
   B: Yes, sir.

PAIR WORK • *Have conversations like the one on page 42.*

A: Good morning, _____.

B: Good morning, _____. Here's a message from _____.

A: Ah, yes. Please call _____. Tell _____ the meeting is at _____.

B: Yes, sir/ma'am.

1. Otis and Gloria
   them

2. Maria
   her

3. Johnnie
   him

4. Anne

5. Tino and
   Barbara

6. Nick

7. Fred and Barney

8. Mr. Moto

9. Mrs. Golo

Listen and repeat.

twenty-one

twenty-two

twenty-three

twenty-four

twenty-five

twenty-six

twenty-seven

twenty-eight

twenty-nine

thirty

forty

fifty

sixty

seventy

eighty

ninety

one hundred

two hundred ten

three hundred forty

four hundred sixty

PAGE SUMMARY
NEW VOCABULARY: Two- and three-digit numbers

▶**FUNCTIONS**
Using numbers

▶**NEW ELEMENTS**
The numbers are all new.

▶**GRAMMAR**
None

▶**IDEAS FOR INSTRUCTION**

New Vocabulary
Have the students listen to and repeat after the tape. When the students have begun saying the words correctly, write some numbers on the board and ask for four to six volunteers to come to the board. When you call out one of the numbers, each student should attempt to point out the number first.

Expansion Activity
Play the game of "Rhythm." On large pieces of paper, with dark felt-tip pens, write different two- or three-digit numbers, one for each student. Ask the students to form a circle with the number either pinned to the front of their shirts or at their feet on the floor. When everyone is ready, start the rhythm, counting out six beats: Each person makes two light slaps on the tops of his or her own thighs, two hand claps, and then two finger-snappings. At the first finger snap, the first person says his or her own number and then, on the second snap, the number of another student. Then the second student does the same thing, first his or her own number and then the number of a third student. Start this game off slowly! Let it build speed as the students become more familiar with the process.

▶**PRONUNCIATION TIPS**
Teach students the difference between the pronunciation of *thirteen* and *thirty, fourteen* and *forty,* etc. The "teen" numbers have a strong stress and a secondary stress. The last syllable of the *-ty* numbers gets no stress.

thirteen	**thir**ty
fourteen	**for**ty
fifteen	**fif**ty
sixteen	**six**ty
seventeen	**seven**ty
eighteen	**eigh**ty
nineteen	**nine**ty

PAGE SUMMARY

CONVERSATION and **PAIR WORK:** Asking and answering questions about prices

▶**FUNCTIONS**
Buying furniture

▶**NEW ELEMENTS**
bed couch desk dresser **lamp price so**fa **salesman** "**Have** a nice **day**."

▶**GRAMMAR**
Review

▶**IDEAS FOR INSTRUCTION**

Conversation
Listen to the tape. After three times, ask two students to act out the conversation. If possible, provide some prop to be a lamp and a wallet full of green colored paper as money.

Expansion Activity
Make price tags for various items about the classroom. Give the students "play money," which you can make out of strips of colored paper, to buy the furniture. Items to tag in your classroom: chalk, the board itself, desks, bookcase, teacher's desk, chairs.

▶**PRONUNCIATION TIPS**
There are no surprises in the conversation.

▶**ANSWERS**

Pair Work

1. A: That's a beautiful lamp.
   B: You're right.
   A: How much is it?
   B: Seventy-eight dollars.
   A: That's a good price. Here you are.
   B: Thank you. Have a nice day.
2. A: That's a beautiful table.
   B: You're right.
   A: How much is it?
   B: One hundred and sixty dollars.
   A: That's a good price. Here you are.
   B: Thank you. Have a nice day.
3. A: That's a beautiful chair.
   B: You're right.
   A: How much is it?
   B: Forty-five dollars.
   A: That's a good price. Here you are.
   B: Thank you. Have a nice day.
4. A: That's a beautiful desk.
   B: You're right.
   A: How much is it?
   B: Three hundred dollars.
   A: That's a good price. Here you are.
   B: Thank you. Have a nice day.
5. A: That's a beautiful easy chair.
   B: You're right.
   A: How much is it?
   B: Two hundred and twenty-five dollars.
   A: That's a good price. Here you are.
   B: Thank you. Have a nice day.

6. A: That's a beautiful sofa.
   B: You're right.
   A: How much is it?
   B: Four hundred and eighty dollars.
   A: That's a good price. Here you are.
   B: Thank you. Have a nice day.
7. A: That's a beautiful bed.
   B: You're right.
   A: How much is it?
   B: Five hundred dollars.
   A: That's a good price. Here you are.
   B: Thank you. Have a nice day.
8. A: That's a beautiful dresser.
   B: You're right.
   A: How much is it?
   B: Two hundred and ninety dollars.
   A: That's a good price. Here you are.
   B: Thank you. Have a nice day.

Listen and practice.

MR. BASCOMB: That's a beautiful lamp.

SALESMAN: You're right.

MR. BASCOMB: How much is it?

SALESMAN: Seventy-eight dollars.

MR. BASCOMB: That's a good price. Here you are.

SALESMAN: Thank you. Have a nice day.

PAIR WORK • *Have similar conversations.*

A: That's a beautiful _____.

B: You're right.

A: How much is it?

B: _____ dollars.

A: That's a good price. Here you are.

B: Thank you. Have a nice day.

1. lamp   2. table   3. chair   4. desk

5. easy chair   6. sofa   7. bed   8. dresser

 *Listen and repeat.*

1

It's six o'clock.

5

It's fifteen minutes past eight.
It's (a) quarter past eight.

2

It's seven o'clock.

6

It's thirty minutes past eight.
It's half past eight.

3

It's ten minutes past seven.
It's seven ten.

7

It's fifteen minutes to ten.
It's (a) quarter to ten.

4

It's twenty minutes past seven.
It's seven twenty.

8

It's five minutes to ten.

TIME: Reading time from an analog clock on the half and quarter hours

▶**FUNCTIONS**

Telling time

▶**NEW ELEMENTS**

half **past**
fifteen **min**utes past the **hour**
half past the **hour**
quarter to the **hour**
quarter after the **hour**
It's **seven** **ten** (7:10).

▶**GRAMMAR**

Past and *after* both refer to times in the first sweep
of the hands, between 12 and 6. Between the 6 and
12 the time is told by *to* the hour.

▶**IDEAS FOR INSTRUCTION**

Time

Have students listen to the tape and practice the
different ways of telling time. You can stop the tape
after they have heard it several times and ask them
for other ways of saying the same time.

Expansion Activity

Bring paper plates, markers, a hole punch, and a
butterfly tack to make clock faces in class. When
students have finished their clocks, call out a time
and have the students hold up their clocks with
that time showing.

▶**PRONUNCIATION TIPS**

If the person knows the approximate time, the
actual hour may not be stated. In this case, the
stress is in an interesting place.

A: What **time** is it?
B: It's **half** **past**.

A: What **time** is it?
B: It's quarter **after**.

PAGE SUMMARY

PAIR WORK: Telling time accurate to the minute
NEW VOCABULARY: Times of day

▶FUNCTIONS

Asking for and telling the time

▶NEW ELEMENTS

after**noon**   evening   **mid**night
morning   **noon**

▶GRAMMAR

There are several ways to tell time. The most modern is to say the two numbers as if reading a digital clock: 4:10 = four ten. However, at midday and in the middle of the night, the words *noon* and *midnight* prevail.

▶IDEAS FOR INSTRUCTION

Pair Work

Ask students to do the Pair Work after you have gone over 1, 2, and 3 with them in class.

Repeat the new vocabulary section at the bottom of the page to be sure that the students have the right rhythm in the sentences.

▶PRONUNCIATION TIPS

See answers below.
It's **noon.**
It's **mid**night.
It's **sev**en o'**clock** in the **eve**ning.

▶ANSWERS

Pair Work

2. "It's **ten** thirty-**five.**" *or* "It's **twen**ty-five minutes to e**lev**en."
3. "It's **nine** o'**clock.**
4. "It's **one-twenty.**" *or* "It's **twenty** past **one.**"
5. "It's **one** for**ty-five.**" *or* "It's **quar**ter to **two.**"
6. "It's **eight-thir**ty." *or* "It's **half** past **eight**."

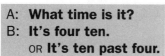

A: **What time is it?**
B: **It's four ten.**
    OR **It's ten past four.**

N E W   V O C A B U L A R Y   •   TIMES OF DAY

 Listen and repeat.

It's noon.

It's midnight.

Morning is from
midnight to noon.

Afternoon is
from noon to six.

Evening is from
six to midnight.

Listen and practice.

PAGE SUMMARY
CARTOON STORY: Reporting a fire

▶**FUNCTIONS**
Reporting an emergency

▶**NEW ELEMENTS**
across (the street)
ad**dress**
e**mer**gency
fire
fire de**part**ment
house
near
on **fire**

▶**GRAMMAR**
Idiom: be on fire
across as a preposition

▶**IDEAS FOR INSTRUCTION**
This page begins the Review Section for Chapter 3.

Cartoon Story
Use the tape to introduce the first part of the Cartoon Story. After hearing it a number of times, students should role-play the action of the Cartoon Story.

▶**PRONUNCIATION TIPS**
A: He**llo**?/ (rising) **Fire**/ De**part**ment?/ (rising intonation)
B: What **is** it,\ ma'am?/ (first falling and then rising intonation)
A: My **house** is on **fire.**\ (falling)
B: What's your ad**dress**?\
A: It's **one eighty-three Map**le Street.\
B: Is that near the post office?/ (rising)
A: **Yes.**\ It's a**cross** the **street.**\

▶**FUNCTIONS**

Reporting an emergency

▶**NEW ELEMENTS**

all **right**
dangerous
hurry
little
one (as pronoun)
out**side** (adverb)
right a**way**
wait for (someone)
worry

▶**GRAMMAR**

The superlative *too* + adjective
    ("No fire is too big for us.")
Alternatives with *or* ("Is it a big fire or a little
    one?")
Use of *one* as a pronoun ("Is it a big fire or a
    little one [fire]?")

▶**IDEAS FOR INSTRUCTION**

Cartoon Story

Practice this dialogue several times with the tape,
and then ask students to role-play the parts.

▶**PRONUNCIATION TIPS**

Practice these sentences for the rhythm of
language.

It's all **right. Don't wor**ry.
Be **care**ful. That's **dang**erous!
Please hurry!
It's a **litt**le **fire.** Not a **big one.** (*One* is used as a
    pronoun here.)
Please **wait** for me out**side.**
Please **come** right a**way.**

STORY QUESTIONS

1. Why is Mrs. Golo worried?
2. What's her address?
3. Is her house far from the post office?
4. Is the post office on Lime Street?
5. Is it a big fire or a little one?
6. Is Mrs. Golo in the house now?
7. Is it dangerous?
8. What is the phone number for emergencies in the United States? in your country?

PRACTICE 1 • *Make commands.*

These glasses are dirty. (wash)
Wash them.

Maria isn't ready. (wait for)
Wait for her.

1. The door is open. (close)
2. There's Barbara. (talk to)
3. Tino is at home. (call)
4. I'm your friend. (listen to)
5. Here's Mrs. Golo. (ask)
6. Mr. and Mrs. Lee are in France. (write to)
7. Those are beautiful pictures. (look at)
8. Peter is a very good dancer. (dance with)

PRACTICE 2 • *Make commands. Use a verb with each of the words.*

book **Open the book.** OR **Close the book.**

sentence **Read the sentence.** OR **Repeat the sentence.**

Mrs. Golo **Ask Mrs. Golo.** OR **Listen to Mrs. Golo.**

1. door
2. teacher
3. picture
4. Maria
5. magazine
6. window
7. letter
8. question
9. fire department

PAIR WORK • *Ask and answer questions about the picture on page 51. Use **between, next to,** and **across . . . from** in your answers.*

the State Bank/City Park
A: **Excuse me, where's the State Bank?**
B: **It's across the street from City Park.**
A: **Thank you.**

the Rex Theater/Mom's Cafe
A: **Excuse me, where's the Rex Theater?**
B: **It's next to Mom's Cafe.**
A: **Thank you.**

the barber shop/the flower shop and the supermarket
A: **Excuse me, where's the barber shop?**
B: **It's between the flower shop and the supermarket.**
A: **Thank you.**

1. the church/City Park
2. the parking lot/the supermarket and the Grand Hotel
3. the flower shop/the barber shop
4. the drug store/the church and the gas station
5. the Grand Hotel/Olson's Department Store
6. the gas station/the drug store
7. Mom's Cafe/the Rex Theater and the State Bank
8. the book store/the post office
9. the supermarket/the church

PAGE SUMMARY
STORY QUESTIONS: Follow-up of cartoon story
PRACTICE 1 and **2:** Making commands
PAIR WORK: Review of prepositions of location

▶ **FUNCTIONS**
Giving directions and commands; giving location

▶ **NEW ELEMENTS**

ask	**drug** store	read
barber	**dry**	re**peat**
be**tween**	**far** from	**shop**
ca**fe**	**Mom**	su**permark**et
church	**park**ing **lot**	**the**ater
city **park**	**phone**	**wash**
country	**num**ber	**worr**ied
de**part**ment	**pic**ture	
store	**ques**tion	

▶ **GRAMMAR**
Review

▶ **IDEAS FOR INSTRUCTION**

Story Questions
After the class has gone over the Cartoon Story, you can use the Story Questions as a comprehension quiz.

Questions 1 and 2 of the Story Questions ask for information. These are best done together as a class. The first question, in particular, needs to be addressed as a class discussion. Questions 3–7 are Yes/No questions and can be answered simply. Discuss the eighth question, as emergency numbers are important and likely to be different. In the U.S. the emergency number for all emergencies is 911. In most communities, a person does not call the police or the fire department at all; one calls 911.

Practice 1
The cause and effect relationship of meaning and the pronoun substitution and case change from subject to object are both part of this exercise. Write on the blackboard:

These glasses are dirty. Wash ___the glasses___.

_____ are dirty. Wash _____.

Under these glasses write "they". Then write "they → them" and under the glasses write "them" in the blank.

Do the same thing for the second example sentence:

Maria isn't ready. Wait for _____.
She isn't ready.
she → her   Wait for her.

Have the students do the same thing on the board with 1–8.

Practice 2
Students need to understand that only a certain number of words can co-occur with any one word. On the board, write: book, sentence, and Peter. Write in a column to the left of those two words, a list of verbs that the students know, but be aware that their answers may vary from these examples:

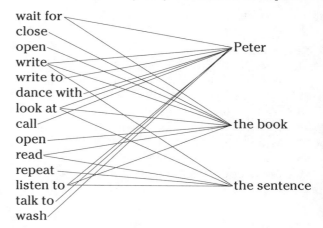

Then draw lines from the verbs to the nouns that work with them:

Wait for, write to, dance with, look at, call, listen to, talk to, and maybe even _wash_ all work with _Peter._
   Close, open, and _read_ work with _the book._
   Write, repeat, read, and _listen to_ work with _the sentence._

Have the students try the same thing with numbers 1–9 in the book.

▶ **ANSWERS**
See page T-51.

►ANSWERS

Story Questions

1. She's worried because her house is on fire.
2. It's 183 Maple Street.
3. No, it's across the street.
4. No, it's on Maple Street.
5. It's a very big fire.
6. Yes, she is.
7. Yes, it is.
8. (In the United States:) 911.

Practice 1

1. Close it.
2. Talk to her.
3. Call him.
4. Listen to me.
5. Ask her.
6. Write to them.
7. Look at them.
8. Dance with him.

Practice 2

1. Open, close, wash the door.
2. Wait for, write to, dance with, look at, call, listen to, talk to the teacher.
3. Look at the picture.
4. Wait for, write to, dance with, look at, call, listen to, talk to Maria.
5. Open, close, read the magazine.
6. Open, close, wash the window.

7. Open, close, read, wait for, listen to the letter.
8. Write, listen to, look at the question.
9. Wait for, call, listen to, talk to the fire department.

Pair Work

1. A: Excuse me, where's the church?
   B: It's across from City Park.
2. A: Excuse me, where's the parking lot?
   B: It's between the supermarket and the Grand Hotel.
3. A: Excuse me, where's the flower shop?
   B: It's next to the barber shop.
4. A: Excuse me, where's the drugstore?
   B: It's between the church and the gas station.
5. A: Excuse me, where's the Grand Hotel?
   B: It's across from Olson's Department Store.
6. A: Excuse me, where's the gas station?
   B: It's next to the drugstore.
7. A: Excuse me, where's Mom's Cafe?
   B: It's between the Rex Theater and the State Bank.
8. A: Excuse me, where's the book store?
   B: It's next to the post office.
9. A: Excuse me, where's the supermarket?
   B: It's across from the church.

WRITTEN EXERCISE • *Choose a command for each picture.*

Give me your money!   Dance with me!   Take me to the airport!
Don't worry!   Don't sit down!   Don't leave me!
Eat your dinner!   Don't touch me!   Answer the phone!

PAGE SUMMARY
WRITTEN EXERCISE: Choosing appropriate commands based on pictures

▶**FUNCTIONS**
Giving orders or commands

▶**NEW ELEMENTS**
answer (v.)
touch

▶**GRAMMAR**
Review

▶**IDEAS FOR INSTRUCTION**

Written Exercise
Read each of the commands. Ask students to find the situation that fits. Then have them write out the answers.

Expansion Activity
This series of pictures could be used for mini role-plays. Students can review and respiral what they have learned. Assign a picture to a group of students and ask them to make a dialogue about the situation. Ask them to perform the role-play for the rest of the class.

▶**PRONUNCIATION TIPS**
See Answers.

▶**ANSWERS**

Written Exercise
1. **An**swer the **phone**.
2. **Don't touch** me.
3. **Eat** your **din**ner!
4. **Don't** sit **down**!
5. **Give** me your **mon**ey!
6. **Don't leave** me!
7. **Take** me to the **air**port!
8. **Don't wor**ry!
9. **Dance** with me!

PAGE SUMMARY

CONVERSATIONS and **PAIR WORK:** Inquiring about prices
READING and **FREE RESPONSE:** Talking about your favorite store

---

▶**FUNCTIONS**

Asking about prices
Talking about a store (hours, atmosphere)

▶**NEW ELEMENTS**

every **day**   free re**sponse**
friendly
hours
socks

▶**GRAMMAR**

Review

▶**IDEAS FOR INSTRUCTION**

Conversations

Have the students listen to the tape and then repeat.

Prereading Activity

If students don't know what a department store is, name one the students are likely to know.
Say: _____ is a department store. Ask students if it is good and if it is expensive to help prepare them for this reading.

Reading

Listen to the tape of the reading and have the students read along with the voice on the tape. Have the students practice reading to each other in pairs. Discuss the questions with the class as a whole.

The students will need to know that some clothing items are considered to come in pairs and are therefore treated like plurals.

Singular (it)	Plural (they)
one sock	socks
dress	
one shoe	shoes
coat	
shirt	
	pants
sweater	
hat	

From a picture file, select items that fit both singular and plural models. Hold up one picture. Ask the students to choose one of the two options:

These are **nice. Buy** them.
It's **nice. Buy** it.

▶**PRONUNCIATION TIPS**

Practice pronouncing prices.

It's **se**venty-**five dol**lars.
They're **six dol**lars.
It's **nine**ty-**eight dol**lars.
They're **eigh**ty-**five dol**lars.
It's **one hund**red and **six**ty-**nine dol**lars.
It's **for**ty-**five dol**lars.
They're **eigh**ty **dol**lars.
It's **se**venty-**five dol**lars
It's **fif**ty **dol**lars.

▶**ANSWERS**

Pair Work

1. A: How much are these socks?
    B: They're six dollars.
2. A: How much is this dress?
    B: It's ninety-eight dollars.
3. A: How much are these shoes?
    B: They're eighty-five dollars.
4. A: How much is this coat?
    B: It's one hundred and sixty-nine dollars.
5. A: How much is this shirt?
    B: It's forty-five dollars.

6. A: How much are these pants?
    B: They're eighty dollars.
7. A: How much is this sweater?
    B: It's seventy-five dollars.
8. A: How much is this hat?
    B: It's fifty dollars.

Free Response

Answers will vary.

Listen and practice.

PAIR WORK • *Have similar conversations.*

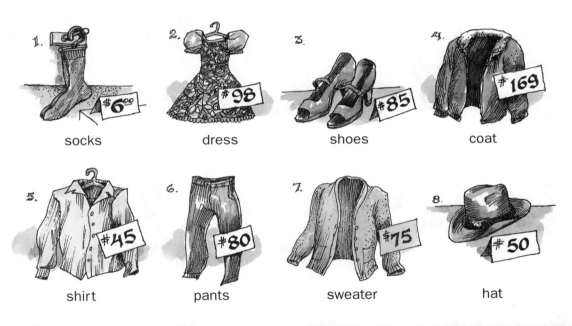

1. socks
2. dress
3. shoes
4. coat

5. shirt
6. pants
7. sweater
8. hat

READING

Olson's Department Store is on Star Avenue. It's open every day from nine to five. It's a very good store. It's not expensive and the salespeople are very friendly.

FREE RESPONSE

1. What's the name of your favorite store?
2. Where is it?
3. What hours is the store open?
4. Is it expensive?
5. Are the salespeople friendly?

GRAMMAR SUMMARY

IMPERATIVE

Close the door!
Open the window!

Negative Imperative

Don't	close the door! open the window!

With Noun Objects

Look at	Peter. Maria. Barbara and Tino. Johnnie and me. the clock.

With Object Pronouns

Look at	him. her. them. us. it.

With Two Objects

Give	Jimmy Linda the children Albert and me the dog	an apple.

With Object Pronouns

Give	him her them us it	an apple.

TIME

What time is it?	It's	six seven	o'clock.
		ten minutes twenty minutes	past seven.
		(a) quarter half	past eight.
		(a) quarter five minutes	to ten.

Question with HOW MUCH

How much	is the watch? are the books?	It's twenty-five dollars. They're ten dollars.

Review Chapter

4

Listen and practice.

CHAPTER 4

PAGE SUMMARY

CARTOON STORY: Three-page story reviewing Chapters 1–3

▶FUNCTIONS

Greetings, giving commands

▶NEW ELEMENTS

page 56:
- **as**pir**in**
- **mouth**
- **mouth**wash
- **Oh, my . . .**
- **pain**
- **teeth**

page 57:
- a**fraid**
- front **desk**
- **move**
- **nurse**
- **pay**
- "**Tell** her I'm **bus**y."
- "**You**'re in **good hands**."

page 58:
- **bill**
- **brush** (verb)
- **den**tal **floss**
- **huh?**
- **more**
- **use**

▶GRAMMAR

The expressions "It's **good** for your **teeth**" and "They're **good** for **pain**" are featured in this story.

▶IDEAS FOR INSTRUCTION

Cartoon Story

Use the tape to introduce the story. Play through all three pages. Then play one frame at a time, pausing to have the students repeat each sentence.

You can also divide the class into three sections. Have each section role-play one part: Dr. Molar, Miss Tracy, and Mr. Wilson. Emphasize the intonation and natural flow of speech, with each word smoothly flowing into the next.

Expansion Activities

1. When the class feels comfortable with the dialogue, groups of students can try to write their own role-plays for visits to the dentist's office, possibly based on their real experiences. As with any independent student oral work, encourage students to use realia.

2. This activity follows up on the pronunciation tip presented below. Form a circle with your students. Ask one student to begin calling the names of the people to his or her right, using the rising intonation. Each student should call three names for practice. Explain that any other intonation is considered rude and abrupt.

Intercultural Awareness

Discuss the benefits (and risks) of taking aspirin. Then ask students to fill in the blank: "_____ is good for pain." You can expect a number of different answers for this sentence.

▶PRONUNCIATION TIPS

This story presents nouns of direct address occurring in all three possible positions: at the beginning, in the middle, and at the end of an utterance.

> **Don't move**, Mr. **Wil**son./
> Get **up**, Mr. **Wil**son./ **Pay** Miss Tracy at the **front desk**.
> **Miss Tracy**,/ **please** leave the **room**.

When the name is being "called" (as in each of these examples except "Pay Miss Tracy . . ."), the intonation rises slightly at the end of the name. One way to practice this is to use counting as a model for calling.

Count slowly with your students to get the right lilt in the voice for a noun of direct address: one/ [rising], two/ [rising], three\ [falling, sign of the end of the utterance].

Then call the students' names in this way: Ann/ [rising], Jim/ [rising], Mark/ [rising], and Pat\ [falling indicates end of utterance].

Huh?/ with a rising intonation means "What did you say?"

PAGE SUMMARY

STORY QUESTIONS: Follow-up to cartoon story
FREE RESPONSE: Visiting the dentist
WRITTEN EXERCISE: Completing a form with personal information

---

▶FUNCTIONS

Giving information

▶NEW ELEMENTS

be in **good hands**
in**form**ation
occu**pa**tion
sugar
telephone
What's _____ for?

▶GRAMMAR

The kinds of questions that are asked on patient information forms with one-word signals.

▶IDEAS FOR INSTRUCTION

Story Questions

Ask the story questions, alternating between two groups of students. Accept short answers as natural use of language.

Free Response

Have students work in small groups to answer these questions. When the groups are finished, check the answers by having each group volunteer one answer.

Expansion Activity

To prepare for the written exercise, have pairs of students interview each other. One student can act as a receptionist, asking questions of a "new patient."

▶ANSWERS

Story Questions

1. At the dentist's office.
2. Ten o'clock.
3. The woman at the front desk/ the receptionist.
4. Dr. Molar.
5. Not good.
6. Next to the mouthwash.
7. It's good for pain.
8. At the front desk.
9. No, it's for the dentist.
10. Yes, he is.
11. Yes, he's in good hands.
12. Five hundred dollars.
13. It's good for your teeth.
14. [a matter of opinion]

Free Response

Answers will vary.

Written Exercise

Answers will vary.

STORY QUESTIONS

1. Where is Mr. Wilson?
2. What time is it?
3. Who is Miss Tracy?
4. What is the dentist's name?
5. How are Mr. Wilson's teeth?
6. Where is the aspirin?
7. What is aspirin good for?
8. Where is the telephone?
9. Is the call for Miss Tracy?
10. Is Dr. Molar busy?
11. Is Mr. Wilson in good hands?
12. How much is Mr. Wilson's dental bill?
13. What is dental floss good for?
14. Is Miss Tracy a good nurse?

FREE RESPONSE

1. Is your dentist like Dr. Molar?
2. What is your dentist's name?
3. Where is your dentist's office?
4. Is your dentist cheap or expensive?
5. Are you afraid when you are at the dentist's?
6. Is sugar good or bad for your teeth?

WRITTEN EXERCISE • *Print your name, address, telephone number, and occupation.*

Please complete this form.

• PATIENT INFORMATION FORM •

name: Johnnie Wilson

address: 802 Oak Street
street

Wickam City
city

California 90720
state   zip

phone: 425-9063

occupation: Businessman

• PATIENT INFORMATION FORM •

name: _____

address: _____
street

_____
city

_____
state   zip

phone: _____

occupation:

_____

PAIR WORK • *Ask and answer questions.*

A: Where are Joe and Eddie?
B: They're at the park.

A: Are they businessmen?
B: No, they aren't. (They're bums.)

A: Are they hot or cold?
B: They're cold.

A: Where's the cat?
B: It's in the tree.

A: Is it fat or thin?
B: It's fat.

A: Is it happy?
B: Yes, it is.

1. _____ Maria?
   _____ a doctor or a teacher?
   _____ ugly?

2. _____ Nick?
   _____ a mechanic?
   _____ old or young?

3. _____ Barbara and Anne?
   _____ teachers or secretaries?
   _____ busy?

4. _____ Tino?
   _____ banker?
   _____ tall or short?

PAGE SUMMARY

PAIR WORK: Asking and responding to questions containing *or*

▶FUNCTIONS
Describing things
Indicating location

▶NEW ELEMENTS
bums
busy
restaur**ant**

▶GRAMMAR
Questions with alternative answers
   signaled by *or*
Are they hot or cold?
Is it fat or thin?

▶IDEAS FOR INSTRUCTION

Pair Work
Ask that students practice the examples in pairs while you walk around the classroom and listen. Then have them fill in the blanks for questions 1–10 (on this page and page 61). Work with the students on the intonation. (See the **Pronunciation Tips** below.)

   When they have finished this exercise, have students write location questions (Where is/are . . . ?) and description questions ("Are they/ Is she or he . . . ?" and "Is/Are . . . or . . . ?") like the ones in the book. Then they can ask the questions of other students in the class.

Expansion Activities
1. You can have students play "Twenty Questions." Start the game by finding a familiar object in the room. Don't tell the students what it is, but tell them that they can ask you twenty Yes/No questions to determine what the object is and where it is in the room. After the students understand the game, choose a student to select an object and come to the front of the room to answer the questions.

2. A variation on this idea is to have a scorekeeper, who tallies the questions. Another useful variation is to ask one or two students to write the questions that are asked on the board. The game is over when either twenty questions have been asked or someone guesses the answer.

▶PRONUNCIATION TIPS
Questions that offer alternatives for the listener require a special intonation pattern. Like other Yes/No questions, the alternatives question at first has a rising intonation, but after *or* the intonation falls.

   Are they **hot** / or **cold**?\
   Is he **old** / or **young**?\

▶ANSWERS

Pair Work
1. A: **Where's** Maria?
   B: She's at the hospital.
   A: Is she a **doc**tor or a **teach**er?
   B: She's a **doc**tor.
   A: Is she **ug**ly?
   B: **No,** she **is**n't.
2. A: Where's **Nick**?
   B: He's at the gar**age.**
   A: Is he a me**chan**ic?
   B: Yes, he **is.**
   A: Is he **old** or **young**?
   B: He's **young.**

3. A: Where are **Bar**bara and **Anne**?
   B: They're at the **bank.**
   A: Are they **teach**ers or **sec**retar**ies**?
   B: They are **sec**retar**ies.**
   A: Are they **busy**?
   B: **Yes,** they **are.**
4. A: Where's **Tino**?
   B: He's at the **rest**aurant.
   A: Is he a **bank**er?
   B: No, he **is**n't.
   A: Is he **tall** or **short**?
   B: He's **tall.**

PAGE SUMMARY

PAIR WORK: (*continued*)

▶NEW ELEMENTS
None

▶GRAMMAR
Review

▶ANSWERS

Pair Work (continued)

5. A: Where's the **clock**?
   B: It's **next** to the **chair**.
   A: Is it **big** or **small**?
   B: It's **big**.
   A: Is it **old**?
   B: **Yes**, it **is**.

6. A: **Where** are the **app**les?
   B: They're on the **tab**le.
   A: Are they **red** or **green**?
   B: They're **red**.
   A: Are they **small**?
   B: **No,** they **aren't**.

7. A: **Where**'s the **wom**an?
   B: She's at the **bus stop**.
   A: Is she **young** or **old**?
   B: She's **old**.
   A: Is she **hap**py?
   B: **No,** she **isn't**.

8. A: **Where** are the **boys**?
   B: They're at the **park**.
   A: Are they **friends**?
   B: **Yes,** they **are**.
   A: Are they **clean** or **dir**ty?
   B: They're **dirty**.

9. A: **Where** are Mr. and Mrs. **Bas**comb?
   B: They're at the **res**taur**ant**.
   A: Are they **rich** or **poor**?
   B: They're **rich**.
   A: Are they a**fraid**?
   B: **Yes,** they **are**.

10. A: **Where**'s the Mer**ced**es?
    B: It's on the **street**.
    A: Is it **black** or **white**?
    B: It's **black**.
    A: Is it **cheap**?
    B: No, it **isn't**.

5. _____ the clock?
   _____ big or small?
   _____ old?

6. _____ the apples?
   _____ red or green?
   _____ small?

7. _____ the woman?
   _____ young or old?
   _____ happy?

8. _____ the boys?
   _____ friends?
   _____ clean or dirty?

9. _____ Mr. and Mrs. Bascomb?
   _____ rich or poor?
   _____ afraid?

10. _____ the Mercedes?
    _____ black or white?
    _____ cheap?

🔲 *Listen and practice.*

NANCY: Who's that?

GLORIA: His name's Tony Romero.

NANCY: He looks nice. Where's he from?

GLORIA: Spain.

NANCY: What's his occupation?

GLORIA: I'm not sure. I think he's a singer.

PAIR WORK • *Have similar conversations.*

A: Who's that?

B: _____.

A: He/she looks nice. Where's he/she from?

B: _____.

A: What's his/her occupation?

B: I'm not sure. I think he/she _____.

1. Laila Hassan/doctor

2. Nobu Moto/businessman

3. Fanta Mutombo/teacher

4. Diego Garcia/artist

5. Mary Wood/secretary

6. Ravi Patel/waiter

7. Natalya Romanov/dancer

8. Wong Wei/pilot

9. Antonia Morales/banker

PAGE SUMMARY

CONVERSATION and **PAIR WORK**: Discussing people's characteristics and occupations

▶**FUNCTIONS**

Asking questions about people and their occupations

▶**NEW ELEMENTS**

I'm **not sure.**
I **think** he's a **sing**er.
nice (adjective)
sure

▶**GRAMMAR**

The embedded clause after *I think* may seem troublesome at first. However, the concept can be explained in two parts:

I think something. + He's a singer. → I think he's a singer.

▶**IDEAS FOR INSTRUCTION**

Conversation

Play the tape two or three times before students move on to the Pair Work. Students take turns asking and answering questions. Once they have mastered the conversation, they can ask questions about their classmates and have their partners answer the questions. They can also vary the dialogue by adding new questions or respiraling questions from earlier chapters.

Expansion Activity

Assign each number 1–9 to a group of people. Three in a group is ideal, but this plan will work even if a group has only two people.

Group 1 selects one person to be Laila Hassan. "She" introduces herself to the class:

Hello, I'm Laila Hassan.
I'm a doctor.
I'm from Morocco.

Then the second student comes in.

I'm (real name) .
This is Laila Hassan. Laila is a doctor from Morocco.

Then advance to number 2.

Hello, I'm Nobu Moto.
I'm a businessman.
I'm from Japan.

The third student introduces him/herself and Nobu Moto:

Hello, I'm (real name) .
And this is Nobu Moto. He's a businessman from Japan.

Then advance to number 3, continuing in the same way until all of the students have participated and all of the characters have been introduced.

Then have the students role-play using the Pair Work exercise.

▶**PRONUNCIATION TIPS**

Note this intonation pattern because there is a hold where the arrow is.

I **think** → he's a **sing**er.
I **think** → she's a **danc**er.

PAGE SUMMARY
NEW VOCABULARY: Fast food
PAIR WORK 1: Asking about prices
CONVERSATION and **PAIR WORK 2:** Ordering food in a restaurant

▶**FUNCTIONS**
Ordering food

▶**NEW ELEMENTS**
apple **pie**
anything
cheese
doughnut
fast food
hamburger
hot dog
ice cream
orange juice
sandwich
soda

▶**GRAMMAR**
Different ways of expressing prices: two dollars and fifty cents, seventy-five cents, a dollar, three fifty.

Anything else? (Use of *else* after an indefinite pronoun—something, whenever, whoever.)

▶**IDEAS FOR INSTRUCTION**

Practice
Read the menu items over several times. Ask the students to point to the pictures of the food items as you call out the names of the foods from the menu.

Conversation
Use the tape to introduce the dialogue.

Pair Work 2
Students use the menu to order food.

Expansion Activity
You can make some paper money and use it (or real coins) to learn to count out money in English. For this exercise, you will need only one-dollar bills and quarters (twenty-five-cent coins). Plumbing washers or other currency can be substituted.

From a picture file, you can select pictures of the food or bring in plastic replicas of the foods and make a pretend fast food restaurant. Students should take turns being the waiter/waitress and the customer.

▶**PRONUNCIATION TIPS**
Students in pairs should practice ordering food.

A: How **much** is a **so**da?
B: **Six**ty **cents.**

Other prices are pronounced this way:

two dollars
three dollars and **fif**ty cents
three dollars
seventy-five **cents**
a **dol**lar
sixty **cents**
a **dol**lar and **fif**ty **cents**

NEW VOCABULARY • FAST FOOD

PRACTICE • *Find the names on the menu.*

> Number 1: **soda**

PAIR WORK 1 • *Ask about the prices.*

> 1: soda
>
> A: **How much is a soda?**
> B: **Seventy-five cents.**

Joe's Cafe

Hot Dog $2.00
Hamburger ... $3.50
Cheese Sandwich . $3.00

Soda .... $.75
Orange Juice .. $1.00
Coffee .... $.60

Doughnut .... $.75
Ice Cream ... $1.50
Apple Pie $2.00

CONVERSATION

Listen and practice.

Hello.

Hello. A cheese sandwich, please.

Anything else?

Yes, an orange juice.

PAIR WORK 2 • *Have similar conversations.*

A: Hello.

B: Hello. _____, please.

A: Anything else?

B: Yes, _____.
   OR No, that's all.

Listen and practice.

PAIR WORK • *Have similar conversations. Pay attention to street names.*

A: Take me to the Crest Theater.
B: On Rock Street?
A: No, it's on Dixon Avenue.
B: Here we are.
A: Thank you. How much is that?
B: Eleven dollars and forty-five cents.

1. Grand Hotel
   Baker Street?
   $9.25

2. State Bank
   Main Street?
   $8.30

3. post office
   Lime Street?
   $10.00

4. Rex Theater
   Sunset Avenue?
   $6.75

5. library
   Central Avenue?
   $7.90

6. hospital
   Dalton Avenue?
   $12.60

PAGE SUMMARY

CARTOON STORY and **PAIR WORK:** Talking to a taxi driver about destination and fare

---

▶FUNCTIONS
Giving and taking directions

▶NEW ELEMENTS
taxi (in picture, on top of car; Barney is a taxi driver)
Bus station
Here we **are.**
Take me to . . .

▶GRAMMAR
More numbers in money expressions: eleven dollars and forty-five cents

▶IDEAS FOR INSTRUCTION

Cartoon Story
Play the tape to emphasize the correct intonation. Two of the expressions—"That's right!" and "Here we are"—are so common that the intonation itself can relay the message.

Pair Work
Identify places in town where your students might like to go. Include the same ones that are in the exercise, such as the post office, the library, the bank, and the hospital. You might also include some other popular sites.

Expansion Activity
Make a map yourself or have the students make their own maps. Then they can practice the conversation and make up their own answers. If students working with only one partner create maps, the pairs could exchange maps with several questions attached, and thus they would experience the direction giving and taking in the same exercise.

▶PRONUNCIATION TIPS
That's right!/ (often said with a slightly rising intonation)
Here we **are.**/ (starts higher than usual, with a kind of low point in the middle of the expression, as if giving reassurance)

▶ANSWERS

Pair Work
1. A: Take me to the Grand Hotel.
   B: On Baker Street?
   A: No, it's on Star Avenue.
   B: Here we are.
   A: Thank you. How much is that?
   B: Nine dollars and twenty-five cents.
2. A: Take me to the State Bank.
   B: On Main Street?
   A: That's right.
   B: Here we are.
   A: Thank you. How much is that?
   B: Eight dollars and thirty cents.
3. A: Take me to the post office.
   B: On Lime Street?
   A: No, it's on Bond Street.
   B: Here we are.
   A: Thank you. How much is that?
   B: Ten dollars.
4. A: Take me to the Rex Theater.
   B: On Sunset Avenue?
   A: No, it's on Main Street.
   B: Here we are.
   A: Thank you. How much is that?
   B: Six dollars and seventy-five cents.
5. A: Take me to the library.
   B: On Central Avenue?
   A: That's right.
   B: Here we are.
   A: Thank you. How much is that?
   B: Seven dollars and ninety cents.
6. A: Take me to the hospital.
   B: On Dalton Avenue?
   A: No, it's on Clark Street.
   B: Here we are.
   A: Thank you. How much is that?
   B: Twelve dollars and sixty cents.

PAGE SUMMARY
CONVERSATION and **PAIR WORK:** Buying a ticket for a trip and reading a schedule

---

▶FUNCTIONS
Asking for and giving information

▶NEW ELEMENTS
de**par**ture
desti**na**tion
next (adjective)
one way
round trip
ticket
new

▶GRAMMAR
The word *next*, which has been used as a preposition, is introduced here as an adjective ("When is the next bus?").

▶IDEAS FOR INSTRUCTION

Expansion Activity
To familiarize students with the format, have them write in the cost of the tickets next to *Time* and *Destination* on the schedule. Point out the difference in price between one-way and round-trip tickets. A one-way ticket may be more expensive than half of a round-trip ticket.

Give each pair of students a card to make into a ticket. They can then make their own tickets for trips to nearby and distant places. Assign them a place to go to and directions as to whether it should be a one-way or round-trip ticket. Have them assign costs to the tickets. On the board, write a schedule for departure and a list of the destinations that you assigned. Then, in whole class arrangement, each group writes the cost of the trip that they made a ticket for. There are sure to be great discrepancies in costs and distances—a natural opportunity for negotiation of reasonable prices.

Ask students to create a role-play of the conversation to perform for the whole class. Encourage them to use other conversation ideas from earlier chapters.

▶PRONUNCIATION TIPS
Practice **one way** and **round trip** in isolation because "a one-way ticket" and "a round-trip ticket" will be different: a **one-way tick**et and a **round-trip tick**et.

Practice the names of these cities:

Los Angeles
San Fran**cis**co
San Di**e**go
Portland
Se**att**le
Las **Veg**as
Denver
Chi**ca**go
New **York**

Listen and practice.

SANDY: One ticket to Los Angeles, please.

MR. LEE: One way or round trip?

SANDY: Round trip. How much?

MR. LEE: Seventy-five dollars and forty cents.

SANDY: When is the next bus?

MR. LEE: At seven-thirty.

PAIR WORK • *Have similar conversations.*

A: One ticket to _____, please.

B: One way or round trip?

A: _____. How much?

B: _____.

A: When is the next bus?

B: _____.

```
INFORMATION: DEPARTURES
Time • Destination
7:30 —— Los Angeles
8:00 —— San Francisco
8:25 —— San Diego
9:10 —— Portland
9:40 —— Seattle
10:00 —— Las Vegas
10:35 —— Denver
11:10 —— Chicago
11:45 —— New York
```

1. Grayline Bus Company
from: Wickam City
to: Los Angeles
Ticket: Round Trip
Price: $75 40

2. Grayline Bus Company
from: Wickam City
to: San Francisco
Ticket: One Way
Price: $13 00

3. Grayline Bus Company
from: Wickam City
to: San Diego
Ticket: Round Trip
Price: $94 25

4. Grayline Bus Company
from: Wickam City
to: Portland
Ticket: One Way
Price: $51 65

5. Grayline Bus Company
from: Wickam City
to: Seattle
Ticket: Round Trip
Price: $188 00

6. Grayline Bus Company
from: Wickam City
to: Las Vegas
Ticket: One Way
Price: $32 50

7. Grayline Bus Company
from: Wickam City
to: Denver
Ticket: Round trip
Price: $209 00

8. Grayline Bus Company
from: Wickam City
to: Chicago
Ticket: One Way
Price: $176 50

9. Grayline Bus Company
from: Wickam City
to: New York
Ticket: Round trip
Price: $298 00

WRITTEN EXERCISE • *Choose a command for each picture.*

Come in!   Don't be afraid!   Sit down!
Don't talk!   Close the window!   Don't touch those cookies!
Hurry up!   Don't bring the cat!   Wait for me!

PAGE SUMMARY
WRITTEN EXERCISE: Matching affirmative and negative imperatives to pictures

▶**FUNCTIONS**
Giving commands

▶**NEW ELEMENTS**
cookies

▶**GRAMMAR**
Review

▶**IDEAS FOR INSTRUCTION**

Written Exercise
Read all of the expressions in the exercise with the students.

Expansion Activity
The students might be able to expand these one-picture contexts into several lines of a role-play.

▶**PRONUNCIATION TIPS**
Come in.
Don't talk!
Hurry up!
Don't be a**fraid**!
Close the **win**dow!
Don't bring the **cat**!
Sit down!
Don't touch those **cook**ies!
Wait for **me**!

▶**ANSWERS**

Written Exercise
3. Don't bring the cat!
4. Close the window!
5. Don't talk!
6. Wait for me!
7. Come in!
8. Sit down!
9. Don't be afraid!

PAGE SUMMARY
WRITTEN EXERCISE: Review of object pronouns
FREE RESPONSE: Discussing food, colors, locations, store hours, home, family, and fears

▶FUNCTIONS
Giving directions

▶NEW ELEMENTS
a**part**ment
animal
over **there**
snake
spider
rat

▶GRAMMAR
Review

▶IDEAS FOR INSTRUCTION

Written Exercise
This practice with commands shows a basic "cause" and "effect" format. This kind of hidden agenda item is good for making students aware of one of the basic rhetorical patterns of English in an oblique way: when an American says "Here's my phone number," for example, he or she is inviting you to call.

Review the object pronouns with the students by walking around the room and indicating different students:

> Here's **Rick.** He's a **good guy.**
> There's Ma**ri**a. She's really **smart.**
> Those two men are **Gil** and **Al.** Do you **know** them?

Free Response
Ask students to do the questions as if they were conducting an interview. Arrange students in triads: One student from each group asks another. The third writes down the responses. After doing five questions, students can switch roles. As an extra activity, tally all of the responses.

▶PRONUNCIATION TIPS
Remind students that object pronouns usually do not take the stress.

> **Take** him this **mes**sage.

▶ANSWERS

Written Exercise
1. We're thirsty. Please bring __us__ a bottle of soda.
2. That's a bad apple. Don't eat __it__.
3. The dishes are dirty. Please wash __them__.
4. Look! There's Mr. Bascomb. That's __him__ over there.
5. His wife is in the hospital. Please take __her__ these flowers.
6. Here's my phone number. Call __me__ next week.
7. We aren't ready. Please wait for __us__.
8. There's Peter and Maria. Let's talk with __them__.
9. Maria is very pretty. Look at __her__.
10. Peter is hungry. Bring __him__ a sandwich.
11. Take the sandwich and put __it__ on the table.
12. I'm very busy. Please help __me__.

Test (on pg. 68)
1. c	4. a	7. c	10. c
2. b	5. b	8. a	11. b
3. d	6. d	9. d	12. a

13. d	15. c	17. c	19. b
14. b	16. a	18. a	20. d

WRITTEN EXERCISE • *Complete the sentences using object pronouns:* **her, him, it, them, me,** *and* **us.**

> Mr. Watkins is in his office. Take *him* this message.
>
> I'm your friend. Listen to *me* .

1. We're thirsty. Please bring _____ a bottle of soda.

2. That's a bad apple. Don't eat _____.

3. The dishes are dirty. Please wash _____.

4. Look! There's Mr. Bascomb. That's _____ over there.

5. His wife is in the hospital. Please take _____ these flowers.

6. Here's my phone number. Call _____ next week.

7. We aren't ready. Please wait for _____.

8. There's Peter and Maria. Let's talk with _____.

9. Maria is very pretty. Look at _____.

10. Peter is hungry. Bring _____ a sandwich.

11. Take the sandwich and put _____ on the table.

12. I'm very busy. Please help _____.

FREE RESPONSE

1. Are you hungry?
2. What is your favorite fruit?
3. Are oranges cheap or expensive?
4. Are apples good for you? soda?
5. How much is a bottle of soda?
6. How is your family?
7. Is your family at home now?
8. Where are your friends?
9. Where is your house/apartment?
10. What color is your room?
11. Is your street beautiful?
12. Where is the post office? library?
13. Is the post office open now? bank? library?
14. Are you busy in the morning?
15. What is your favorite animal?
16. Are you afraid of rats? spiders? snakes?

fruit

horse

lion

rat

spider

snake

1. _____ books are expensive.
   a. This   c. Those
   b. Them   d. They

2. Where are the glasses?
   _____ on the shelf.
   a. They   c. There
   b. They're d. These

3. This is Miss Jones.
   _____ is a secretary.
   a. It   c. Her
   b. He   d. She

4. _____ is Nick? He's at the garage.
   a. Where c. Who
   b. What   d. How

5. _____ is that woman?
   She's Nancy Paine.
   a. Where c. What
   b. Who   d. How

6. What color is your car? It's _____.
   a. big   c. expensive
   b. new   d. red

7. Mr. Bascomb isn't poor.
   He's _____.
   a. happy c. rich
   b. tall   d. good

8. Those shoes aren't old.
   They're _____.
   a. new   c. big
   b. young d. cheap

9. Those are my post cards.
   Don't take _____.
   a. it   c. they
   b. that   d. them

10. There's Maria. Let's talk with _____.
    a. him   c. her
    b. she   d. them

11. Call Mr. Poole. Give _____ the information.
    a. he   c. her
    b. him   d. it

12. The tephone is _____ the living room.
    a. in   c. to
    b. on   d. at

13. The girls are _____ the bus stop.
    a. in   c. to
    b. on   d. at

14. Those men are tourists.
    They're _____ England.
    a. of   c. for
    b. from d. with

15. California is a beautiful _____.
    a. street c. state
    b. city   d. country

16. My _____ is 205 Oak Street.
    a. address   c. office
    b. telephone number d. business

17. How much are those magazines?
    a. They're on the table.
    b. There are five of them.
    c. They're two dollars each.
    d. They're three years old.

18. How old is that clock?
    a. It's twenty years old.
    b. It's two o'clock.
    c. It's two hundred dollars.
    d. It's expensive.

19. Aspirin is good for _____.
    a. work   c. teeth
    b. pain   d. dinner

20. New York is a _____ city.
    a. small   c. cheap
    b. English d. modern

(See page T-67 for answers.)

Chapter

5

TOPICS
Morning routines
Locations
Leisure activities
Colors
Clothes

GRAMMAR
Present continuous
Wh- questions

FUNCTIONS
Describing actions
Describing people's dress
Talking on the telephone

Listen and repeat.

It's Monday morning. Mr. and Mrs. Bascomb are getting up.

1. He's wearing pajamas.

2. She's wearing a nightgown.

3. He's brushing his teeth.

4. _____ her hair.

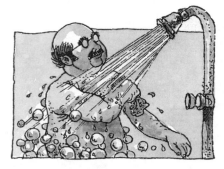

5. He's taking a shower.

6. _____ a bath.

7. He's making coffee.

8. _____ tea.

CHAPTER 5

PAGE SUMMARY

STRUCTURE: Present continuous, morning routines

►FUNCTIONS

Talking about what others are doing

►NEW ELEMENTS

bath	take a **bath**
get	take a **show**er
hair	
make	
Monday	
nightgown	
pa**jam**as	
tea	
wear	

►GRAMMAR

Present continuous tense in the third person singular:

'**s** (is) verb + ing

Idioms: take a **bath**
       take a **show**er

►PRELIMINARY ORAL WORK

Present Continuous

Teach verbs that can be easily demonstrated: drink, eat, walk, sit, stand, write, read, etc.

Teacher:	I'm sitting.
	I'm standing.
	I'm walking to the door.
	You're sitting, you're sitting, etc. (Point to different students.)
	What am I doing?
Students:	You're walking to the door.
Teacher:	Right. Now I'm looking at a book. What am I doing?
Students:	You're looking at a book.
Teacher:	Right. Now look. I'm wearing a (blue shirt, black skirt, etc.) (Point to yourself.) You're wearing a (white shirt, black skirt, etc.) (Point to different students.) What am I wearing?
Students:	You're wearing a _____.
Teacher:	What are you wearing? (Point to a student.)
Student:	I'm wearing a _____.

►IDEAS FOR INSTRUCTION

Structure

Have students listen to the tape. After they have listened to it several times, have them repeat what they hear. Explain that the present continuous tense is used when we talk about something that is happening at the time of speaking. Then have them fill in the blanks on both pages. They can practice the sentences either as a large group or in pairs.

Expansion Activity

Have the students tell what they are doing now by using the following times as prompts.

6:00
7:00
8:00
9:00
10:00
11:00
12:00

Example:

6:00	It's six o'clock. And I am sleeping now.
7:00	It's seven o'clock. And I am getting up now.
8:00	It's eight o'clock. And I am eating breakfast now.
9:00	It's nine o'clock. And I am sitting in class now.
10:00	It's ten o'clock. And I am studying English now.
11:00	It's eleven o'clock. And I am getting hungry now.
12:00	It's twelve o'clock. And I am having lunch now.

►PRONUNCIATION TIPS

Practice these two idioms:

He's **tak**ing a **bath.**
She's **tak**ing a **show**er.

►ANSWERS

Structure

See page T-71.

PAGE SUMMARY
STRUCTURE: Present continuous *(continued)*

▶FUNCTIONS
Talking about what others are doing

▶NEW ELEMENTS
husband
kiss
milk
wife

▶ANSWERS

Structure
(pages 70 and 71, with Pronunciation Tips)

1. He's **wear**ing pa**jam**as.
2. She's **wear**ing a **nightgown.**
3. He's **brush**ing his **teeth.**
4. She's **brush**ing her **hair.**
5. He's **tak**ing a **show**er.
6. She's **tak**ing a **bath.**
7. He's **mak**ing **coff**ee.
8. She's **mak**ing **tea.**
9. He's **put**ting **milk** in his **cof**fee.
10. She's **put**ting **sugar** in her **tea.**
11. He's **read**ing a maga**zine.**
12. She's **read**ing the **news**paper.
13. He's **eat**ing an **egg.**
14. She's **eat**ing an **orange.**
15. He's **kiss**ing his **wife.**
16. She's **kiss**ing her **hus**band.

9. He's putting milk in his coffee.

10. _____ her tea.

11. He's reading a magazine.

12. _____ the newspaper.

13. He's eating an egg.

14. _____ an orange.

15. He's kissing his wife.

16. _____ her husband.

Listen and repeat.

1. Peter and Maria are sitting in a snack bar.

2. Barbara and Tino are sitting in a coffee shop.

3. They're watching a football game.

4. _____.

5. They're drinking soda.

6. _____.

7. They're talking to Otis.

8. _____.

PAGE SUMMARY

STRUCTURE: Present continuous; describing common activities

▶**FUNCTIONS**

Talking about what others are doing

▶**NEW ELEMENTS**

coffee **shop**
Coke
drink (v.)
football game
snack bar

▶**GRAMMAR**

Present continuous tense

▶**IDEAS FOR INSTRUCTION**

Structure

Use the tape to reinforce the new tense form.

Expansion Activity

The people in the pictures are doing things in addition to the activities that are being prompted. Ask the students to say as much as they can about each picture. For example:

Peter and Maria are waiting for some food.
Peter and Maria are talking to each other.

▶**PRONUNCIATION TIPS**

Watch for the right intonation with these phrases.

football game
snack bar
coffee **shop**

▶**ANSWERS**

Structure

See page T-73.

PAGE SUMMARY

STRUCTURE: Present continuous *(continued)*

▶FUNCTIONS

Talking about what others are doing

▶NEW ELEMENTS

cashier
darts
play (v)
say (v)

▶GRAMMAR

Present continuous tense

▶IDEAS FOR INSTRUCTION

Expansion Activity

Ask students to role-play the story of Peter and Maria and the story of Barbara and Tino.

▶PRONUNCIATION TIPS

The emphasis in the word ca**shier** is on the second syllable.

▶ANSWERS

Structure

(pages 72 and 73)

1. Peter and Maria are sitting in a snack bar.
2. Barbara and Tino are sitting in a coffee shop.
3. They're watching a football game.
4. They're watching the cat.
5. They're drinking soda.
6. They're drinking coffee.
7. They're talking to Otis.
8. They're talking to Mr. Bascomb.
9. They're playing darts.
10. They're playing cards.
11. They're looking at the clock.
12. They're looking at the bill.
13. They're paying the cashier.
14. They're paying the waiter.
15. They're saying "good-bye" to Otis.
16. They're saying "good-bye" to Mr. Bascomb.

9. They're playing darts.

10. _____.

11. They're looking at the clock.

12. _____.

13. They're paying the cashier.

14. _____.

15. They're saying "good-bye" to Otis.

16. _____.

PAIR WORK • *Ask and answer questions.*

1. A: Where's Mr. Bascomb?
   B: He's in the bathroom.
   A: What's he doing?
   B: He's taking a shower.

2. A: Where are Barbara and Tino?
   B: They're at Mom's Cafe.
   A: What are they doing?
   B: They're drinking coffee.

3. _____ Anne?
   _____ doing?

4. _____ Fred and Barney?
   _____ doing?

5. _____ Jimmy and Linda?
   _____ doing?

6. _____ Mrs. Bascomb?
   _____ doing?

7. _____ Nick?
   _____ doing?

8. _____ Otis and Gloria?
   _____ doing?

PAGE SUMMARY

PAIR WORK: Using *where* and *what* to initiate questions

▶**FUNCTIONS**

Asking where people are and telling what they are doing

▶**NEW ELEMENTS**

bathroom
do

▶**GRAMMAR**

Contrasting simple present and present continuous:

Where *is* he?   What *is* he *doing*?

▶**PRELIMINARY ORAL WORK**

Question form:

Teacher: What are you wearing? Listen. What are you wearing? Everyone!
Students: What are you wearing?
Teacher: _____, ask _____, "What are you wearing?"
Student 1: _____, what are you wearing?
Student 2: I'm wearing a black dress.

▶**IDEAS FOR INSTRUCTION**

Pair Work

The contrast between where or who a person is and what that person does is easily explained with personal examples.

I am a teacher. I am here in class. I am teaching this class now.
You are students. You are here, too. You are studying English.

Review the first two examples with your students. Then ask them to do the rest in pairs.

▶**PRONUNCIATION TIPS**

Where **are** you?
What's she **do**ing?
What are you **do**ing?

▶**ANSWERS**

Pair Work

3. A: Where's Anne?
    B: She's at/in the library.
    A: What's she doing?
    B: She's reading a book.
4. A: Where are Fred and Barney?
    B: They're in the park.
    A: What are they doing?
    B: They're playing cards.
5. A: Where are Jimmy and Linda?
    B: They're at home in the living room.
    A: What are they doing?
    B: They're watching television.

6. A: Where is Mrs. Bascomb?
    B: She's in the kitchen.
    A: What's she doing?
    B: She's making tea.
7. A: Where is Nick?
    B: He's at the garage.
    A: What's he doing?
    B: He's eating a sandwich.
8. A: Where are Otis and Gloria?
    B: They're at the bus stop.
    A: What are they doing?
    B: They're waiting for a bus.

PAGE SUMMARY

WHAT'S HAPPENING HERE? The present continuous tense

▶ **FUNCTIONS**
Describing scenes

▶ **NEW ELEMENTS**
happen

▶ **GRAMMAR**
None

▶ **IDEAS FOR INSTRUCTION**

Prereading Activity

What's Happening Here?
Start by asking students what they usually do on Saturday nights. Where do they go, and who are they with? These simple present tense questions will prepare them for the ideas in the readings and the follow-up questions.

Encourage students to predict what the first story is about by examining picture 1. Ask them to describe the scene. You may decide to have them write their ideas on the board.

Students should continue to look at picture 1 while you read or play the tape of the first story. To get the most out of this listening activity, students should not read the story on page 76 at this point. Have the students listen to the story until they have gained full comprehension by connecting the words to the picture. If the students' ideas are on the board, you could ask them to point out the ideas that are closest to the actual story.

Then move to page 76 and work on the story questions and pair work related to picture 1. Complete these before moving on to picture 2.

▶ **PRONUNCIATION TIPS**
What's **hap**pening here?

1

2

1. *Talk about the pictures.*
2. *Listen to the stories.*
3. *Answer the story questions.*

READING

1 It's Saturday night at the Student Club. Jimmy and Linda are dancing and Tony's watching them. Albert's standing by the table. He's eating a sandwich. Bill and Jane are talking to each other and Karen's walking to the door. It's eleven o'clock and she's going home.

1. What night is it?
2. What are Jimmy and Linda doing? (b)
3. What's Tony doing? (a)
4. Where's Albert standing? (c)
5. What's he eating?
6. What are Bill and Jane doing? (d)
7. What's Karen doing? (e)
8. Where's she going?

2 Sam and Mabel Brown are in a small restaurant. They're sitting at a table in the corner. Sam's calling the waiter and Mabel's looking at the menu. The waiter's standing at the counter. He's reading a newspaper.

1. Where are Sam and Mabel?
2. Are they standing or sitting?
3. Who's Sam calling?
4. What's Mabel looking at?
5. Where's the waiter?
6. What's he doing?

PRESENT CONTINUOUS Affirmative	
Karen's walking to the door.	We're reading the newspaper.
She's _____.	They're _____.
John's _____.	You're _____.
He's _____.	I'm _____.

PAIR WORK • *Ask and answer questions about the stories.*

A: Is Albert eating an apple? (a sandwich)
B: **No, he's eating a sandwich.**

1
1. Is Linda dancing with Albert? (with Jimmy)
2. Is Tony watching Karen? (Jimmy and Linda)
3. Is Karen walking to the table? (to the door)
4. Is she going to a movie? (home)
5. Is she wearing a long dress? (a short dress)

2
1. Are Sam and Mabel sitting in a coffee shop? (in a restaurant)
2. Is Mabel looking at Sam? (at the menu)
3. Is Sam calling the cashier? (the waiter)
4. Is the waiter standing by the table? (by the counter)
5. Is he reading a magazine? (a newspaper)

PAGE SUMMARY

READING 1 and **2**: Two stories and follow-up questions
PAIR WORK 1 and **2**: Asking and responding to questions about the stories

---

▶**FUNCTIONS**
Describing scenes

▶**NEW ELEMENTS**
counter
dance
door
each other
long
night
watch (v)

▶**GRAMMAR**
A summary of the present continuous tense in the affirmative

Use of the empty subject *it*:

What night is it?
It's eleven o'clock.

▶**IDEAS FOR INSTRUCTION**

Readings 1 and **2**
Play the tape and have students read silently along with it. Ask them to circle any unfamiliar words. Discuss the words or demonstrate them.

Expansion Activity
In addition to the questions following the readings, you can ask these questions:

1. 1. Who is dancing? (Jimmy and Linda. *or* Jimmy and Linda are dancing.)
   2. Who's watching them? (Tony. *or* Tony is watching them.)

3. Who's standing by the table? (Albert. *or* Albert's standing by the table.)
4. Who's eating a sandwich? (Albert. *or* Albert's eating a sandwich.)
5. Who are talking to each other? (Bill and Jane. *or* Bill and Jane are talking to each other.)
6. Who's walking to the door? (Karen. *or* Karen is walking to the door.)

2. 1. Who are in a small restaurant in the story? (Sam and Mabel are. *or* Sam and Mabel are in a small restaurant.)
   2. Who's calling the waiter? (Sam. *or* Sam's calling the waiter.)
   3. Who's looking at the menu? (Mabel. *or* Mabel's looking at the menu.)
   4. Who's standing by the counter? (The waiter. *or* The waiter's standing by the counter.)
   5. Who's reading a newspaper? (The waiter. *or* The waiter's reading a newspaper.)

▶**PRONUNCIATION TIPS**
With the empty subject *it*, the other content words are the likely ones for stress.

Q: What **night** is it?
A: It's **Sat**urday **night.**

Q: What **time** is it?
A: It's el**ev**en o'**clock.**

▶**ANSWERS**

Reading 1
1. It's Saturday night.
2. They're dancing.
3. He's watching them.
4. Albert's standing by the table.
5. He's eating a sandwich.
6. They're talking to each other.
7. She's walking to the door.
8. She's going home.

Reading 2
1. Sam and Mabel are at a small restaurant.
2. They're sitting.
3. Sam's calling the waiter.
4. Mabel's looking at the menu.
5. The waiter's at the counter.
6. He's reading the newspaper.

Pair Work 1
1. No, she's dancing with Jimmy.
2. No, he's watching Jimmy and Linda.
3. No, she's walking to the door.
4. No, she's going home.
5. No, she's wearing a short dress.

Pair Work 2
1. No, they're sitting in a restaurant.
2. No, she's looking at the menu.
3. No, he's calling the waiter.
4. No, he's standing by the counter.
5. No, he's reading a newspaper.

PAGE SUMMARY
CONVERSATION: Present continuous

▶**FUNCTIONS**

Asking where others are and what others are doing

▶**NEW ELEMENTS**

clean (v)
cut
grass
home
mother
to**day**
sister
Sunday
rest (v)
work (v)

▶**GRAMMAR**

Questions with present continuous tense

> Is she **wash**ing the **dish**es?/
> Is your **fath**er **home**?/

▶**IDEAS FOR INSTRUCTION**

Conversation

Use the tape to provide an example. Then have the students read the conversation, taking the parts of Albert and Jimmy.

Expansion Activity

Have the students act out washing the dishes, cleaning a window, cutting the grass, and resting. One at a time, students rise and mime one of these actions. The others ask the teacher or a student, who has been appointed the judge, questions like these:

> Is she cutting the grass?
> Is he resting?

▶**PRONUNCIATION TIPS**

Note the intonation patterns and practice the rising intonation:

> Is she **wash**ing the **dish**es?/
> Is your **fath**er **home**?/

Listen and practice.

ALBERT: Hi, Jimmy. Where's your sister?

JIMMY: At home. She's helping my mother.

ALBERT: Is she washing the dishes?

JIMMY: No, she isn't.

ALBERT: What's she doing?

JIMMY: She's cleaning the windows.

ALBERT: Is your father home?

JIMMY: Yes. He's cutting the grass.

ALBERT: Why aren't you working, too?

JIMMY: It's Sunday. I'm resting today.

PRACTICE • *Read the first sentence aloud. Then make a negative sentence for each picture.*

1. **Linda is cleaning the windows.
   She isn't cleaning the floor.**

2. **Jimmy and Albert are talking about Linda.
   They aren't talking about Karen.**

3. Otis is reading a newspaper.
   _____ a magazine.

4. Mr. and Mrs. Bascomb are having breakfast.
   _____ dinner.

5. Barbara and Tino are drinking lemonade.
   _____ orange juice.

6. Jenny is wearing jeans.
   _____ a dress.

7. Peter is dancing with Maria.
   _____ with Nancy.

8. The women are playing baseball.
   _____ basketball.

PAGE SUMMARY

PRACTICE: Making present continuous statements negative

▶FUNCTIONS

Expressing what a person isn't doing in contrast to what she or he is doing

▶NEW ELEMENTS

a**bout**
baseball
basket**ball**
breakfast
floor
jeans

▶GRAMMAR

She*'s* cleaning the windows.
She *isn't* cleaning the floor.

They *are* talking about Linda.
They *aren't* talking about Karen.

▶PRELIMINARY ORAL WORK

Negative form:

Teacher:	(Point to a student who is doing nothing.) Is _____ writing on the wall? (pause) No, _____ isn't writing on the wall. Listen. _____ isn't writing on the wall. Everyone!
Students:	_____ isn't writing on the wall.
Teacher:	_____, is _____ writing in his notebook?
Student:	No, _____ isn't writing in his notebook.

▶IDEAS FOR INSTRUCTION

Practice

Go over the examples with students, and then have them work on the rest. If there seems to be some difficulty, do several more of the items with them. Or turn to two students in your classroom who are talking and say, "A is talking to B. He/she isn't talking to C."

Expansion Activity

Play a charade game. Write actions on slips of paper, enough for each member of the class to have one. Here are some possible actions to write on slips of paper:

wash the dishes	have lunch
brush his/her teeth	wash the car
drink coffee	wear jeans
clean the floor	play football
dance with Tino	watch the game
read a book	buy a magazine
talk about the class	do the homework
cut his/her hair	wash her glasses
ask about	
(a person in the class)	

Draw the slips and have each student act one out. The protocol is to have the first student stand up and act out what is on the slip (for example, washing the dishes). The students should respond with, "He's washing the dishes. He's not washing the _____." They should supply something else that can be washed, such as "his car."

▶PRONUNCIATION TIPS

The words in contrast will be stressed.

Anne and **Ot**is are **talk**ing to **each oth**er.
They **aren't talk**ing with **you.**

▶ANSWERS

Practice

3. He isn't reading a magazine.
4. They aren't having dinner.
5. They aren't drinking orange juice.
6. She isn't wearing a dress.
7. He isn't dancing with Nancy.
8. They aren't playing basketball.

▶**FUNCTIONS**
Describing a scene and actions

▶**NEW ELEMENTS**

cook (v)	**draw**
family	**game**
hill	**lunch**
pre**pare**	**shine**
sing (v)	**smile** (v)
sun	the **past**

▶**GRAMMAR**
Review of present continuous tense Compound structures

<u>Sam and Mabel</u> are preparing lunch.
  (2 subjects)
Mabel is making <u>sandwiches and lemonade</u>.
  (2 direct objects)
He's <u>smiling and thinking</u> about the past.
  (2 verbs)
<u>The sun is shining</u> and <u>the birds are singing</u>.
  (2 sentences)

▶**IDEAS FOR INSTRUCTION**
This page begins the Review Section for Chapter 5.

Prereading Activity
Discuss what students see in the picture. Then, play the tape and have students follow along. Ask what each person is doing:

1. What's the Brown family doing?
2. What's Sam Brown doing?
3. What's Mable Brown doing?
4. What's Linda doing?
5. What's Jimmy doing?
6. What's the old man doing?

Then have the students read the paragraph about the Brown family picnic, circling unfamiliar words. Make sure that they know all of the words.

▶**PRONUNCIATION TIPS**
In sentences with compound structures, both parts will be stressed:

Sam and **Mab**el are **pre**paring **lunch.**
Mabel is **mak**ing **sand**wiches and **lem**on**ade.**
He's **smil**ing and **think**ing about the **past.**
The **sun** is **shin**ing → and the **birds** are **sing**ing.

It's a beautiful Sunday. The sun is shining and the birds are singing. The Brown family is in the park. Sam and Mabel are preparing lunch. Sam is cooking hot dogs. Mabel is making sandwiches and lemonade. Linda is sitting by a tree drawing pictures. Jimmy is playing football. An old man is sitting on the hill watching the game. He's smiling and thinking about the past.

STORY QUESTIONS

1. Where is the Brown family?
2. Are Sam and Mabel preparing lunch?
3. Is Sam cooking hamburgers?
4. What is Mabel making?
5. Where is Linda?
6. What's she doing?
7. Is Jimmy playing basketball?
8. What is the old man doing?

PAIR WORK • *Ask and answer questions using these verbs:* **buy, eat, drink, make, play, read, watch,** *and* **wear.**

1. Mabel/sandwiches?	2. the boys/basketball?	3. Linda/a pear?
A: **Is Mabel making sandwiches?**	A: **Are the boys playing basketball?**	
B: **Yes, she is.**	B: **No, they aren't. They're playing football.**	

4. Otis and Gloria/TV?   5. Maria/a green dress?   6. Fred and Barney/lemonade?

7. Mr. Moto/a newspaper?   8. Mr. and Mrs. Golo/a clock?   9. Anne/a piano?

PAGE SUMMARY

STORY QUESTIONS: Follow-up questions to the reading
PAIR WORK: Asking and answering questions using common verbs

▶ FUNCTIONS
Asking and talking about what other people are doing

▶ NEW ELEMENTS
buy
pi**ano**
TV or TV

▶ GRAMMAR
Questions with the present continuous tense

Practice with these verbs: buy, eat, drink, make, play, read, watch, and wear.

▶ IDEAS FOR INSTRUCTION

Story Questions
Continue working on the story by asking the Story Questions. If possible, students should attempt to answer the questions without looking at the picture or the reading text.

Expansion Activity
Initiate a discussion about picnics in different cultures:

What do people eat on picnics?
Where do they go for picnics?
Who do they have picnics with?

Write students' answers on the board. Make two lists:

How picnics are the same in my culture
How picnics are different in my culture

Pair Work
Prepare the students by going over the two examples.

▶ PRONUNCIATION TIPS
The adjective noun sequence is normally "a **green dress**." If the question is whether it is one color or another, the stress may be more on the adjective: "Not a **red dress.**→ A **green dress**."

▶ ANSWERS

Story Questions
1. The Brown family is in (or at) the park.
2. Yes, they are.
3. No, he's cooking hot dogs.
4. Mabel is making sandwiches and lemonade.
5. Linda is sitting by a tree.
6. She's drawing pictures.
7. No, he isn't.
8. He's sitting on the side of the hill. He's thinking about the past. He's smiling.

Pair Work
3. A: Is Linda eating a pear?
   B: No, she isn't. She's eating an apple.
4. A: Are Otis and Gloria watching TV?
   B: Yes, they are.
5. A: Is Maria wearing a green dress?
   B: No, she isn't. She's wearing a yellow dress.
6. A: Are Barney and Fred drinking lemonade?
   B: No, they aren't. They're drinking coffee.
7. A: Is Mr. Moto reading a newspaper?
   B: Yes, he is.
8. A: Are Mr. and Mrs. Golo buying a clock?
   B: No, they aren't. They're buying a radio.
9. A: Is Anne playing a piano?
   B: No, she isn't. She's playing a guitar.

PAGE SUMMARY

PAIR WORK 1: Asking and answering questions about the people in the picture (What are they wearing?)

PAIR WORK 2: Asking questions about students in the class

WRITTEN EXERCISE: Describing what others are doing (Dictation)

PAIR WORK 3: Asking and answering questions about the people in the picture (What are they doing?)

▶FUNCTIONS

Asking questions about what people are doing
Answering the questions

▶NEW ELEMENTS

waving
wearing

▶GRAMMAR

Wh– questions in the present continuous tense

▶IDEAS FOR INSTRUCTION

Pair Work 1

Assign one or two students to describe what each person is wearing in the picture.

Pair Work 2

Students should describe their partners and another pair of students.

Written Exercise

This exercise can be used effectively as a recall builder. After the students have listened to the story several times, ask one student to repeat the first sentence. Then the next student adds the second sentence and repeats sentences 1 and 2. The third student adds sentence 3 and then repeats the 3 sentences, and so on. Then all students write the story on pieces of paper.

Pair Work 3

The students can form a competition: which pair can make up the most sentences about the actions in the picture?

"Peter and Maria are walking. They are holding hands. They are looking into each other's eyes. They are talking with each other." (and so on)

▶TAPESCRIPT FOR WRITTEN EXERCISE

It's Sunday afternoon. There are a lot of people at the corner of Sunset and Main. Jenny and Marty are sitting in a tree. They're waving to Barbara and Tino, who are riding their bicycles. Peter and Maria are walking on the sidewalk. They're smiling and holding hands. Johnnie is standing next to the tree. He's eating an apple. Otis and Gloria are having a conversation. They're talking about the new movie at the Plaza Theater. Suzi is buying a ticket for the movie. It's a nice day and everyone is having a good time.

| red | orange | yellow | green | blue | brown | beige | gray | white |

PAIR WORK 1 • *Ask and answer questions about the people in the picture.*

1. Jenny
   A: What is Jenny wearing?
   B: She's wearing a yellow blouse and a red skirt.

2. Marty
   A: What is Marty wearing?
   B: He's wearing a white shirt and blue pants.

PAIR WORK 2 • *Ask and answer the same question about the other students in your class.*

WRITTEN EXERCISE • *Listen to the story about the picture. Listen again and write the story.*

PAIR WORK 3 • *Ask and answer questions about the picture.*

A: What are Jenny and Marty doing?
B: They're waving to Barbara and Tino.

Listen and practice.

JACK: Hi, Sam. What are you doing?

SAM: I'm working. What are you doing?

JACK: Nothing . . . just relaxing.

SAM: Oh, what a sweet life!

PAIR WORK • *Have similar conversations.*

A: Hi, _____. What are you doing?

B: _____. What are you doing?

A: Nothing . . . just relaxing.

B: Oh, what a sweet life!

PAGE SUMMARY

CONVERSATION and **PAIR WORK:** Discussing activities using the present continuous

▶**FUNCTIONS**

Talking on the telephone

▶**NEW ELEMENTS**

homework
kitchen
life
nothing
paint (v)
re**lax**
re**pair**
sweet

▶**GRAMMAR**

Idioms

Q: What are you doing?
A: Nothing . . . just relaxing.
Oh, what a sweet life!

▶**IDEAS FOR INSTRUCTION**

Conversation

The students should listen to the tape, repeat the conversation, and then act it out.

Expansion Activity

Make a list of other things that students have to do:

study my English lesson
prepare lunch
wash my clothes
clean my room

Then plan other conversations like the ones in the book.

▶**PRONUNCIATION TIPS**

A: What are you **do**ing?
B: **Noth**ing . . . just **relax**ing.
A: **Oh,** what a **sweet** <u>**life**</u>!

▶**ANSWERS**

Pair Work

1. A: Hi, _____. What are you doing?
   B: I'm paying the bills. What are you doing?
   A: Nothing . . . just relaxing.
   B: Oh, what a sweet life!
2. A: Hi, _____. What are you doing?
   B: I'm cleaning the floor. What are you doing?
3. A: Hi, _____. What are you doing?
   B: I'm painting the kitchen. What are you doing?
4. A: Hi, _____. What are you doing?
   B: I'm doing my homework. What are you doing?

5. A: Hi, _____. What are you doing?
   B: I'm helping my brother. What are you doing?
6. A: Hi, _____. What are you doing?
   B: I'm cleaning the windows. What are you doing?
7. A: Hi, _____. What are you doing?
   B: I'm making dinner. What are you doing?
8. A: Hi, _____. What are you doing?
   B: I'm washing the dishes. What are you doing?
9. A: Hi, _____. What are you doing?
   B: I'm repairing my car. What are you doing?

GRAMMAR SUMMARY

PRESENT CONTINUOUS Affirmative		
He She It	's (is)	
I	'm (am)	watching television.
You We They	're (are)	

Negative		
He She It	isn't (is not) 's not	
I	'm not (am not)	watching television.
You We They	aren't (are not) 're not	

Interrogative		
Is	he she it	
Am	I	watching television?
Are	you we they	

Short Answers					
Yes,	he she it	is.	No,	he she it	isn't.
	I	am.		I	'm not.
	you we they	are.		you we they	aren't.

Questions with WHAT, WHO, WHERE	
What 's (is) Albert eating?	A sandwich.
Who 's (is) Linda dancing with?	Jimmy.
Where 's (is) Sam going?	To the garage.

Chapter

TOPICS
Physical characteristics
Small talk

GRAMMAR
"To have"
Possessive adjectives
Possessive of nouns
"Whose . . . ?"

FUNCTIONS
Identifying possessions
Describing people
Getting and giving personal information

CHAPTER 6

PAGE SUMMARY
CARTOON STORY: *To have*

► FUNCTIONS
Talking about people
Describing people

► NEW ELEMENTS
cute
classic
yeah (informal for *yes*)

► GRAMMAR
you have / you don't have
Do you have . . . ?

► PRELIMINARY ORAL WORK
Bring objects to class: magazine, bottle, orange, radio, etc.

Teacher: I have a magazine. I have a pen, etc. What do you have? (Point to a student's book.)
Student: I have a book.

Question form:
Teacher: What do you have? Listen. What do you have? Everyone!
Students: What do you have?
Teacher: _____, ask _____, "What do you have?"
Student 1: _____, what do you have?
Student 2: I have a pen.

Negative form:
Teacher: I have a coat. But I don't have a hat. (Point to your head.) And I don't have an umbrella. _____, do you have an umbrella? (Make sure she doesn't have one.)
Student: No, I don't have an umbrella.

Yes/No questions:
Teacher: Do you have an umbrella? Listen. Do you have an umbrella? Everyone!
Students: Do you have an umbrella?
Teacher: _____, ask _____, "Do you have an umbrella?"
Student 1: _____, do you have an umbrella?
Student 2: Yes, I have an umbrella.

Students might say *Yes, I do have* or *Yes, I have.* This would be a good time to mention short answers:

Yes I do.
No, I don't.

Do the same patterns with *we* and *they*.

► IDEAS FOR INSTRUCTION

Cartoon Story
Use the tape for listening practice. Divide the class into three sections, one group to repeat Tino's lines, another to be Nick, and a third to say Louie's lines.

Expansion Activity
Change the conversation and have the students use their own names in the conversation. Have them brainstorm things to say about people. For example, what can they say about people's *hair* (blond, brown, black, dark, light, gray, silver, straight, curly, short, long)? What can they say about people's *eyes* (big, blue, brown, green, dark)?

Then do pair work; have them make up sentences about their partners, using *you are* and *you have.* Here are some examples:

You are a beautiful girl/handsome man/lovely woman.
You are a good student/good driver/wonderful person.
You have nice hair.
You have a wonderful family.

► PRONUNCIATION TIPS
There is an intonation pattern that can be taught here very effectively. It is used when there is a series of words that are emphasized:

<u>**What**</u> a <u>**great**</u> <u>**car**</u>!
  3   2   1

Each word is said distinctly and separately with emphasis. There is also a sense of the first word getting the highest pitch and each following word going just a little bit lower (like going down the steps).

(She has) <u>**long**</u> <u>**blond**</u> <u>**hair**</u> . . . and <u>**blue**</u> <u>**eyes**</u>.
          3   2   1   2   1

There is a contrast in frame 7 of the cartoon story—what Louie doesn't have and what he does have. "Louie **doesn't** have a **girlfriend,** but he **has** a **class**ic **car.**" (Ordinarily, the *doesn't* will get a secondary stress, but *has* would not.)

Listen and practice.

TO HAVE Affirmative	
Louie has a great car.	You have good friends.
He _____.	They _____.
Nancy _____.	We _____.
She _____.	I _____.

WRITTEN EXERCISE • *Complete the sentences with* **have** *or* **has**.

Barney _*has*_ a red taxi.
Mr. and Mrs. Brown _*have*_ a large refrigerator.

1. They _____ a friend named Jack.

2. He _____ two brothers.

3. You _____ a nice family.

4. Tino _____ a girlfriend named Barbara.

5. She _____ a beautiful smile.

6. I _____ a new radio.

7. We _____ a good library.

8. Mrs. Bascomb _____ a rich husband.

9. He _____ an important job.

10. They _____ an expensive car.

a refrigerator

a radio

PAIR WORK • *Ask and answer questions.*

> a brother
> A: **Do you have a brother?**
> B: **Yes, I do.** OR **No, I don't.**

1. a sister
2. a clock
3. a watch
4. a cat
5. a dog
6. a guitar
7. a computer
8. a camera
9. a football
10. a bicycle

a computer

a camera

PAGE SUMMARY

WRITTEN EXERCISE and **PAIR WORK:** Using *have*

▶ FUNCTIONS
Talking about possessions

▶ NEW ELEMENTS
camera
in**tell**igence
re**frig**er**a**tor

▶ GRAMMAR
The third person singular form of *have* is *has:*

He has . . .	You have . . .
She has . . .	They have . . .
It has . . .	We have . . .
	I have

▶ PRELIMINARY ORAL WORK

Introduce Third-Person Singular
Teacher:	_____ has a watch. (Point to a student wearing a watch.) Listen. _____ has a watch. Everyone!
Students:	_____ has a watch.
Teacher:	What does _____ have?
Students:	_____ has a watch.

▶ IDEAS FOR INSTRUCTION

Grammar Box
Write these two forms of *have* on the board with examples:

Look at Peter. *He has* a red shirt.
Look at Anna. *She has* a pink blouse.
There's a glass of water. *It has* no color.
You have a question.
They have a question, too.
We *have* an answer.
I have an answer, too.

Expansion Activity
Ask students to interview a partner. Each should then introduce the partner by telling the class who the partner has in his/her family and what things the partner has. Example: "My partner has two sisters, a mom and a dad. She also has a dog. She has a radio, a TV, and her own room."

▶ PRONUNCIATION TIPS
Practice the flow of the intonation in these two expressions.

Yes, I do.
No, I don't.

▶ ANSWERS

Written Exercise
1. They __have__ a friend named Jack.
2. He __has__ two brothers.
3. You __have__ a nice family.
4. Tino __has__ a girlfriend named Barbara.
5. She __has__ a beautiful smile.
6. I __have__ a new radio.
7. We __have__ a good library.
8. Mrs. Bascomb __has__ a rich husband.
9. He __has__ an important job.
10. They __have__ an expensive car.

Pair Work
1. A: Do you have a sister?
   B: Yes, I do./ No, I don't.
2. A: Do you have a clock?
   B: Yes, I do./ No, I don't.
3. A: Do you have a watch?
   B: Yes, I do./ No, I don't.
4. A: Do you have a cat?
   B: Yes, I do./ No, I don't.
5. A: Do you have a dog?
   B: Yes, I do./ No, I don't.
6. A: Do you have a guitar?
   B: Yes, I do./ No, I don't.
7. A: Do you have a computer?
   B: Yes, I do./ No, I don't.
8. A: Do you have a camera?
   B: Yes, I do./ No, I don't.
9. A: Do you have a football?
   B: Yes, I do./ No, I don't.
10. A: Do you have a bicycle?
    B: Yes, I do./ No, I don't.

PAGE SUMMARY
CONVERSATION: Using *have*

▶**FUNCTIONS**

Getting and giving information about possessions (do you have . . . ?)

▶**NEW ELEMENTS**

pencil
piece
paper
stamp

▶**GRAMMAR**

A piece of paper (how to ask for one item of an uncountable noun)

Do is used to form questions with have.

Don't is used to form negative statements with have.

▶**IDEAS FOR INSTRUCTION**

Conversation

Play the tape several times; then ask for volunteers to read the two parts.

Expansion Activity

Brainstorm a list of items in your classroom, and write them on the board:

book	pencil
dictionary	piece of paper
encyclopedia	envelope
stamps	letter
pen	computer

Have students practice asking other students for items. To make this a game, have one student ask for an item and the other student guess why the first student wants it.

▶**PRONUNCIATION TIPS**

There are two strong accents in this question:

Do you have a **piece** of **pap**er?

Listen and practice.

ANNE: Barbara, give me your pen, please.

BARBARA: I don't have a pen. Here's a pencil.

ANNE: Thank you. Do you have a piece of paper?

BARBARA: Here you are. Is it for a letter?

ANNE: That's right. Do you have an envelope?

BARBARA: Yes. But I don't have stamps.

ANNE: That's OK, I have stamps.

BARBARA: Oh, really? That's good.

TO HAVE Interrogative	
Do you have an envelope?	Does Anne have a pen?
_____ they _____?	_____ she _____?
_____ we _____?	_____ John _____?
_____ the girls _____?	_____ he _____?

WRITTEN EXERCISE 1 • *Complete the questions with **do** or **does**.*

> *Do* they have a computer?
> *Does* Albert have a telephone?

a telephone   a computer

1. _____ we have a dictionary?

2. _____ she have a bicycle?

3. _____ you have a sister?

4. _____ I have your address?

5. _____ Nick have a garage?

6. _____ you have a guitar?

7. _____ Maria have a brown hat?

8. _____ they have an apartment?

9. _____ he have a lamp?

10. _____ we have stamps?

TO HAVE Negative	
We don't have a clock.	Linda doesn't have a car.
They _____.	She _____.
You _____.	Jimmy _____.
I _____.	He _____.

WRITTEN EXERCISE 2 • *Complete the sentences with **don't** or **doesn't**.*

> They *don't* have a piano.
> Joe *doesn't* have a television.

a piano   a television (TV)

1. We _____ have a computer.

2. Barbara _____ have a pen.

3. I _____ have a dictionary.

4. They _____ have a telephone.

5. He _____ have a camera.

6. You _____ have an umbrella.

7. I _____ have a bicycle.

8. She _____ have a car.

9. Louie _____ have a girlfriend.

10. We _____ have your phone number.

PAGE SUMMARY

WRITTEN EXERCISE 1: Using *do* and *does* in questions
WRITTEN EXERCISE 2: Using *do* and *does* in negative sentences

▶FUNCTIONS
Getting and giving personal information

▶NEW ELEMENTS
None

▶GRAMMAR
Do is used with I, you, we, and they
Does is used with she, he, and it

▶PRELIMINARY ORAL WORK

Question form:
Teacher:	What does _____ have?
	Listen. What does _____ have?
Students:	What does _____ have?
Teacher:	_____, ask _____, "What does _____ have?"
Student 1:	_____, what does _____ have?
Student 2:	_____ has a watch.

Negative form:
Teacher:	_____ has a watch. But he (she) doesn't have a clock. Listen. _____ doesn't have a clock.
Students:	_____ doesn't have a clock.
Teacher:	_____, does _____ have a radio? (Be sure the student doesn't have one.)
Student 1:	No, _____ doesn't have a radio.

Yes/No questions:
Teacher:	Does _____ have a radio? Listen. Does _____ have a radio?
Students:	Does _____ have a radio?
Teacher:	_____, ask _____, "Does _____ have a radio?"
Student 1:	_____, does _____ have a radio?
Student 2:	No, _____ doesn't have a radio.

▶IDEAS FOR INSTRUCTION

Written Exercise 1
Present things that you and students have as preparation for the written exercise.

> I have a **yel**low **pencil**. Do **you** have a **yel**low **pen**cil **too**?

Expansion Activities
1. Pair the students. Have them ask their partner the questions in the written exercise, changing the questions so that they are directed at the partner.

Example: Do you have a dictionary?
  Do you have a bicycle?

2. Have students ask questions similar to these questions about classmates, but using other words. In preparation, brainstorm what students have:

  a hat a backpack a coat gloves a raincoat

Examples: Does the teacher have chalk?
  Does Amy have a backpack?

▶PRONUNCIATION TIPS
Review the intonation of Yes/No questions. It is important for students to be aware that the rising intonation at the end of a sentence alone can carry the meaning of a question:

Do you have a **yel**low **pen**cil?/
A **yel**low **pen**cil?/

In an expanded exercise, you can suggest an interchange like this:

A: I have a **yel**low **pen**cil.\ Do **you** have a **yel**low **pen**cil **too**?/
B: A **yel**low **pen**cil?/ Yes.\ **Here** it is.\

▶ANSWERS

Written Exercise 1
1. __Do__ we have a dictionary?
2. __Does__ she have a bicycle?
3. __Do__ you have a sister?
4. __Do__ I have your address?
5. __Does__ Nick have a garage?
6. __Do__ you have a guitar?
7. __Does__ Maria have a brown hat?
8. __Do__ they have an apartment?
9. __Does__ he have a lamp?
10. __Do__ we have stamps?

Written Exercise 2
1. We __don't__ have a computer.
2. Barbara __doesn't__ have a pen.
3. I __don't__ have a dictionary.
4. They __don't__ have a telephone.
5. He __doesn't__ have a camera.
6. You __don't__ have an umbrella.
7. I __don't__ have a bicycle.
8. She __doesn't__ have a car.
9. Louie __doesn't__ have a girlfriend.
10. We __don't__ have your phone number.

PAGE SUMMARY

PAIR WORK: Using short answers with *do* or *does* and providing long answers when necessary

▶**FUNCTIONS**
Discussing possessions

▶**NEW ELEMENTS**
handbag
wallet

▶**GRAMMAR**
Continuation of questions with *to have*

▶**PRELIMINARY ORAL WORK**

Short Answer Form
Ask Yes/No questions.

Teacher: Does _____ have a dictionary?
            Yes, she (he) does. No, she (he)
            doesn't, etc.

Get students to ask each other questions using the verb *to have*.

▶**IDEAS FOR INSTRUCTION**

Expansion Activity
Play a game that has the same rules as "Authors." For each group of 4-6 players, a set of cards will be needed. The teacher or the students themselves can prepare picture cards of a limited number of objects known to the students. Here are some examples of cards that are easily made by cutting up a catalogue and pasting the pictures on cards:

four pictures of coats
four pictures of pairs of shoes
four pictures of hats
four pictures of shirts
four pictures of socks
four pictures of handbags

The object of the game is to get all four like pictures. Note that the pictures do not have to be the same, just pictures of the same kind of objects. Distribute all of the cards to the students so that each student has at least four. Students should hold the cards so that other students cannot see them.

Play the game like this:
Student A asks any other student (Student B), "Do you have a card with a coat?"

Student B answers, "Yes," and gives the card to Student A or "No," and the turn passes to the next student. If Student A gets a "Yes" answer and a card, then Student A continues, asking another student for another particular card.

A student must have one of the four cards of a group in his or her hand in order to ask other students for that kind of card. When a student has all four cards, he or she lays them on the table. Play continues until all of the groups of four cards are on the table. The student with the greatest number of sets wins.

This game can also be played with a regular deck of cards.

▶**ANSWERS**

Pair Work 1

3. A: Does Maria have a bottle?
   B: No, she doesn't. She has a vase.
4. A: Does Barbara have a computer?
   B: Yes, she does.
5. A: Does Albert have an apple?
   B: No, he doesn't. He has a pear.
6. A: Does Simon have a rabbit?
   B: No, he doesn't. He has a chicken.

7. A: Does Mrs. Golo have an umbrella?
   B: Yes, she does.
8. A: Does Barney have a truck?
   B: No, he doesn't. He has a taxi.
9. A: Does Anne have a guitar?
   B: Yes, she does.

PAIR WORK • *Ask and answer questions.*

1. A: Does Tino have
      a wallet?
   B: Yes, he does.

2. A: Does Mrs. Bascomb
      have a wallet?
   B: No, she doesn't.
      She has a handbag.

3. Does Maria have
   a bottle?

4. Does Barbara have
   a computer?

5. Does Albert have
   an apple?

6. Does Simon have
   a rabbit?

7. Does Mrs. Golo
   have an umbrella?

8. Does Barney have
   a truck?

9. Does Anne have
   a guitar?

PAIR WORK • *Ask and answer questions.*

A: Do Mr. and Mrs. Wankie have a house?
B: **No, they don't. (They have an apartment.)**

A: Do they have a telephone?
B: **Yes, they do.**

1. Do they have a radio?
2. Do they have a piano?
3. Do they have a clock?
4. Do they have a bookcase?
5. Do they have a computer?
6. Do they have a camera?
7. Do they have a television?
8. Do they have a dog?
9. Do they have a cat?

▶**FUNCTIONS**
Talking about what people have and do not have

▶**NEW ELEMENTS**
None

▶**GRAMMAR**
Do they have . . . ?
Short answers: Yes, they do. *or* No, they don't.

▶**IDEAS FOR INSTRUCTION**

Pair Work
This exercise can be done in a circle. Each student asks the person to his or her right. Encourage students to scramble the order of the questions.

Expansion Activity
Have students make up questions about the classroom. You can then make a game out of the questions. Have the students divide into two groups, team A and team B. A student from each team stands up. The student from team A asks the other student a question. If the student can answer the question, team B gets two points. If not, team A gets a point. Then, team B can try to answer the question again; if a student from team B can answer the question, the team gets a point. If team B cannot answer the question, then team A gets a second point. Keep playing until all of the questions have been asked or until the end of the class.

▶**PRONUNCIATION TIPS**
Remember the rising intonation of the Yes/No question.

▶**ANSWERS**

Pair Work
1. A: Do they have a radio?
   B: Yes, they do.
2. A: Do they have a piano?
   B: No, they don't.
3. A: Do they have a clock?
   B: Yes, they do.
4. A: Do they have a bookcase?
   B: No, they don't.
5. A: Do they have a computer?
   B: Yes, they do.
6. A: Do they have a camera?
   B: Yes, they do.
7. A: Do they have a television?
   B: No, they don't.
8. A: Do they have a dog?
   B: Yes, they do.
9. A: Do they have a cat?
   B: No, they don't.

PAGE SUMMARY
STRUCTURE: Possessive adjectives

▶ **FUNCTIONS**

Talking about possessions

▶ **NEW ELEMENTS**

our   their

▶ **GRAMMAR**

The possessive adjective precedes the word it modifies.

my pencil	our class	your book
her desk	his homework	their pens

▶ **PRELIMINARY ORAL WORK**

Possessive Adjectives

Teacher:	I have a book. (Hold up a book.) It's my book. It's your pen, notebook, etc. (Point to objects that belong to students.) Whose book is this? (Hold up your book.)
Students:	It's your book.
Teacher:	Right. It's my book. Whose book is this? (Pick up a student's book.)
Student:	It's my book.
Teacher:	It's her book. (Point to a female student.) Whose book is it?
Students:	It's her book.

Do the same pattern with *our* and *their*.

Teacher:	We have a clock. (Point to the clock on the wall.) Listen. Whose clock is that? Everyone!
Students:	Whose clock is that?
Teacher:	_____, ask _____ and _____, "Whose clock is that?"
Student 1:	_____ and _____, whose clock is that?
Students 2 & 3:	It's our clock.

Have students ask each other questions about different objects in the room, using the word *whose*.

▶ **IDEAS FOR INSTRUCTION**

Structure

After playing the tape several times, ask students to repeat. You might cue which one you want them to repeat by stating only one word, such as "homework." In the book, "He is doing his homework" is the sentence about homework.

Expansion Activity

Use the *Jazz Chants* principle introduced by Carolyn Graham (Oxford University Press). Establish a strong 1-2-3-4 beat, and read the sentences in the chant in a natural intonation.

Example:

What's he doing?
What's he doing?
   He's doing his homework.
   He's doing his homework.
What's she doing?
What's she doing?
   She's washing her hair.
   She's washing her hair.
What're we doing?
What're we doing?
   We're washing our car.
   We're washing our car.
What're they doing?
What're they doing?
   They're painting their house.
   They're painting their house.
What're you doing?
What're you doing?
   I'm brushing my teeth.
   I'm brushing my teeth.
What are you doing?
What are you doing?
   You're looking at your books.
   You're looking at your books.
Why are we doing this?
Why are we doing this?
   TO LEARN!

▶ **PRONUNCIATION TIPS**

Unless there is a contrast of whose homework it is (or to whom anything belongs), the possessive adjective will not be stressed:

A: This is **my home**work.
B: No, it's **his home**work.

Listen and repeat.

1.

2.

3.

4.

5.

6.

	POSSESSIVE ADJECTIVES
I have a book.	It's **my** book.
You have a book.	It's **your** book.
He has a book.	It's **his** book.
She has a book.	It's **her** book.
We have a book.	It's **our** book.
They have a book.	It's **their** book.

WRITTEN EXERCISE 1 • *Complete the sentences with **my, your, his, her, our,** or **their.***

Peter has a clock in ____*his*____ apartment.

1. Maria has a piano in _____ apartment.

2. Mr. and Mrs. Brown have a television in _____ living room.

3. I have an umbrella in _____ car.

4. We have a good library in _____ city.

5. She has a radio in _____ room.

6. You have a beautiful vase in _____ kitchen.

7. I have a pen in _____ pocket.

8. He has a newspaper in _____ desk.

WRITTEN EXERCISE 2 • *Complete the sentences.*

They're painting ____*their*____ house.

1. I'm waiting for _____ sister.

2. She's talking with _____ friends.

3. They're doing _____ homework.

4. Is Jimmy helping _____ mother?

5. Linda is talking with _____ father.

6. He's cleaning _____ shoes.

7. Are you thinking about _____ family?

8. We're thinking about _____ friends.

PAGE SUMMARY

WRITTEN EXERCISE 1 and **2**: Practice using possessive adjectives

---

▶FUNCTIONS
Talking about possessions

▶NEW ELEMENTS
pocket

▶GRAMMAR
Possessive adjectives

▶IDEAS FOR INSTRUCTION

Written Exercise 1
Students should attempt the first part of the exercise on their own. Check to see that they have gotten the sentences right.

Written Exercise 2
If students completed the first exercise successfully, assign this one for homework or do it in class as a dictation.

Expansion Activity
You can make up other cloze exercises that use possessive adjectives or you can have the students make up sentences. Put them together for the next class as homework.

▶PRONUNCIATION TIPS
The possessive adjective does not take stress under ordinary circumstances.

> **Pet**er has a **clock** in his a**part**ment.

▶ANSWERS

Written Exercise 1
1. Maria has a piano in ___her___ apartment.
2. Mr. and Mrs. Brown have a television in ___their___ living room.
3. I have an umbrella in ___my___ car.
4. We have a good library in ___our___ city.
5. She has a radio in ___her___ room.
6. You have a beautiful vase in ___your___ kitchen.
7. I have a pen in ___my___ pocket.
8. He has a newspaper in ___his___ desk.

Written Exercise 2
1. I'm waiting for ___my___ sister.
2. She's talking with ___her___ friends.
3. They're doing ___their___ homework.
4. Is Jimmy helping ___his___ mother?
5. Linda is talking with ___her___ father.
6. He's cleaning ___his___ shoes.
7. Are you thinking about ___your___ family?
8. We're thinking about ___our___ friends.

PAGE SUMMARY
CONVERSATION and **PAIR WORK:** Using *whose* to inquire about ownership

▶FUNCTIONS
Asking about ownership

▶NEW ELEMENTS
whose
glasses

▶GRAMMAR
Whose takes the place of a possessive adjective in a question about ownership. Any of the possessive pronouns or a person's name with *'s* (or if plural, just an apostrophe) on the end of it can substitute for it in the answer:

Whose car is that? / That's my car. \ That's mine. \ That's Jim's car. \ That's the Browns' car. \

▶IDEAS FOR INSTRUCTION

Conversation
The tape provides a clear example. Play it several times for the students to focus on and repeat.

Pair Work
The students will benefit from class presentation of the two examples to get the rhythm of the question.

Expansion Activity
Ask each student to put a personal item in one large bag. Make sure that the students know the names of all of the objects by writing the names of them as they are pulled one at a time out of the bag. Then replace all of the items in the bag.

Then ask the students to write down the items as you or one of the students pulls each item from the bag. The students should also write down the name of the person who is thought to own the item. As you pull each item out, hold it up and place it on the table, 1, 2, 3, . . . In that way the order of the items will be maintained.

After you have finished pulling out the items, hold each one up and ask who owns it. Write the owner's name on the board next to the item name or the number of the item. Then have the students compare the list that they wrote with the list on the board. Each time an item is held up, ask "Whose _____ is this?" The student(s) who has the most correct answers wins the game.

▶PRONUNCIATION TIPS
Whose does not ordinarily take the stress.

Whose **house** is that?
Whose **glass**es are these?

When an item belongs to a specific person, that person's name will get the stress.

That's **Bar**bara's **coat.**

▶ANSWERS

Pair Work

3. A: Whose watch is this?
   B: It's Barney's watch.
4. A: Whose bicycles are those?
   B: They're the boys' bicycles.
5. A: Whose camera is this?
   B: It's Maria's camera.
6. A: Whose dog is that?
   B: It's the Browns' dog.

7. A: Whose pencils are these?
   B: They're Jimmy's pencils.
8. A: Whose hat is this?
   B: It's Sam's hat.
9. A: Whose umbrellas are those?
   B: They're the girls' umbrellas.

Listen and practice.

JIMMY: Whose car is that?

ALBERT: It's Mr. Smith's car.

PAIR WORK • *Ask and answer questions.*

1. A: **Whose house is that?**
   B: **It's the Golos' house.**

2. A: **Whose glasses are these?**
   B: **They're Anne's glasses.**

3. Whose _____ is this?
   _____ Barney's _____.

4. Whose _____ are those?
   _____ the boys' _____.

5. Whose _____ is this?
   _____ Maria's _____.

6. Whose _____ is that?
   _____ the Brown's _____.

7. Whose _____ are these?
   _____ Jimmy's _____.

8. Whose _____ is this?
   _____ Sam's _____.

9. Whose _____ are those?
   _____ the girls' _____.

PAIR WORK • *Complete the conversations.*

PAGE SUMMARY
PAIR WORK: Inquiring about ownership using *whose* and possessive adjectives

▶**FUNCTIONS**
Discussing ownership

▶**NEW ELEMENTS**
None

▶**GRAMMAR**
Continuation of *whose* and possessive adjectives

▶**IDEAS FOR INSTRUCTION**

Pair Work
Because this is the same practice with fewer prompts, the students should be able to do it without much difficulty. Have two students act out the two sample exchanges. Remind them of the use of *this* and *these* for objects in hand and *that* and *those* for objects pointed to.

Expansion Activity
Have the students practice asking and answering questions using possessive adjectives by having them make up questions about other people in the classroom. Then students can ask the questions of a partner or in a small group.

▶**ANSWERS**

Pair Work
3. A: Whose envelopes are those?
   B: They're her envelopes.
4. A: Whose guitar is this?
   B: It's my guitar.
5. A: Whose cat is that?
   B: It's their cat.
6. A: Whose pens are these?
   B: They're his pens.

PAGE SUMMARY
PAIR WORK: (*continued*)

▶**FUNCTIONS**
Same

▶**NEW ELEMENTS**
None

▶**GRAMMAR**
Same

▶**IDEAS FOR INSTRUCTION**
Follow the suggestions given for page 94.

▶**ANSWERS**

Pair Work (continued)

7. A: Whose handbag is this?
    B: It's her handbag.
8. A: Whose magazines are those?
    B: They're our magazines.
9. A: Whose shoes are these?
    B: They're his shoes.

10. A: Whose umbrella is that?
     B: It's your umbrella.
11. A: Whose flowers are those?
     B: They're my flowers.
12. A: Whose ball is this?
     B: It's their ball.

Mr. Brown is a family man. He has a wife, Mabel, and two children. Their names are Jimmy and Linda. The Browns have a small house with a red roof. Their house is near the library. Mr. Brown has a car and his wife also has a car. His car is orange and her car is blue. Right now, Mr. Brown is washing his car. His dog, Fenwick, is at his side. Mrs. Brown is working in the garden. She's planting vegetables. Linda is helping her mother in the garden. Jimmy isn't home. He's playing football with his friends.

PAGE SUMMARY

READING: Review of *to have* and possessive adjectives

▶ **FUNCTIONS**

Describing and assigning ownership

▶ **NEW ELEMENTS**

also
plant (v)
right <u>now</u>
roof
side
vegeta**bl**es

▶ **GRAMMAR**

Idiom: at his **side**

Compound sentence: Mr. Brown has a car and
his wife also has a car.

Compound object: He has a wife, Mabel, and two
children. (wife and children)

Other compounds: Their names are Jimmy and
Linda.

Appositives (repetition of the same meaning
between commas):

He has a wife, Mabel, and two children.
His dog, Fenwick, is at his side.

▶ **IDEAS FOR INSTRUCTION**

This page begins the Review Section for Chapter 6.

Prereading Activity

Ask individual students to volunteer individual
sentences about what they see in the picture. Ask
questions to get the process started. Then ask more
able students to volunteer groups of sentences
about the picture. Build to extensive descriptions
by more able students.

Reading

Discuss the picture. Then, ask students to read
silently. Ask these questions:

1. Who is the man in the reading? (Mr. Brown)
2. Is he married? (yes)
3. Who is Mabel? (his wife)
4. Do they have children? (yes)
5. What are their names? (Linda and Jimmy)
6. What are they doing?
   a. Mr. Brown is washing his car.
   b. Mrs. Brown and Linda are working in their
      garden.
   c. Jimmy is playing football.

Then play the tape of the reading.

Expansion Activity

Give students a picture like the one in the book.
Then have them write their own stories. After all of
the stories have been written, have each student
go to the front of the classroom and read his or her
story to the class.

▶ **PRONUNCIATION TIPS**

Mabel
Linda
Jimmy
Mr. **Brown**

When *also* is used in a full sentence, it generally
gets extra stress:

Mr. **Brown** has a car and his wife **<u>also</u>** has a **car**.

PAGE SUMMARY

STORY QUESTIONS: Follow-up questions about the reading
PAIR WORK: Using *have* with prepositional phrases

▶**FUNCTIONS**
Getting and giving personal information

▶**NEW ELEMENTS**
fish
hand
mirror
sailboat
month

▶**GRAMMAR**
Questions with Wh- words and *have* as the verb:

What do they have in their gar**age**?

▶**IDEAS FOR INSTRUCTION**

Story Questions
After students have finished the reading on page 96, have them close their books. Ask the story questions, many of which have been asked in slightly different forms.

Expansion Activity
Play a version of "Charades." Students mime actions that require using their hands. Make a list of things for them to do; then, ask them to choose one from a pile and perform the action. The rest of the students should try to guess what the action is and what item is being used.

Examples: Brushing your hair.
Washing your face.
Brushing your teeth.
Reading a book.
Writing a letter.

You can make up other things for the students to do.

▶**PRONUNCIATION TIPS**
Remember the stress patterns of adjective noun and noun-noun combinations.

living **room**
small **cars**
sailboat

▶**ANSWERS**

Story Questions
1. Yes, he does.
2. Their names are Linda and Jimmy.
3. No, they don't.
4. Their house is near the library.
5. Yes, they do.
6. His car is orange.
7. Her car is blue.
8. They have a dog.
9. His name is Fenwick.
10. He's washing his car.
11. She's working in her garden.
12. She's helping her mother.
13. No, he's playing football with his friends.

Pair Work
4. A: What does Johnnie have in his pocket?
   B: He has a pen.
5. A: What does the dog have in his mouth?
   B: He has a ball.
6. A: What does Anne have in her handbag?
   B: She has an umbrella.
7. A: What do the Bascombs have in their living room?
   B: They have a piano.
8. A: What does Simon have in his hat?
   B: He has a rabbit.
9. A: What does Jenny have in her hand?
   B: She has an apple.

STORY QUESTIONS

1. Does Mr. Brown have children?
2. What are their names?
3. Do the Browns have a big house with a white roof?
4. Where is their house?
5. Do Mr. and Mrs. Brown have small cars?
6. What color is his car?
7. What color is her car?
8. Do the Browns have a dog or a cat?
9. What's the dog's name?
10. What's Mr. Brown doing now?
11. What's Mrs. Brown doing?
12. What's Linda doing?
13. Is Jimmy helping, too?

PAIR WORK • *Ask and answer questions.*

1. Barbara/hand

A: **What does Barbara have in her hand?**
B: **She has a mirror.**

2. cat/mouth

A: **What does the cat have in its mouth?**
B: **It has a fish.**

3. Golos/garage

A: **What do the Golos have in their garage?**
B: **They have a sailboat.**

4. Johnny/pocket

5. dog/mouth

6. Anne/handbag

7. Bascombs/living room

8. Simon/hat

9. Jenny/hand

Listen and repeat.

Barbara has blond hair.

Nancy has brown hair.

Suzi has black hair.

Barney is short.

Otis is average height.

Mr. Poole is tall.

Linda is about twenty.

Sam is in his forties.

Mrs. Morley is in her seventies.

PRACTICE • *Describe these people.*

Number 1: Barbara   **She's *short,* she has *blond hair,* and she's *about twenty-five.***

1. Barbara   2. Mr. Poole   3. Sam   4. Barney   5. Miss Hackey   6. Suzi   7. Mrs. Morley

FREE RESPONSE

1. Describe someone in your family.
2. Describe your best friend.
3. Describe a famous person.
4. Describe your favorite movie star.
5. Describe the president of the United States.

PAGE SUMMARY
DESCRIBING PEOPLE and **PRACTICE:** Using adjectives to describe people
FREE RESPONSE: Describing people

▶FUNCTIONS
Describing people's ages and physical stature

▶NEW ELEMENTS
average
best
best friend
des**cribe**
height
people
president
someone

▶GRAMMAR
There are two ways of expressing approximate ages:

1. to be in one's twenties/thirties/forties/fifties/sixties/seventies . . .

She's in her **sev**enties. (She is between seventy and seventy-nine.)

2. to be about (any age)

He's about **sev**enty. (He's sixty-eight or sixty-nine—or maybe he's seventy-two.)

▶IDEAS FOR INSTRUCTION

Describing People
Ask students to listen to the tape. Then find people in the class who fit the various descriptions. You can use pictures from the picture file to illustrate the target concepts.

Expansion Activity
This may be a good time to do a summary exercise to practice describing people. Have the students play a game similar to "Musical Chairs." Start by playing some music. Then have students walk around the room, looking closely at the other students. When you stop the music, each student should pair up with the closest student. They should stand back to back. Then, when you point at the pair, each partner should try to describe what the other partner looks like: his or her clothing, hair color, age. If both describe their partner accurately, they stay in the game. If the student cannot describe his or her partner accurately, that student leaves the game. Continue the game until only a few students are left.

▶PRONUNCIATION TIPS
She's in her **twen**ties.
They're about **thir**ty-**five**.

▶ANSWERS

Practice
Examples:

2. Mr. Poole is tall, he has brown hair, and he's about thirty-five.
3. Sam is average height, he has brown hair, and he's in his forties.
4. Barney is short, he has brown hair, and he's in his fifties.
5. Miss Hackey is tall, she has blond hair, and she's about twenty-nine.
6. Suzi is average height, she has black hair, and she's about thirty.
7. Mrs. Morley is average height, she has gray hair, and she's in her seventies.

PAGE SUMMARY
SMALL TALK, WRITTEN EXERCISE, FREE RESPONSE, and **ROLE PLAY:** Making small talk

▶FUNCTIONS
Describing people and places

▶NEW ELEMENTS
One thing "is like" something else
drink (n)
intro**duce**
ori**g**inal
party
phone
your**self**

▶GRAMMAR
to be like

In asking for a description, a person can ask for a comparison.

A: What's New York like?
B: It's like every big city.

Sometimes, however, people answer with just adjectives, without the comparison:

A: What's Santiago like?
B: It's a wonderful city. The people are very friendly.

Explain that either way is acceptable.

▶IDEAS FOR INSTRUCTION
Small Talk
Ask students to compare these things to something else or to describe them:

1. What's an apple like? It's _____.
2. What's this class like? It's _____.
3. What's _(a person in the class)_ like?
    She's . . . / He's . . .

Then have the students do the written exercise.

Expansion Activity
Play the "Name Game" as a follow-up to the role-play. You choose a famous person and pretend to be that person. Then, students ask you questions to try to figure out who you are. You can only answer yes or no to the questions. When a student has figured out who you are, that student can come to the front of the classroom and answer questions about a famous person whom they have chosen to be.

▶PRONUNCIATION TIPS
The word before the *like* gets the stress.

What's an **app**le like?
What's an **orange** like?
What's **Anne** like?

▶ANSWERS
Written Exercise
2. Where are you from?
3. Who's your favorite singer?
4. What time is it?
5. Where are you going?
6. What's your phone number?
7. Who's that woman?
8. What's her job?
9. How old is she?

Free Response
Answers will vary.

SMALL TALK

WRITTEN EXERCISE • *Write a question for each answer.*

1. (What's your name?)   (My name is Nobu.)

2. (   )   (I'm from Tokyo.)

3. (   )   (My favorite singer is Michael Jackson.)

4. (   )   (It's nine o'clock.)

5. (   )   (I'm going home.)

6. (   )   (My phone number is 260-5347.)

7. (   )   (That woman is Maria Miranda.)

8. (   )   (She's a doctor.)

9. (   )   (She's twenty-seven.)

FREE RESPONSE

1. What nationality are you?
2. What city are you from?
3. What's it like?
4. How is your family?
5. Do you have any brothers or sisters?
6. Where are they?
7. What are they doing now?
8. Are you having a good time?
9. Are you thirsty?
10. What is your favorite drink?

ROLE PLAY • *You're at a party. Introduce yourself to four people. Ask them some of the questions above and ask some original questions.*

GRAMMAR SUMMARY

TO HAVE Affirmative

He She	has	
I You We They	have	a car.

Negative

He She	doesn't (does not)	
I You We They	don't (do not)	have a car.

Interrogative

Does	he she	
Do	I you we they	have a car?

Short Answers

Yes,	he she	does.	No,	he she	doesn't.
	I you we they	do.		I you we they	don't.

POSSESSIVE ADJECTIVES

It's	my your our their his her	house.

Questions with WHOSE

Whose	radio is this? pens are these?

Whose	house is that? bicycles are those?

POSSESSIVE OF NOUNS

It's Mrs. Golo's radio.
They're Linda's pens.

It's the Browns' house.
They're the girls' bicycles.

Chapter 7

TOPICS

Food and drinks

The home and furniture

GRAMMAR

There is/there are

Some/any

Countables and uncountables

"To like," "to want," "to need"

FUNCTIONS

Asking about quantity

Expressing preferences in food

Expressing satisfaction/dissatisfaction

Expressing likes/dislikes

Expressing want-desire

Expressing need

🔊 *Listen and repeat.*

There's a dog under the table.
_____ chair by the table.
_____ typewriter on the table.
_____ lamp behind the typewriter.
_____ vase next to the typewriter.
_____ rose in the vase.
_____ cup in the front of the vase.

PRACTICE • *Answer the questions about the picture.*

Is there a typewriter on the table?	Is there a book on the table?
Yes, there is.	**No, there isn't.**

1. Is there a cup on the table?
2. Is there a glass on the table?
3. Is there a bottle on the table?
4. Is there a vase on the table?
5. Is there a rose in the vase?

6. Is there a chair by the table?
7. Is there a magazine on the chair?
8. Is there a dog under the table?
9. Is there a cat under the table?

PAIR WORK • *Ask and answer questions about your classroom.*

flag

map

flag
A: **Is there a flag in the room?**
B: **Yes, there is.**
OR **No, there isn't.**

1. clock
2. television
3. computer
4. wastebasket
5. radio
6. map
7. flag
8. calendar
9. newspaper
10. table

· JANUARY ·

Sunday	Monday	Tuesday	Wednesday	Thursday	Friday	Saturday
		1	2	3	4	5
6	7	8	9	10	11	12

calendar

PAGE SUMMARY

STRUCTURE and **PRACTICE:** Using *there is* to identify objects and their location
PAIR WORK: Asking about items in the classroom

►FUNCTIONS

Describing a house, a room, a scene

►NEW ELEMENTS

rose
typewriter
flag
calendar
map

►GRAMMAR

There is + (singular noun).
Is there + (singular noun)?
Yes, there is. / No, there isn't.

►PRELIMINARY ORAL WORK

There is/There are
Teach *there is* and *there are* with prepositions:

Teacher:	There's a book on the desk. (Point to a book.) What is there on the desk?
Students:	There's a book on the desk. (Correct the students if they say "It's a book.")
Teacher:	What is there on the table? (Point to different objects.)
Students:	There's a coat, umbrella, etc.

Teach the short answer form by asking Yes/No questions:

Teacher:	Is there a book on the table? (pause) Yes, there is.
Students:	Yes, there is.
Teacher:	Is there a book on the table now? (Take all objects off the table.) No, there isn't. Is there an umbrella on the table?
Students:	No, there isn't.

►IDEAS FOR INSTRUCTION

Structure
Point out that each of the sentences in the structure section could be rewritten by removing *there* and relocating *is* and that the basic meaning would be retained.

There's a dog under the table. = A dog *is* under the table.

There's a chair by the table. = A chair *is* by the table.

The focus of the sentence changes, however. Note that most English speakers will use *there*.

Expansion Activity
Use realia to heighten the interest of the lesson. Bring in a variety of items and put them on the desk. Then ask students questions about the items, or have them make up questions about the items on the desk and ask their partners for the answers. Suggested items: a paper rose, an alarm clock, a vase, a cup, a pair of glasses, a stuffed toy dog, a stuffed toy cat, a plastic bowl.

►PRONUNCIATION TIPS

The emphasis is on the real subject of the sentence, not on *There's*.

There's a **chair** by the **tab**le.

►ANSWERS

Practice
1. Yes, there is.
2. No, there isn't.
3. No, there isn't.
4. Yes, there is.
5. Yes, there is.
6. Yes, there is.
7. No, there isn't.
8. Yes, there is.
9. No, there isn't.

Pair Work
Answers will vary according to the environment.

PAGE SUMMARY

STRUCTURE and **PRACTICE:** Using *there are* to describe the location of people and objects
PAIR WORK: Responding to questions with *how many* using *there are*

▶ **FUNCTIONS**
Describing an outdoor scene

▶ **NEW ELEMENTS**

side**walk**	in **front** of the **the**ater	
month	**minute**	hour
page	**chap**ter	

▶ **GRAMMAR**
There are + (plural noun).
Are there + (plural noun)?
Yes, there are. / No, there aren't.
About any: Yes, there are (some).
           No, there aren't (any).

Any is used to express a general feeling of lack or anticipated lack. *Some* expresses the positive alternative. If a person asks, "Are there some cookies?" he/she thinks that there may be some. If that person thinks that the cookies have been eaten, he/she is likely to ask, "Are there any cookies?"

    many: Yes, there are (many, a lot).
         No, there aren't (many, just one or two).
    How many . . . ? (The answer is a number.)

Similarly, *many* is used in questions. *Many* is also used in negative answers more naturally than in positive answers:

    There are a lot of cookies. *or* There aren't many.

▶ **PRELIMINARY ORAL WORK**
Teacher: There are some magazines on the chair. What's on the chair?
Students: There are some magazines on the chair. (Correct students if they say "They are magazines.")
Teacher: What's on the chair? (Point to different plural objects)
Students: There are some pens, envelopes, etc.
Teacher: Are there any magazines on the chair? Yes, there are. Are there any pens on the chair?

Students: Yes, there are.
Teacher: Are there any pens on the chair now? (Take all objects off the chair.) No, there aren't. Are there any magazines on the chair?
Students: No, there aren't.

Bring in different prepositions.

How Many
Teacher: There are four bottles on the table. How many bottles are there on the table?
Students: There are four bottles on the table.
Teacher: How many bottles are there on the table? Listen. How many bottles are there on the table? Everyone!
Students: How many bottles are there on the table?

Get students to ask each other questions using *how many*.

▶ **IDEAS FOR INSTRUCTION**
Structure
Use the tape to introduce the structure. Ask students to point to the items that are being identified on the tape. If you can, make an enlargement transparency of the scene and ask a student to point out the cars, the people at the bus stop, the bicycles under the trees, the children in front of the theater, and the tables and chairs on the sidewalk, as the tape is playing.

Expansion Activity
After students are comfortable with *there is/are*, have them think about their ideal classroom. Tell them that the room is empty and they can choose what to put in the room. You can have students work in pairs or in small groups.

▶ **PRONUNCIATION TIPS**
The *be* verb gets the stress in the short answers.

    Yes, there **are**.   **No**, there **aren't**.

▶ **ANSWERS**
Practice
1. No, there aren't.
2. Yes, there are.
3. No, there aren't.
4. Yes, there are.
5. No, there aren't.
6. Yes, there are.
7. Yes, there are.
8. No, there aren't.
9. Yes, there are.

Pair Work
1. There are twelve months in a year.
2. There are twenty-four hours in a day.
3. There are sixty minutes in an hour.
4. There are _____ people in my family.
5. There are eight chapters in this book.
6. There are 148 pages in this book.

Listen and repeat.

There are some cars in the street.

_____ people at the bus stop.

_____ birds on the sidewalk.

_____ bicycles under the tree.

_____ children in front of the theater.

_____ tables and chairs on the sidewalk.

PRACTICE • *Answer the questions about the picture.*

> Are there any cars in the street?
> **Yes, there are.**
>
> Are there any buses in the street?
> **No, there aren't.**

1. Are there any trucks in the street?
2. Are there any people at the bus stop?
3. Are there any people at Joe's Cafe?
4. Are there any birds on the sidewalk?
5. Are there any birds in the tree?
6. Are there any bicycles under the tree?
7. Are there any tables and chairs on the sidewalk?
8. Are there any glasses on the tables?
9. Are there any children in front of the theater?

PAIR WORK • *Ask and answer questions.*

> A: How many days are there in a week?
> B: **There are seven days in a week.**

1. How many months are there in a year?
2. How many hours are there in a day?
3. How many minutes are there in an hour?
4. How many people are there in your family?
5. How many chapters are there in this book?
6. How many pages are there in this book?

PRACTICE 1 • *Complete the sentences.*

There's a bus in the street. **It's a** school bus.

1. _____ garden in the front yard. _____ vegetable garden.
2. _____ fence around the garden. _____ wire fence.
3. _____ table near the garden. _____ picnic table.

There are some cans on the sidewalk. **They're** trash cans.

1. _____ trees next to the house. _____ peach trees.
2. _____ cartons on the table. _____ milk cartons.
3. _____ boots on the steps. _____ cowboy boots.

PRACTICE 2 • *Answer the questions about the picture.*

What's in the street?	What's on the sidewalk?
There's a bus in the street.	**There are some cans on the sidewalk.**
What kind of bus is it?	What kind of cans are they?
It's a school bus.	**They're trash cans.**

1. What's next to the house?
   What kind of trees are they?

2. What's in the front yard?
   What kind of garden is it?

3. What's around the garden?
   What kind of fence is it?

4. What's near the garden?
   What kind of table is it?

5. What's on the table?
   What kind of cartons are they?

6. What's on the steps?
   What kind of boots are they?

PAGE SUMMARY

PRACTICE 1: Using *there is/there are* to describe what is contained in the picture
PRACTICE 2: Asking for specific information using *what kind of*

▶ FUNCTIONS
Describing a scene around a house

▶ NEW ELEMENTS

Noun-noun	Adjective-noun
sidewalk	**wire fence**
trash can	**front yard**
school bus	
peach tree	**school**
picnic table	**can** (n)
cowboy boots	**around** (preposition)

▶ GRAMMAR
What is there + (prepositional phrases of location)?
There is + ?→ *is there* in a question whether it is
a Yes/No question or a Wh- word question

▶ PRELIMINARY ORAL WORK

There's a/It's a

Teacher:	What is there on the table? (Point to an object.)
Students:	There's a bottle on the table.
Teacher:	Right. What kind of bottle is it?
Students:	It's a milk bottle.

Bring in other objects. Ask about their size, shape, color, etc.

There are/They are

Teacher:	What's on the table? (Point to plural objects.)
Students:	There are some shoes on the table.
Teacher:	What kind of shoes are they?
Students:	They're tennis shoes.

▶ IDEAS FOR INSTRUCTION

Expansion Activity
Have students ask and answer questions about the areas around their homes. You can start by asking questions similar to those in Practice 2. Then, encourage them to make up their own questions to ask their partners or members of their small groups.

▶ PRONUNCIATION TIPS
Noun-noun compounds like those in the New Elements section show a different stress pattern from adjective-noun constructions. The noun-noun combinations stress the first word. The adjective-noun constructions stress the noun:

Noun-noun	**cow**boy **boots**
Adjective-noun	**big boots**

Read the contrasting forms aloud:

There's a **nice gard**en. It's a **veg**etable **gard**en.
There's a **yell**ow **bus**. It's a **school bus**.
There's an **orange can**. It's a **trash can**.
There's a **wide walk** to the house. It's a **sidewalk**.
There's a **beau**tiful **tree** in the yard. It's a **peach tree**.
There are some **cart**ons on the table. They're **milk cart**ons.
There are **big boots** on the step. They're **cow**boy **boots**.

▶ ANSWERS

Practice 1
1. There's a garden in the front yard. It's a vegetable garden.
2. There's a fence around the garden. It's a wire fence.
3. There's a table near the garden. It's a picnic table.

1. There are some trees next to the house. They're peach trees.
2. There are some cartons on the table. They're milk cartons.
3. There are some boots on the steps. They're cowboy boots.

Practice 2
1. What's next to the house? **There are some trees.** What kind of trees are they? **They're peach trees.**
2. What's in the front yard? **There's a garden.** What kind of garden is it? **It's a vegetable garden.**
3. What's around the garden? **There's a fence.** What kind of fence is it? **It's a wire fence.**
4. What's near the garden? **There's a table.** What kind of table is it? **It's a picnic table.**
5. What's on the table? **There are some cartons.** What kind of cartons are they? **They're milk cartons.**
6. What's on the steps? **There are some boots.** What kind of boots are they? **They're cowboy boots.**

PAGE SUMMARY

PAIR WORK: Using *some* to indicate quantity

▶ **FUNCTIONS**

Describing objects on a table
Asking about quantity

▶ **NEW ELEMENTS**

un**count**able (n)

bread	**but**ter
carton	**cer**eal
jar	**bag**
rice	**box**
bowl	**soup**
mustard	to**ma**to **juice**
juice	to**ma**to

▶ **GRAMMAR**

There is . . .
Some + uncountable noun

▶ **PRELIMINARY ORAL WORK**

Countables/Uncountables

Countable nouns are the names of objects—both singular and plural—that can be counted: book, chair, hat, etc.

Bring various countable and uncountable objects to class. Start with uncountable objects:

Teacher: There's some cereal on the table. (Point to cereal.) There's some sugar, flour, etc. What's on the table? (Point to an object.)

Students: There's some cereal on the table.

Remove the uncountable objects and replace them with single countable objects:

Teacher: There's a book on the table. (Point to a book.) There's a clock, umbrella, etc.

Teacher: What's on the table? (Point to an object.)

Students: There's a book on the table.

Put plural countable objects on the table:

Teacher: There are some magazines on the table. (Point to magazines.) There are some pens, erasers, etc. What's on the table? (Point to objects of same category.)

Students: There are some magazines on the table.

Put various countable and uncountable objects on the table and ask questions at random so students will have to respond using *there's a, there's some,* or *there are some.*

▶ **IDEAS FOR INSTRUCTION**

Grammar Box

Read the sentences in the box. Use them as dictation stimuli.

There's some **bread** on the **tab**le.
There's some **cheese** on the **tab**le.
There's some **but**ter on the **tab**le.
There's some **milk** on the **tab**le.

Expansion Activity

Have the students brainstorm countable and uncountable items that are found in a kitchen or a classroom. Then see if they can decide why the items are countable or uncountable. (Sometimes there is logic behind it, but other times whether a noun is countable or not is more arbitrary.)

▶ **PRONUNCIATION TIPS**

Note that the noun in contrast gets the emphasis. Under ordinary circumstances, the sentence might very well get this intonation:

There's some **milk** on the **tab**le.

▶ **ANSWERS**

Pair Work

2. A: What's in the box?
   B: There's some cereal in the box.
3. A: What's in the pitcher?
   B: There's some lemonade in the pitcher.
4. A: What's in the bowl?
   B: There's some soup in the bowl.
5. A: What's in the cup?
   B: There's some coffee in the cup.

6. A: What's in the dish?
   B: There's some ice cream in the dish.
7. A: What's in the jar?
   B: There's some mustard in the jar.
8. A: What's in the bag?
   B: There's some rice in the bag.
9. A: What's in the can?
   B: There's some tomato juice in the can.

UNCOUNTABLES

There's some bread on the table.

_____ cheese _____ .

_____ butter _____ .

_____ milk _____ .

PAIR WORK • *Ask and answer questions.*

1. a carton of milk

2. a box of cereal

3. a pitcher of lemonade

A: **What's in the carton?**
B: **There's some milk in the carton.**

4. a bowl of soup

5. a cup of coffee

6. a dish of ice cream

7. a jar of mustard

8. a bag of rice

9. a can of tomato juice

GROUP WORK • *Think of five uncountable food items that aren't on this page and make a list. Make another list of five countable food items. They can be items in your kitchen or in the market.*

Uncountable food item: **sugar**   Countable food item: **apple**

WRITTEN EXERCISE • *Complete the sentences using* **there's a,** **there's some,** *or* **there are some.**

There's a plate on the table.

There are some cookies on the plate.

1. _____ coffeepot on the table.

_____ coffee in the coffeepot.

2. _____ bread on the table.

_____ knives next to the bread.

3. _____ bottle on the table.

_____ orange juice in the bottle.

4. _____ sandwiches on the table.

_____ cheese next to the sandwiches.

5. _____ dish on the table.

_____ cherries in the dish.

Note: knife ⟶ knives   wife ⟶ wives   life ⟶ lives

PAGE SUMMARY
WRITTEN EXERCISE: Countable and uncountable nouns

▶FUNCTIONS
Describing things; asking about quantity

▶NEW ELEMENTS
plate
coffeepot
knife, knives
cherry, cherries

▶GRAMMAR
There is . . .
There are . . .
Some + countable plurals and
        uncountables

▶IDEAS FOR INSTRUCTION

Written Exercise
Ask students to point to the items on the picture of
the table as you call out the items.

  a. cheese
  b. orange juice
  c. coffeepot
  d. bread
  e. knives
  f. cherries
  g. cookies
  h. plate or dish

Then ask where each of the items are: "Where
are there some knives?" (Answer: "There are some
knives on the table next to the bread." or "There
are some knives on the table next to the sandwiches.") Point out that the sentences are expand-
able by adding other prepositional phrases to the
one that is provided in the book.

This Written Exercise can be assigned as homework.

Expansion Activity
Have students write their own sentences using the
items from the brainstorm session (see page 105).
Then have them share their ideas with a partner or
in a small group.

▶PRONUNCIATION TIPS
Remind students that the natural place for emphasis in these sentences is on one of the nouns.

There are some **cookies** on the **plate** next to the
bread on the **table** in the **kitchen**.

The plurals of nouns that end with *-ife* are irregular:

life → lives
wife → wives
knife → knives

▶ANSWERS

Written Exercise
1. <u>There's a</u> coffeepot on the table.
   <u>There's some</u> coffee in the coffeepot.
2. <u>There's some</u> bread on the table.
   <u>There are some</u> knives next to the bread.
3. <u>There's a</u> bottle on the table.
   <u>There's some</u> orange juice in the bottle.
4. <u>There are some</u> sandwiches on the table.
   <u>There's some</u> cheese next to the sandwiches.
5. <u>There's a</u> dish on the table.
   <u>There are some</u> cherries in the dish.

PAGE SUMMARY

WRITTEN EXERCISE: Identifying containers for uncountable nouns (bag, jar, bottle, bunch, can)

▶**FUNCTIONS**

Describing things: countables and uncountables in containers

▶**NEW ELEMENTS**

ba**na**na, ba**na**nas
bunch
cherry **sod**a
corn flakes
ketchup
mayon**naise**
olives, **ol**ives
onion, **on**ions
po**ta**to, po**ta**toes

▶**GRAMMAR**

Countable nouns (in comparison with uncountables)
Ways to measure amounts of nouns using *of* expressions

▶**IDEAS FOR INSTRUCTION**

Expansion Activity
The best way to teach the concept of containers or amounts is to bring to class a bunch of socks tied with a string at one end, an empty jar, a paper bag, a cloth bag, a bottle, a box for crackers or corn flakes, and a can.

What do you buy in a . . . ?

Write across the top on the board in a single row:

BUNCH   JAR   BAG   BOTTLE
BOX   CAN   CARTON

Under each category title, write the names of foods that can be purchased in these containers. One item may be under more than one category. Cookies, for example, can be bought in a box or a bag. Other possibilities for foods include mass nouns, such as rice, milk, sugar, flour, coffee, and tea.

▶**PRONUNCIATION TIPS**

The stress goes on the food, unless it is in contrast.

I want a **bag** of **app**les. (I want a **box** of **ap**ples, not a **bag**.)

▶**ANSWERS**

Written Exercise

4. a __bottle__ of orange juice
5. a __box__ of corn flakes
6. a __can__ of cherry soda
7. a __bag__ of apples
8. a __bunch__ of carrots
9. a __box__ of cookies
10. a __can__ of onion soup
11. a __bottle__ of ketchup
12. a __jar__ of mayonnaise

WRITTEN EXERCISE • *Fill in the blanks with* **bag, bottle, box, bunch, can,** *or* **jar.**

1.

a *bunch* of bananas

2.

a *jar* of olives

3.

a *bag* of potatoes

4.

a _____ of orange juice

5.

a _____ of corn flakes

6.

a _____ of cherry soda

7.

a _____ of apples

8.

a _____ of carrots

9.

a _____ of cookies

10.

a _____ of onion soup

11.

a _____ of ketchup

12.

a _____ of mayonnaise

Listen and repeat.

PAIR WORK I • *Talk about food.*

ham	hot dogs
fish	hamburgers
chicken	spaghetti
roast beef	pizza

A: What do you like?

B: I like _____. What about you?

A: I like _____.

PAIR WORK 2 • *Talk about drinks.*

coffee	orange juice
tea	lemonade
milk	cherry soda

A: Do you like _____?

B: Yes, I do.

  OR No, I don't. I prefer _____.

GROUP WORK • *Work in groups of four or five. One student asks the other students to name their favorite food and drink. What is the most popular food and drink in your group? Tell the class.*

PAGE SUMMARY

CONVERSATION: Introduction of the verb *to like*
PAIR WORK 1 and **2** and **GROUP WORK:** Talking about food and drinks

---

▶ FUNCTIONS
Expressing preferences and satisfaction

▶ NEW ELEMENTS
cake	like (v)
pizza	prefer
delicious	roast beef
everything	spaghetti
ham	

▶ GRAMMAR
To like
Do you like . . . ?
What do you like . . . ?

▶ PRELIMINARY ORAL WORK

Like

Teacher: Every morning I have three cups of coffee for breakfast. I like coffee for breakfast. (Smile to show satisfaction.) What do you like for breakfast, coffee or tea? (Point to a student.)

Student: I like coffee for breakfast.

Teacher: _____, what do you like for breakfast?

Student: I like orange juice for breakfast.

Ask students what they like for breakfast, lunch, dinner, etc. Ask them what kind of movies, sports, music they like.

Question form:

Teacher: What do you like for breakfast? Listen. What do you like for breakfast? Everyone!

Students: What do you like for breakfast?

Teacher: _____, ask _____, "What do you like for breakfast?"

Student 1: _____, what do you like for breakfast?

Student 2: I like tea for breakfast.

Negative form:

Teacher: I don't like Coca-Cola for breakfast. Do you like Coca-Cola for breakfast? (Point to a student.)

Student 1: No, I don't like Coca-Cola for breakfast.

Yes/No questions:

Teacher: Do you like Coca-Cola? Listen. Do you like Coca-Cola? Everyone!

Students: Do you like Coca-Cola?

Teacher: _____, ask _____, "Do you like Coca-Cola?"

Student 1: _____, do you like Coca-Cola?

Student 2: Yes, I like Coca-Cola.

Teach short answers: *Yes, I do. No, I don't.*
Do the same patterns with *we* and *they.*

▶ IDEAS FOR INSTRUCTION

Conversation

Ask students to identify these foods in the picture:

> ham, roast beef, chicken, fish,
> fruit, cake, pie, soda, cheese

Then, play the tape so they can hear all the names of foods pronounced with another voice. Ask them to repeat the sentences.

Expansion Activity

Have the class work in small groups and make up dialogues about different kinds of food and drinks. Then have the groups act out the dialogue for the rest of the class.

▶ PRONUNCIATION TIPS

Remind students that questions that start with Wh- words have normal falling intonation.

> How's the **cake**? \

Questions that can be answered with *yes* or *no* have a rising intonation.

> Do you like **cher**ry **soda**?/

▶ ANSWERS

Pair Work 1
Example:
    A: What do you like?
    B: I like spaghetti. What about you?
    A: I like roast beef.

Pair Work 2
Example:
    A: Do you like lemonade?
    B: Yes, I do.

    A: Do you like cherry soda?
    B: No, I don't. I prefer coffee.

PAGE SUMMARY

CONVERSATION and **PAIR WORK:** Describing likes and dislikes for food and drink

▶ **FUNCTIONS**

Expressing food preferences
Expressing satisfaction or
   dissatisfaction

▶ **NEW ELEMENTS**

<u>french fries</u>
<u>verb</u>

▶ **GRAMMAR**

to like a food
Question form: What does a person like?
                  What do they like?
(Do you want) more . . . ?

▶ **PRELIMINARY ORAL WORK**

Introduce the third-person singular. Draw a picture on the blackboard of a person eating an ice cream cone.

Teacher:	Tom likes ice cream. What does he like?
Students:	He likes ice cream.

Call attention to the "s" in the third-person singular.

Question form:

Teacher:	What does he like? Listen. What does he like? Everyone!
Students:	What does he like?
Teacher:	_____, ask _____, "What does he like?"
Student 1:	_____, what does he like?
Student 2:	He likes ice cream.

▶ **IDEAS FOR INSTRUCTION**

Conversation

Discuss the pictures. Then play the tape several times so that the students become familiar with it. Ask them to repeat the utterances after the voice on tape.

Expansion Activities

1. Have students describe their favorite foods and their favorite restaurants to the rest of the class.

2. In pairs, have them make up conversations that they might have in their favorite restaurants. The pairs can then do the conversations for the rest of the class.

▶ **PRONUNCIATION TIPS**

The "More coffee?" question is a cut-off version of the whole question:

Do you want **more cof**fee?/

As such, it need only have the rising intonation pattern.

▶ **ANSWERS**

Pair Work

3. A: What does Johnnie like?
   B: He likes french fries.
4. A: What do Barney and Fred like?
   B: They like sandwiches.
5. A: What does Anne like?
   B: She likes tomato soup.
6. A: What do Mr. and Mrs. Farley like?
   B: They like pizza.
7. A: What do Jenny and Marty like?
   B: They like ice cream.
8. A: What does Mr. Bascomb like?
   B: He likes coffee.
9. A: What does Maria like?
   B: She likes cheese.

Listen and repeat.

PAIR WORK • *Ask and answer questions about the customers in Mom's Cafe. Use the verb to like.*

1. Suzi
A: **What does Suzi like?**
B: **She likes apple pie.**

2. Otis and Gloria
A: **What do Otis and Gloria like?**
B: **They like lemonade.**

3. Johnnie
4. Barney and Fred
5. Anne
6. Mr. and Mrs. Farley
7. Jenny and Marty
8. Mr. Bascomb
9. Maria

Listen and practice.

ROLE PLAY • *You are in a restaurant. Student A (waiter or waitress) asks Student B (customer) what he or she wants for lunch. The customer chooses from the following:*

coffee	ham sandwich	mayonnaise
milk	cheese sandwich	mustard
orange juice	roast beef sandwich	ketchup
lemonade	hot dog	
cherry soda	hamburger	

A: What do you want for lunch, _____?

B: I want some _____ and a _____.

A: Do you want _____ on your _____?

B: Yes, please. OR No, thanks. I don't like _____.

PAGE SUMMARY

CARTOON STORY: Ordering lunch
ROLE PLAY: Ordering food at a restaurant

▶ FUNCTIONS

Expressing preferences in food
Making requests

▶ NEW ELEMENTS

want (v)	**No, thanks.**/
waitress	**Yes,** I **do.**\
customer	**Yes, please.**/

▶ GRAMMAR

some, to want, to like (I want . . . , I like . . . ,
   I don't like . . .)
Questions with *do*: What do you want?
                       Do you want . . . ?
Short answers: Yes, I do. (No, I don't.)

▶ PRELIMINARY ORAL WORK

Negative form:

Teacher: (Make an unhappy face) I don't like fish. Do I like fish?
Students: No, you don't like fish.

Teach Yes/No questions and the short answer form.

Want

Teacher: I'm thirsty. (Mime being thirsty.) I want a glass of water. What do I want? Students: You want a glass of water.

Ask students what they want when they're thirsty.

▶ IDEAS FOR INSTRUCTION

Cartoon Story

Listen to the cartoon story on the tape. When the students feel comfortable, ask them to mime the words, and then ask for volunteers to do a role play, first with the tape, and then independently.

Expansion Activity

Make up a list of things that are done in the kitchen. Put these things on separate pieces of paper. Then have the students pick one of the things to do and mime the action for the rest of the class. The class should try to guess what the student is doing. The student that guesses the right answer can be the next student to mime an action.

Examples: Making a sandwich. Washing dishes.
             Eating soup.

▶ PRONUNCIATION TIPS

The noun of direct address in the sentence below means that the Wh-word question ends with a falling intonation and then a rising intonation.

   What do you **want** for **lunch,**\ **ma'am**?/

▶ ANSWERS

Role Play
Examples:

A: What do you want for lunch, Mike?
B: I want some milk and a hot dog.
A: Do you want ketchup on your hot dog?
B: No, thanks. I don't like ketchup.

A: What do you want for lunch, Mary?
B: I want some orange juice and a roast beef sandwich.
A: Do you want mustard on your sandwich?
B: Yes, please.

PAGE SUMMARY

NEW VOCABULARY: Vegetables
CONVERSATION and **PAIR WORK:** Buying vegetables
FREE RESPONSE: Talking about buying food

▶FUNCTIONS
Expressing needs and preferences

▶NEW ELEMENTS
al**ready**
carrot, carrots
choose (v)
corn
lettuce
market
radish, radishes
string **beans**
what **kind** of . . . ?
which . . . ?

▶GRAMMAR
Some/any as adjectives and as pronouns
To need
Identification questions: Which, what kind of
Questions with *do*
      What do you need today?
      Do you need . . . ?
Which

▶IDEAS FOR INSTRUCTION

New Vocabulary
Learn the new vocabulary by listening to the tape and having the students point at the vegetables in their books.

Conversation and **Pair Work**
After listening to the conversation on tape, have the students role-play ordering vegetables.

Expansion Activity
The class could play a game called "Fruit Basket Upset." For this activity, though, you can rename it "Salad Bowl Upset." Prepare slips of paper with the names of vegetables on them. Each student draws one of the vegetables on it. There should be several students with the same vegetable name. You have to move the desks to the edge of the room and put the chairs in a circle in the center. There should be one fewer chair than students playing the game. One of the students stands in the middle of the circle. All of the rest of the students are seated on the chairs. The student in the center then calls out the name of one of the vegetables. The students who have the name of that vegetable have to get up and find a new seat, and the person in the center must to try to get a seat at the same time. The student without a seat then has to call out the name of a new vegetable. If the student wants to, he/she can say "Salad Bowl Upset." If the person says "Salad Bowl Upset," all of the students must get up and move to a new chair.

▶PRONUNCIATION TIPS
There are three separate intonation patterns in the sentence below. One is the fall in intonation of "no." The sentence itself "I already **have** some," also has a normal falling intonation. The "thank you" part has a slightly rising intonation.

    No,\ I al**ready** **have** some,\ **thank you.**/

▶ANSWERS

Pair Work
Examples:

A: What do you need today, Mr. Student?
B: I need some carrots and some string beans.
A: Do you need any lettuce?
B: No, I already have some, thank you.

A: What do you need today, ma'am?
B: I need some onions and some radishes.
A: Do you need any corn?
B: No, I already have some, thank you.

Free Response
Answers will vary; however, they should include these elements:

1. Supply the name of a supermarket or grocery store.
2. Choices: fresh vegetables, meat, fish, chicken, fruit, bread, etc.

NEW VOCABULARY • VEGETABLES

 Listen and repeat.

Potatoes · Tomatoes · · Onions · Carrots

Lettuce · · Radishes · String Beans · · Corn ·

CONVERSATION

 Listen and practice.

What do you need today, Mrs. Brown?

I need some potatoes and tomatoes.

Do you need any onions?

No, I already have some, thank you.

PAIR WORK • *Have similar conversations. Choose any vegetables.*

A: What do you need today, _____?

B: I need some _____ and _____.

A: Do you need any _____?

B: No, I already have some, thank you.

FREE RESPONSE

    1. Which market do you go to?   2. What kind of food do you buy?

PAIR WORK I • *The people in the pictures are making salads. Ask and answer questions about them.*

1. Tino
A: **What vegetables is Tino using for his salad?**
B: **He's using cucumbers, mushrooms, peppers, and radishes.**

Vegetables	
carrots	onions
cucumbers	peppers
lettuce	radishes
mushrooms	tomatoes

1. Tino

2. Suzi

3. Otis

4. Maria

PAIR WORK 2 • *Ask and answer questions.*

A: **Whose salad do you like best?**
B: **Maria's salad.***
A: **Why?**
B: **Because it has carrots and radishes, and I love carrots and radishes.**

*If you don't like salad, say "I don't like any of them."

GROUP WORK • *Talk about vegetables.*

1. Do you like vegetables?
2. What's your favorite vegetable?
3. Are there any vegetables you don't like?
4. Which vegetables do you use for salad?
5. Where do you buy vegetables?
6. Do you have a vegetable garden?

PAGE SUMMARY

PAIR WORK 1: Preparing salads
PAIR WORK 2: Expressing preferences
GROUP WORK: Talking about vegetables

►FUNCTIONS
Expressing preferences

►NEW ELEMENTS
any as a pronoun
be**cause**
love (v)
mushroom
pepper
salad
why

►GRAMMAR
To like
Wh- word questions and practice with *do* inversion
The wh-word *why* and the answering subordinating conjunction *because* are used here for the first time:

> A: Why?
> B: Because it has carrots and radishes, and I love carrots and radishes.

This is also the first time a compound sentence-like construction is used with a comma before the coordinating conjunction:

> Because it has carrots and radishes, and I love carrots and radishes.

►IDEAS FOR INSTRUCTION

Pair Work 1 and 2
Use the pictures to stimulate statements about the four people who are making salads.

Expansion Activity
Ask students to write recipes for their favorite salads. Then have them share their recipes with the rest of the class.

►PRONUNCIATION TIPS
Note the intonation pattern of these unusual sentences.

> A: **Why**?\
> B: Be**cause** it has **car**rots and **rad**ishes,\ and I **love** → **car**rots and **rad**ishes.\

►ANSWERS

Pair Work 1
2. Suzi
   A: What vegetables is Suzi using for her salad?
   B: She's using cucumbers, tomatoes, and lettuce.
3. Otis
   A: What vegetables is Otis using for his salad?
   B: He's using tomatoes, mushrooms, and onions.
4. Maria
   A: What vegetables is Maria using for her salad?
   B: She's using radishes, carrots, peppers, and lettuce.

Pair Work 2
Examples:
A: Whose salad do you like best?
B: I like Otis's salad best.
A: Why?
B: Because it has mushrooms in it, and I love mushrooms.

A: Whose salad do you like best?
B: I don't like any of them.
A: Why?
B: Because I don't like any vegetables.

Group Work
Answers will vary.

PAGE SUMMARY

READING: Review of *There is/are, to like,* and *to want*

▶FUNCTIONS
Describing a house, a person

▶NEW ELEMENTS

be**long** to (v)
chase (v)
col**lec**tion, collections
expert
large
moment
pro**fess**or, pro**fess**ors
statue, **sta**tues
tra**di**tional
visitor, **vis**itors
window, windows

▶GRAMMAR
Review of:
> There is . . .
> There are . . .
> to like
> to want

▶IDEAS FOR INSTRUCTION
This page begins the Review Section for Chapter 7.

Reading
Discuss the picture. Then, use the audiotape to introduce the story. After the students have heard the tape several times, have them join the tape voice. Then practice the reading as a choral reading. When the students are familiar with it, assign single sentences to groups of two to four students. Have them emphasize the falling intonation at the end of each sentence.

Expansion Activity
Ask students to write a description of the outside of their ideal house. Encourage them to draw pictures or use pictures from magazines. Then post the descriptions around the room with the drawings or magazine pictures.

▶PRONUNCIATION TIPS
Practice this sentence.

> People **like** him → be**cause** he's very **friend**ly. \
> People **like** him.\ He's very **friend**ly.

There's an old white house on Bunker Hill. It's a traditional American house. It has large windows and a wide green door. There's a statue of a woman in front of the house. And there are red roses in the garden. The trees behind the house are tall and very beautiful. The house belongs to an old professor. He's a butterfly expert. His name is Dr. Pasto. The people of Bunker Hill like him because he's very friendly. He has visitors every day. At the moment, Dr. Pasto is chasing butterflies. He wants them for his collection.

STORY QUESTIONS

1. Describe Dr. Pasto's house. Is it old or new? What color is it?
2. Is there a statue of a man in front of the house?
3. What kind of flowers are in the garden?
4. Where are the trees? What are they like?
5. What is Dr. Pasto doing now?
6. Why do people like Dr. Pasto?
7. How old do you think he is?
8. Do you like Dr. Pasto's house? Why?

PRACTICE • *Answer the questions about the picture.*

> What's in the bathroom? (a mirror)
> **There's a mirror in the bathroom.**
> What's in the bedroom? (some flowers)
> **There are some flowers in the bedroom.**

1. What's in the kitchen? (a stove)
   (some pots)
   (a sink)

2. What's in the living room? (some chairs)
   (a table)
   (a television)

3. What's in the bathroom? (a bathtub)
   (a toilet)
   (a wash basin)

4. What's in the bedroom? (a bed)
   (some flowers)
   (a picture)

PAGE SUMMARY

STORY QUESTIONS: Follow-up questions to reading
PRACTICE: Discussing contents in a house

▶ FUNCTIONS
Describing a house

▶ NEW ELEMENTS
bathroom
bedroom
be **like**
sink
stove
toilet
washbasin

▶ GRAMMAR
To be like
The question inversion from There is . . . →
   Is there . . . ?
There is some . . .

"How old do you think he is?" from "How old is he?" and "What do you think?" (How old, do you think, he is?)

▶ IDEAS FOR INSTRUCTION

Expansion Activity
Ask students to describe the inside of their ideal houses. Have them draw diagrams or use pictures from magazines to show their ideas.

▶ PRONUNCIATION TIPS
   How **old** → (do you think) → he **is**?

Note that the *do you think* clause in the middle of the sentence is spoken like a parenthetical expression, with a lowered intonation but natural stress.

▶ ANSWERS

Story Questions
1. Dr. Pasto's house is an old white house. It's a traditional American house. It has large windows and a wide green door.
2. No, there isn't. There's a statue of a woman in front of the house.
3. There are red roses in the garden.
4. The trees are behind the house. They are tall and very beautiful.
5. He is chasing butterflies.
6. People like him because he's very friendly.
7. He's probably about . . . years old.
8. Yes, I like Dr. Pasto's house because it . . .
   No, I don't like Dr. Pasto's house because it . . .

Practice
1. There's a stove in the kitchen.
   There are some pots in the kitchen.
   There's a sink in the kitchen.
2. There are some chairs in the living room.
   There's a table in the living room.
   There's a television in the living room.
3. There's a bathtub in the bathroom.
   There's a toilet in the bathroom.
   There's a wash basin in the bathroom.
4. There's a bed in the bedroom.
   There are some flowers in the bedroom.
   There's a picture in the bedroom.

PAGE SUMMARY

PAIR WORK 1: Asking *there is/there are* questions about picture on page 114
PAIR WORK 2: Asking questions about contents of a refrigerator
PRACTICE 1 and **2:** Making sentences with *like* and *want*

▶FUNCTIONS

Describing a house, describing what is in the kitchen
Expressing preferences for foods

▶NEW ELEMENTS

af**firm**ative
negative

▶GRAMMAR

Are there any . . . ?
Is there a . . . ?
Short answers: **No,** there **are**n't.
　　　　　　　 Yes, there **is.**

▶IDEAS FOR INSTRUCTION

Pair Work 1
Make a transparency of the house and project it onto the wall with an overhead projector. Then ask a student to point to the items asked about, or to where those items logically belong in the picture.

Pair Work 2
Assign numbers to pairs of students and have them model the dialogue. Ask them to point to the elements that are being asked about.
　　Pair Work 2 works well as a check-up quiz.

Expansion Activity
Ask students to describe what is in their refrigerators at home. Then have them compare their descriptions with a partner or a small group.

▶PRONUNCIATION TIPS

No, there **are**n't.
Yes, there **is.**

▶ANSWERS

Pair Work 1
1. A: Is there a window in the bedroom?
   B: Yes, there is.
2. A: Is there a window in the bathroom?
   B: No, there isn't.
3. A: Is there a mirror in the bathroom?
   B: Yes, there is.
4. A: Are there any chairs in the living room?
   B: Yes, there are.
5. A: Are there any chairs in the bedroom?
   B: No, there aren't.
6. A: Is there a table in the bedroom?
   B: Yes, there is.
7. A: Are there any flowers in the bedroom?
   B: Yes, there are.
8. A: Are there any flowers in the living room?
   B: No, there aren't.
9. A: Is there a sofa in the living room?
   B: No, there isn't.

Pair Work 2
1. Is there any cheese in the refrigerator?
   Yes, there is.
2. Is there any butter in the refrigerator?
   No, there isn't.
3. Are there any eggs in the refrigerator?
   Yes, there are.
4. Is there any bread in the refrigerator?
   No, there isn't.
5. Is there any cake in the refrigerator?
   Yes, there is.
6. Are there any cookies in the refrigerator?
   No, there aren't.
7. Is there any ice cream in the refrigerator?
   Yes, there is.
8. Are there any apples in the refrigerator?
   Yes, there are.
9. Are there any cherries in the refrigerator?
   No, there aren't.
10. Are there any pears in the refrigerator?
    Yes, there are.
11. Is there any lemonade in the refrigerator?
    No, there isn't.
12. Is there any orange juice in the refrigerator?
    Yes, there is.

Practice 1
1. He wants a plate of French fries.
2. They want a cup of coffee.
3. She wants a piece of cheese.
4. I want a bowl of tomato soup.
5. He wants a plate of spaghetti.
6. We want a dish of ice cream.
7. They want a glass of orange juice.
8. She wants a cup of tea.

Practice 2
1. Gloria doesn't like tomato soup. She doesn't want any.
2. We don't like French fries. We don't want any.
3. They don't like onions. They don't want any.
4. Johnnie doesn't like olives. He doesn't want any.
5. I don't like cheese. I don't want any.
6. My friends don't like pizza. They don't want any.
7. Mr. Farley doesn't like chicken. He doesn't want any.
8. We don't like string beans. We don't want any.

PAIR WORK 1 • *Ask and answer questions about the picture on page 114.*

> pots/kitchen
> A: **Are there any pots in the kitchen?**
> B: **Yes, there are.**
>
> television/bedroom
> A: **Is there a television in the bedroom?**
> B: **No, there isn't.**

1. window/bedroom
2. window/bathroom
3. mirror/bathroom
4. chairs/living room
5. chairs/bedroom
6. table/bedroom
7. flowers/bedroom
8. flowers/living room
9. sofa/living room

PAIR WORK 2 • *Ask and answer questions about the contents of the refrigerator.*

> milk
> A: **Is there any milk in the refrigerator?**
> B: **Yes, there is.**
>
> bananas
> A: **Are there any bananas in the refrigerator?**
> B: **No, there aren't.**

1. cheese
2. butter
3. eggs
4. bread
5. cake
6. cookies
7. ice cream
8. apples
9. cherries
10. pears
11. lemonade
12. orange juice

PRACTICE 1 • *Make affirmative sentences with **to want**.*

> Anne likes cake. (a piece)
> **She wants a piece of cake.**
>
> We like lemonade. (a glass)
> **We want a glass of lemonade.**

1. Johnnie likes French fries. (a plate)
2. Fred and Barney like coffee. (a cup)
3. Maria likes cheese. (a piece)
4. I like tomato soup. (a bowl)
5. Peter likes spaghetti. (a plate)
6. We like ice cream. (a dish)
7. They like orange juice. (a glass)
8. Barbara likes tea. (a cup)

PRACTICE 2 • *Make negative sentences with **to like** and **to want**.*

> I/coffee
> **I don't like coffee. I don't want any (coffee).**
>
> Otis/ham
> **Otis doesn't like ham. He doesn't want any (ham).**

1. Gloria/tomato soup
2. We/French fries
3. They/onions
4. Johnnie/olives
5. I/cheese
6. My friends/pizza
7. Mr. Farley/chicken
8. We/string beans

PAIR WORK • *Ask and answer questions using **have**, **like**, and **want**.*

1. Mr. Bascomb/a secretary?

A: **Does Mr. Bascomb have a secretary?**
B: **Yes, he does.**

2. Anne/her job?

A: **Does Anne like her job?**
B: **No, she doesn't.**

3. Anne/a raise?

A: **Does Anne want a raise?**
B: **Yes, she does.**

have   4. Peter/a car?   5. Joe and Eddie/a car?   6. Joe and Eddie/money?

like 7. Barbara and Tino/rock music? 8. Mr. Bascomb/rock music? 9. Mrs. Bascomb/ice cream?

want 10. Jenny/ice cream?   11. Barbara and Tino/ice cream?   12. Barbara and Tino/soda?

PAGE SUMMARY
PAIR WORK: Asking questions using *have, like,* and *want*

▶FUNCTIONS
Expressing preferences and needs, other than foods

▶NEW ELEMENTS
money
music
raise (n)
rock music

▶GRAMMAR
Does he/she like/want/have . . . ?
Yes, he does. No, she doesn't.
Review of *some* and *any*

▶IDEAS FOR INSTRUCTION
Pair Work
Students must understand the differences between three common verbs: have, like, and want. In the pictures for the verb *have* (numbers 4 and 5), the context is clear:

> Peter *has* a car. He looks happy. He *likes* his car. He doesn't *want* a new one.
> Joe and Eddie don't *have* a car. They probably *want* one.

Expansion Activity
Have the students make up lists of things they have, things they like, and things they want. Then have them compare the lists with a partner or a small group.

▶ANSWERS
Pair Work
4. A: Does Peter have a car?
    B: Yes, he does.
5. A: Do Joe and Eddie have a car?
    B: No, they don't.
6. A: Do Joe and Eddie have any money?
    B: No, they don't.
7. A: Do Barbara and Tino like rock music?
    B: Yes, they do.
8. A: Does Mr. Bascomb like rock music?
    B: No, he doesn't.
9. A: Does Mrs. Bascomb like ice cream?
    B: Yes, she does.
10. A: Does Jenny want ice cream?
    B: Yes, she does.
11. A: Do Barbara and Tino want ice cream?
    B: No, they don't.
12. A: Do Barbara and Tino want soda?
    B: Yes, they do.

PAGE SUMMARY
FREE RESPONSE 1: Talking about needs and preferences
WRITTEN EXERCISE: Review of prepositions
FREE RESPONSE 2: Talking about the home and furnishings

▶ **FUNCTIONS**
Expressing needs and preferences
Describing a house or apartment

▶ **NEW ELEMENTS**
athlete
balcony
comfortable
fireplace
plants (n)
popular
sport
team

▶ **GRAMMAR**
Review of Are you . . . ?
Do you . . . ?
What's . . . ?
How old/many . . . ?
Prepositions

▶ **IDEAS FOR INSTRUCTION**

Free Response 1
Form groups of four or five students to discuss the questions. Ask them to generate lists for questions 5, 6, 9, and 10. If students have trouble, brainstorm names of foods and sports. Write them all on the board.

Free Response 2
Review furniture, colors, and words about houses and apartments.

Expansion Activity
After students have attempted the Written Exercise, make lists on the board like these:

about	**in**	**at**
about her job	in his car	at the bank
	in a coffee shop	at the post office
	in Florida	
	in the garden	

of	**for**	**to**
of soup	for lunch	to a friend
	for his collection	to Dr. Pasto

from	**with**	**on**
from 9 to 5	with Tino	on Maple Street

These expressions with prepositions are typical of their uses. Ask students to add more examples of prepositional phrases.

▶ **PRONUNCIATION TIPS**
Remind students that unless there is a specific reason for the stress to be on a preposition, the natural stress pattern puts emphasis on the final noun and secondary stress on another important word:

Barbara is talking about her **job** at the **bank.**

▶ **ANSWERS**

Free Response 1 and 2
Answers will vary.

Written Exercise
1. She's talking __about__ her job __at__ the bank.
2. Albert and Linda are sitting __in__ a coffee shop.
3. She wants a bowl __of__ soup __for__ lunch.
4. Jimmy is buying some stamps __at__ the post office __on__ Maple Street.
5. He's writing a letter __to__ a friend __in__ Florida.
6. The post office is open __from__ nine __to__ five.
7. That old house belongs __to__ Dr. Pasto.
8. He's working __in__ the garden.
9. I'm giving this butterfly __to__ Dr. Pasto __for__ his collection.

FREE RESPONSE I

1. Are you thirsty? Do you want a glass of water?
2. Are you hungry? Do you want a sandwich?
3. Do you like ice cream? cake?
4. Do you like lemonade? coffee?
5. What's your favorite food? drink?
6. What's your favorite sport?
7. Do you like football? basketball? baseball?
8. Is baseball popular in your country?
9. Who is your favorite athlete?
10. What's your favorite team?

a baseball
game

WRITTEN EXERCISE • *Complete the sentences using suitable prepositions.*

Barbara is sitting *with* Tino *in* his car.

1. She's talking _____ her job _____ the bank.

2. Albert and Linda are sitting _____ a coffee shop.

3. She wants a bowl _____ soup _____ lunch.

4. Jimmy is buying some stamps _____ the post office _____ Maple Street.

5. He's writing a letter _____ a friend _____ Florida.

6. The post office is open _____ nine _____ five.

7. That old house belongs _____ Dr. Pasto.

8. He's working _____ the garden.

9. I'm giving this butterfly _____ Dr. Pasto _____ his collection.

FREE RESPONSE 2

1. How old is your house or apartment?
2. How many rooms are there? Are they large or small?
3. What is your living room like? How many windows are there?
4. What color are the walls? Are there any pictures on the walls?
5. Are there any plants or flowers in your home?
6. What is the kitchen like? Is it large or small?
   Is it next to the living room?
7. What is the furniture like? Is it comfortable?
8. Do you have a balcony? a fireplace?
9. What do you need for your house or apartment?
10. What's the best thing about your home?

a balcony

a fireplace

THERE IS/THERE ARE Affirmative

There's (There is)	a bottle	
There are	some glasses	on the table.
There's (There is)	some cake	

Negative

There isn't (There is not)	a bottle	
There aren't (There are not)	any glasses	on the table.
There's isn't (There is not)	any cake	

Interrogative

Is there	a bottle	
Are there	any glasses	on the table?
Is there	any cake	

Short Answers

	there is.			there isn't.
Yes,	there are.	No,		there aren't.
	there is.			there isn't.

NOUNS AS MODIFIERS

It's a	school bus. business letter.
They're	apple trees. office buildings.

TO WANT Affirmative

He She	wants	
I You We They	want	a glass of water.

Negative

He She	doesn't (does not)	
I You We They	don't (do not)	want a glass of water.

Interrogative

Does	he she	
Do	I you we they	want a glass of water?

Short Answers

	he she	does.		he she	doesn't.
Yes,	I you we they	do.	No,	I you we they	don't.

Review Chapter

8

TOPICS
Art exhibition
Popular entertainment
A trip to Paris
Leisure activities

GRAMMAR
Review

FUNCTIONS
Expressing preferences in entertainment
Indicating location
Describing actions
Making suggestions
Offering to help
Expressing need
Apologizing
Expressing disappointment
Expressing gratitude

Today there's an art exhibition in City Park. Otis Jackson has some of his new paintings in the exhibition. He's showing them to the public for the first time. Otis is a very good artist. His paintings are an expression of his strong personality. He's a vegetarian; that's why Otis likes to paint fruit and vegetables. The fruit and vegetables in Otis's paintings are different from ordinary fruit and vegetables. They're very large and have strange shapes and colors.

At the moment Otis is talking to some art lovers, including Dr. Pasto. They're standing around some of his paintings of fruit. Otis is a good talker, and he has some interesting ideas on art.

CHAPTER 8

PAGE SUMMARY
READING: The art exhibition

▶**FUNCTIONS**
Expressing likes
Indicating location of people, objects, and
places
Describing actions

▶**NEW ELEMENTS**
art
different
ex**hib**ition
ex**pres**sion
first
i**de**a
in**clude**
interesting
lover
ordinary
painting
personality
(the) **pub**lic
shape
strange
talker
vegetarian

▶**GRAMMAR**
Review

▶**IDEAS FOR INSTRUCTION**
Reading
Try to get the students engaged in a conversation
about the picture before they do the reading or listen to the tape. Ask them to guess what is happening. What words and concepts do they anticipate?

Expansion Activity
Have students brainstorm ideas about art and
artists and put them on the board. Suggest that
each student write sentences about one of the art
forms or artists. Use these sentences as spring-
boards:

What kind of pictures do you like?
What kind of pictures don't you like?
Do you know the names of some artists?
Who are they?

▶**PRONUNCIATION TIPS**
The syllable before the -*tion*/-*sion* syllable gets the
stress. Practice these words with the class.

ex**hib**ition
ex**pres**sion
in**struc**tion
col**lec**tion
com**pos**ition
pro**nun**ciation

PAGE SUMMARY

READING: The art exhibition *(continued)*
STORY QUESTIONS: Follow-up questions to reading

▶FUNCTIONS

Expressing likes
Indicating location of people, objects, and
    places
Describing actions

▶NEW ELEMENTS

certainly
composi̱tion
en**joy**
for **sale**
sale
why

▶GRAMMAR

I think + clause
"I think I have eighty dollars in my
    wallet."

Here, the students are encountering the statement form of an already familiar question form:

How old <u>do you think</u> he is?

▶IDEAS FOR INSTRUCTION

Reading
Encourage students to role-play the parts of Dr. Pasto and Mr. Jackson after hearing the tape and reading on their own.

Expansion Activities

1. Ask them questions like these to promote understanding and use of the forms:

    A: How much money do you think you have in your pocket/wallet?
    B: I think I have . . .

    A: What movie do you think you like?
    B: I think I like all of them.

2. Have students write questions about preferences in art or artists. Then have them ask their classmates the questions. Each student can then give a presentation about the various answers they received to their questions.

    Do you like light paintings or dark ones?
    What are your favorite colors?
    Are the best paintings realistic?

▶PRONUNCIATION TIPS

Review the pronunciation of more familiar words ending with *-tion* or *-sion*.

    station
    oc**cupa**tion
    preposi̱tion

Note the exception: **televi**sion

▶ANSWERS

Story Questions

1. It's in City Park.
2. Yes, he is.
3. He's a vegetarian.
4. He's talking to Dr. Pasto.
5. "Art is life. My paintings are me."
6. He's looking at a painting of a butterfly.
7. "The Happy Butterfly." *or* It's called "The Happy Butterfly."
8. He likes butterflies. It's a fine painting. The colors are beautiful.
9. He wants eighty dollars for it. Yes, it's a good price.
10. (Answers will vary.)
11. (Answers will vary.)

"Art is life," says Otis. "My paintings are me."

"That's certainly true," says Dr. Pasto. "You and your paintings are very original."

"Thank you, Dr. Pasto."

"This is a fine painting here, Otis. The colors are beautiful."

"You're looking at one of my favorite compositions. It's called 'The Happy Butterfly.'"

"Is it for sale, Otis?"

"Yes, sir."

"How much do you want for it?"

"I'm asking eighty dollars."

"Let's see. I think I have eighty dollars in my wallet. Yes. Here you are, Otis."

"Thank you, Dr. Pasto. You have a good painting there. Enjoy it."

STORY QUESTIONS

1. Where is the art exhibition?
2. Is Otis showing his new paintings today?
3. Why does Otis like to paint fruit and vegetables?
4. Who is Otis talking to?
5. What does Otis say about art?
6. What is Dr. Pasto looking at?
7. What is the painting called?
8. Why does Dr. Pasto like the painting?
9. How much does Otis want for it? Is that a good price?
10. Do you think Otis is a good artist?
11. Do you like to paint? Are you a good artist?

 *Listen and repeat.*

MOVIES: musicals, comedies, westerns, science fiction, dramas.

TV PROGRAMS: dramas, news, sports, cartoons, comedies.

MUSIC: rock, jazz, country western, classical, popular.

BOOKS: mysteries, love stories, biographies, historical books.

PAGE SUMMARY
NEW VOCABULARY: Entertainment

▶**FUNCTIONS**
None

▶**NEW ELEMENTS**
bi**ography**
classical
co**med**y
country **west**ern
drama
en**tertain**ment
his**tor**ical
jazz
love story
musical
mystery
popular
science fiction
sports
star
T**V star**
western

▶**GRAMMAR**
None

▶**IDEAS FOR INSTRUCTION**

New Vocabulary
Discuss the pictures. Then, listen to the tape and repeat.

Expansion Activity
In small groups have the students brainstorm their favorite movies, TV shows, musicians, and books. Then, compare answers as a whole class.

▶**PRONUNCIATION TIPS**
Follow the suggestions in the New Elements section.

PAGE SUMMARY

PAIR WORK 1: Talking about entertainment
PAIR WORK 2: Review of opposites
WRITTEN EXERCISE: Review of object pronouns

▶**FUNCTIONS**

Expressing likes, describing people, answering questions about people, making suggestions

▶**NEW ELEMENTS**

chocolate

▶**GRAMMAR**

Review of object pronouns it, her, him, me, us, them

▶**IDEAS FOR INSTRUCTION**

Pair Work 1

This Pair Work exercise offers a great deal of freedom to create sentences. You could divide the students into two groups, A and B. First have the A's interview the B's about their movie preferences. Then have the B's interview the A's. Have one student from each team write the names of the movies that were given as "favorites" and two other students tally the number of the results of the votes for comedies and dramas. Discuss surveys and interviews and what they mean with the class. For example, if *Jurassic Park* and *Star Wars* get the most votes, then the class as a whole likes science fiction. That means that the class members are intelligent, science-minded. You can use this lesson as an opportunity to get adjective review on the board.

Pair Work 2

This exercise begins with four questions about the characters in the textbook. However, it then becomes an ideal exercise for practicing opposites. Tell the students that they must ask questions that generate a negative answer about characters in the book or members of the class. A member of the other team must answer with a correction. For example,

Team A member:	Is Peter poor?
Team B member:	No, he isn't. He's rich. He drives a nice car and he travels a lot.
Team B member:	Is (Abdul) tall?
Team A member:	No, he isn't. He's short.

▶**PRONUNCIATION TIPS**

The pronouns in the Written Exercise do not take stress.

I'm **com**ing. **Wait** for me.

▶**ANSWERS**

Pair Work 1

Answers will vary.

Pair Work 2

1. Yes, he is.
2. No, he isn't. He's rich.
3. No, they aren't. They're young.
4. Yes, they are.
5. (Individual answer) Yes, I am./ No, I'm not.
6. (Individual answer) Yes, I am./ No, I'm not.
7. Yes, it is. (Unless there is an unusual reason why it is not.)
8. No, they aren't. They're large.
9. Yes, it is. (But there are other countries that are much larger.)
10. No, it isn't. It's cold.

Written Exercise

1. Call the waiter. Ask ___him___ for the menu.
2. We're thirsty. Please bring ___us___ some water.
3. That apple is no good. Don't eat ___it___.
4. Those aren't your magazines. Don't take ___them___.
5. Here's my telephone number. Call ___me___ tonight.
6. We don't have the school's address. Please give ___it___ to ___us___.
7. The students are in the classroom. Mrs. Golo is with ___them___.
8. Mrs. Golo is a good teacher. The students like ___her___.
9. Where's my dictionary? Do you have ___it___?
10. Marty has chocolate on his face. Look at ___him___.

PAIR WORK 1 • *Look at page 122. Ask and answer questions about movies, TV programs, music, and books.*

> A: **What kind of movies do you like?**
> B: **I like comedies and dramas.**
>
> A: **What's your favorite movie?**
> B: **Star Wars.**

PAIR WORK 2 • *Ask and answer questions.*

> A: **Is Peter married?**
> B: **No, he isn't. He's single.**
>
> A: **Are Barbara and Tino nice people?**
> B: **Yes, they are.**

1. Is Mr. Bascomb a banker?
2. Is he poor?
3. Are Jimmy and Linda old?
4. Are they students?
5. Are you a tourist?
6. Are you very busy today?
7. Is the post office open now?
8. Are London and Tokyo small cities?
9. Is the United States a big country?
10. Is it hot in Iceland?

WRITTEN EXERCISE • *Complete the sentences using object pronouns.*

> There's Maria. Let's talk with *her*.
> I'm coming. Wait for *me*.

1. Call the waiter. Ask _____ for the menu.

2. We're thirsty. Please bring _____ some water.

3. That apple is no good. Don't eat _____.

4. Those aren't your magazines. Don't take _____.

5. Here's my telephone number. Call _____ tonight.

6. We don't have the school's address. Please give _____ to _____.

7. The students are in the classroom. Mrs. Golo is with _____.

8. Mrs. Golo is a good teacher. The students like _____.

9. Where's my dictionary? Do you have _____?

10. Marty has chocolate on his face. Look at _____.

PRACTICE • *Answer the questions about the picture.*

1. How many dogs are there in the street?
2. How many firefighters are there on the fire truck?
3. How many children are there in front of the snack bar?
4. How many police officers are there in the street?
5. How many passengers are there in Barney's taxi?
6. How many bicycles are there in front of the movie theater?
7. How many cats are there on the roof?
8. How many birds are there in the picture?
9. How many trees are there in the picture?

PAGE SUMMARY

PRACTICE: Answering questions with *there is/there are* + number + prepositional phrase

▶ FUNCTIONS

Expressing location of people, animals, and objects

▶ NEW ELEMENTS

firefighter
passenger

▶ GRAMMAR

How many . . . ?
many . . .

▶ IDEAS FOR INSTRUCTION

Practice

Prepare students for the exercise by having them talk about the picture. Put their ideas about what is happening on the board. (A woman is coming out of the drugstore. A police officer is standing on the corner. There are birds in the air. There are two bicycles outside the movie theater. And so on.)

Expansion Activity

Give the students copies of similar pictures that have several elements and ask them to write questions that they can ask a partner.

▶ ANSWERS

Practice

1. There are two dogs in the street.
2. There are seven firefighters and one driver on the truck.
3. There are two children in front of the snack bar.
4. There is one police officer on the corner.
5. There are four passengers in Barney's taxi.
6. There are two bicycles in front of the movie theater.
7. There is one cat on the roof.
8. There are five birds in the picture.
9. There are three trees in the picture.

PAGE SUMMARY
WRITTEN EXERCISE: Review of prepositions
PRACTICE: Responding to Yes/No questions
PAIR WORK: Review of present continuous

▶**FUNCTIONS**
Indicating location of people, objects, and places
Describing actions

▶**NEW ELEMENTS**
drugstore
cross (v)
Japanese
pet shop

▶**GRAMMAR**
Where is/are . . . ?
What is/are . . . ?

▶**IDEAS FOR INSTRUCTION**

Written Exercise
Review the students' answers and discuss common
errors.

Expansion Activity
Review the rules regarding emergency vehicles. All
drivers should stop their cars and pull over to the
curb. Children on bicycles should get off the road.
The road should be clear.

▶**PRONUNCIATION TIPS**
drugstore
pet shop
snack bar
movie theater
fire truck

▶**ANSWERS**

Written Exercise
1. It's in front of the green car.
2. It's behind the green car.
3. He's on the corner.
4. They're on the fire truck.
5. They're in Barney's taxi.
6. They're in front of the snack bar.
7. It's across the street from the drugstore.
8. They're in front of the movie theater.
9. It's next to the snack bar.
10. It's on the roof.

Practice
1. Yes, he is.
2. No, he isn't.
3. Yes, he is.
4. No, he doesn't. He has four passengers.
5. No, they aren't. They're Japanese.
6. Yes, they are.
7. No, she isn't. She's opening it.
8. No, they aren't. They're chasing the fire truck.
9. Yes, they are.
10. No, it isn't. It's across the street from the snack bar. It's next to the theater.

Pair Work
1. A: Where's Mr. Bascomb?
   B: He's on the corner.
2. A: What's he looking at?
   B: He's looking at the fire truck.
3. A: What's Barney doing?
   B: He's driving the taxi.
4. A: What are his passengers doing?
   B: They're looking at the fire truck.
5. A: Where's the policeman standing?
   B: He's standing in the street.
6. A: What are the dogs chasing?
   B: They're chasing the fire truck.
7. A: What are the children eating?
   B: They're eating hot dogs.
8. A: What are they looking at?
   B: They're looking at the fire truck.
9. A: What's the old woman doing?
   B: She's leaning out the window and looking at the fire truck.
10. A: Is the young woman leaving the drugstore or the movie theater?
    B: She's leaving the drugstore.

WRITTEN EXERCISE • *Answer the questions about the picture.*

Where are the dogs? _____*They're in*_____ the street.

Where's the green car? _____*It's between*_____ the taxi and the bus.

1. Where's the taxi? _____ the green car.

2. Where's the bus? _____ the green car.

3. Where's Mr. Bascomb? _____ the corner.

4. Where are the firefighters? _____ the fire truck.

5. Where are the Japanese tourists? _____ Barney's taxi.

6. Where are the children? _____ the snack bar.

7. Where's the snack bar? _____ the street from the drugstore.

8. Where are the bicycles? _____ the movie theater.

9. Where's the pet shop? _____ the snack bar.

10. Where's the cat? _____ the roof.

PRACTICE • *Answer the questions about the picture.*

Is Mr. Bascomb crossing the street?
No, he isn't. He's standing at the corner.

Is he looking at the fire truck?
Yes, he is.

1. Is Mr. Bascomb wearing glasses?
2. Is he wearing a hat?
3. Is Barney driving his taxi?
4. Does he have three passengers?
5. Are they Italian?
6. Are the children eating hot dogs?
7. Is the old woman closing the window?
8. Are the dogs chasing the police officer?
9. Are the bicycles in front of the movie theater?
10. Is the drugstore next to the snack bar?

PAIR WORK • *Ask and answer questions.*

A: Where's the cat?
B: **It's on the roof.**

1. Where's Mr. Bascomb?
2. What's he looking at?
3. What's Barney doing?
4. What are his passengers doing?
5. Where's the policeman standing?
6. What are the dogs chasing?
7. What are the children eating?
8. What are they looking at?
9. What's the old woman doing?
10. Is the young woman leaving the drugstore or the movie theater?

CONVERSATION

🔊 *Listen and practice.*

PETER: Do you like jazz?

MARIA: Yes, very much.

PETER: There's a good concert tonight. Are you free?

MARIA: Sure. Let's go.
OR No, I'm sorry. I'm busy tonight.

PAIR WORK • *Have similar conversations.*

1. basketball
   game/this weekend

2. rock and roll
   concert/Saturday night

3. baseball
   game/tomorrow afternoon

4. classical music
   concert/next week

5. boxing
   fight/Friday night

6. jazz
   concert/tonight

7. football
   game/this Sunday

8. country music
   concert/tomorrow

9. soccer
   game/next Saturday

PAGE SUMMARY

CONVERSATION and **PAIR WORK:** Making plans based on likes and dislikes

▶**FUNCTIONS**

Making suggestions
Expressing likes and dislikes

▶**NEW ELEMENTS**

<u>con</u>cert
to<u>**night**</u>
<u>sor</u>ry
<u>**box**</u>ing
<u>**week**</u>end
<u>rock</u> and <u>**roll**</u>
to<u>**morrow**</u>
<u>Fri</u>day
<u>Sat</u>urday
<u>**next**</u> <u>**week**</u>
<u>soc</u>cer

▶**GRAMMAR**

Let's go!
I'm sorry.

▶**IDEAS FOR INSTRUCTION**

Conversation

Use the tape to present the conversation. Then have students role-play the parts.

Expansion Activity

Have the students interview a fellow classmate, a friend, or a relative about what they do on the weekend. Then have them give a presentation about the interview. They should ask at least five questions. You might need to brainstorm the questions with them.

▶**PRONUNCIATION TIPS**

I like <u>**rock**</u> and <u>**roll**</u>.
I like <u>**jazz**</u>.
I like <u>**clas**</u>si<u>cal</u> <u>**mus**</u>ic.

▶**ANSWERS**

Pair Work

Examples:

1. A: Do you like basketball?
   B: Sure!
   A: There's a basketball game this weekend.
      Do you want to go?
   B: Let's go!
5. A: Do you like boxing?
   B: Why?
   A: There's a boxing fight (or boxing match) on
      Friday night. Are you free?
   B: I'm sorry. I can't go.

PAGE SUMMARY

WRITTEN EXERCISE: Review of negative sentences with *like*

▶FUNCTIONS
Expressing negative preferences

▶NEW ELEMENTS
flies (singular, **fly**)

▶GRAMMAR
He or she doesn't like . . .
They don't like . . .

▶IDEAS FOR INSTRUCTION

Expansion Activity
Have students go around the classroom and ask their classmates about things that they do not like. Have them explain why they do not like the items.

You can suggest some unusual foods for this exercise, such as anchovies, clams, and oysters.

▶PRONUNCIATION TIPS
The *don't* and *doesn't* get secondary stress.
Peter **doesn't** like **may**on**naise.**

▶ANSWERS

Written Exercise
3. Mrs. Golo _doesn't like rats_.
4. The students _don't like homework_.
5. Jack _doesn't like cats_.
6. Anne _doesn't like birds_.
7. Mr. and Mrs. Bascomb _don't like cheese_.
8. Dr. Pasto _doesn't like coffee_ (or tea).

WRITTEN EXERCISE • *Make a negative sentence for each picture using the verb to like.*

1. Peter *doesn't like mayonnaise*.

2. Barbara and Tino *don't like flies*.

3. Mrs. Golo _____.

4. The students _____.

5. Jack _____.

6. Anne _____.

7. The Bascombs _____.

8. Dr. Pasto _____.

Listen and practice.

STOREKEEPER: Can I help you, ma'am?

MABEL BROWN: Yes. I'm looking for some bananas.

STOREKEEPER: I'm sorry. There aren't any bananas left.

MABEL BROWN: Oh, that's too bad!

PAIR WORK • *Have similar conversations.*

A: Can I help you, _____?

B: Yes, I'm looking for some _____.

A: You're lucky. We have some nice

_____ today.

OR I'm sorry. There aren't any

_____ left.

B: Oh, that's wonderful!

OR Oh, that's too bad!

1. apples
2. bananas
3. pears
4. peaches
5. pineapples
6. cherries
7. oranges
8. grapes
9. lemons

WRITTEN EXERCISE • *Write a list of things you need to buy at the market.*

PAGE SUMMARY
CONVERSATION and **PAIR WORK:** Buying fruit

▶**FUNCTIONS**
Expressing needs

▶**NEW ELEMENTS**
storekeeper
be **left** (v)
That's too **bad**!
lucky
pineapple
grapes
lemons

▶**GRAMMAR**
To be left, as in "There aren't any bananas left."

▶**IDEAS FOR INSTRUCTION**

Conversation
Ask students to look at the pictures first. What is
the gist of the interchange? Then have them read
the dialogue silently. Were their guesses right?
Next, play the tape and have them repeat.

Expansion Activity
Play the game "Fruit Basket Upset" using the
names of the fruit from this page. (See page 111 for
rules.)

▶**PRONUNCIATION TIPS**
The two words **storekeep**er and **pineapp**le have
the same stress pattern.

▶**ANSWERS**

Pair Work
Examples:

A: Can I help you?
B: Yes, I'm looking for some apples.
A: You're lucky. We have some nice apples today.
B: Oh, that's wonderful!

A: Can I help you?
B: Yes, I'm looking for some peaches.
A: I'm sorry. There aren't any peaches left.
B: Oh, that's too bad!

▶**FUNCTIONS**
Expressing needs

▶**NEW ELEMENTS**
to **need** (v)
gas

▶**GRAMMAR**
To need something

▶**IDEAS FOR INSTRUCTION**

Expansion Activity
Play the game "Consensus." Have students pretend that they are on a deserted island. They can only have five things with them. Students should work alone at first to make lists of things they think that they will need. Then have them work in small groups and compare and revise lists. Then have each group make up a list of five things they think they need, and have the whole class compare lists.

▶**PRONUNCIATION TIPS**

What do **Joe** and **Ed**die **need**?
What do they **need**?

▶**ANSWERS**

Pair Work

3. A: What does Monty need?
   B: He needs some water.
4. A: What do Joe and Eddie need?
   B: They need some shoes.
5. A: What does Gloria need?
   B: She needs an umbrella.
6. A: What do Betty and Bruno need?
   B: They need some food.
7. A: What does Mr. Workman need?
   B: He needs a secretary.

8. A: What do these people need?
   B: They need jobs.
9. A: What does Suzi need?
   B: She needs a coat.
10. A: What do Joe and Eddie need?
    B: They need some money.
11. A: What do you need?
    B: I need _____.

• *Ask and answer questions using the verb* **to need.**

1. Peter

| A: **What does Peter need?** |
| B: **He needs some gas.** |

2. Joe and Eddie

| A: **What do Joe and Eddie need?** |
| B: **They need a car.** |

3.   Monty

4.   Joe and Eddie

5.   Gloria

6.   Betty and Bruno

7.   Mr. Workman

8.   these people

9.   Suzi

10.   Joe and Eddie

11.   you

Listen and practice.

ROLE PLAY • *Student A plays a tourist, Student B plays a concierge, and Student C plays a bellboy. Act out a scene like the one above. Choose any city.*

PAGE SUMMARY
CONVERSATION and **ROLE PLAY:** Checking into a hotel

▶FUNCTIONS
Checking into a hotel

▶NEW ELEMENTS

reservation	**Can** I **help** you?
key	**Yes, sir.**
bags	You're **welcome.**
mademoiselle	
concierge	
bell boy	
act out	
scene	
stay (v)	
how long?	

▶GRAMMAR
"How long are you staying?"
Question about duration.

▶IDEAS FOR INSTRUCTION

Conversation
Discuss the pictures. Then, listen to the tape. Stop after each frame of the cartoon story to discuss what is happening in that scene.

Role Play
Make a list of four or five cities. If you wish have students practice in groups of four: one tourist, one concierge, one bell boy, and one critic to provide feedback.

Expansion Activity
Have the students work in small groups to create their own role-plays. Ask each group to act out the role-play before the whole class. Encourage them to use realia to make the role-play more realistic.

▶PRONUNCIATION TIPS
Pronunciation practice with the French words in English will probably be helpful.

mademoiselle /maèdimazél/
concierge /kòn siy érž

PAGE SUMMARY

CLASS ACTIVITY: Discussing a scene at a Parisian cafe
READING: Understanding the content and format of a postcard
PAIR WORK: Writing a postcard to a friend

▶**FUNCTIONS**
Describing actions

▶**NEW ELEMENTS**
to **write** (v)
charming
to **feel** (v)
partner
a **French**man

▶**GRAMMAR**
Review of present continuous tense
I'm having coffee with a charming Frenchman.
Who is Nancy writing to?
Why is Nancy feeling so good?

▶**IDEAS FOR INSTRUCTION**

Class Activity
Start the lesson with a discussion of what's going on in the picture.

Nancy and **Pierre** are **sitt**ing at a **tab**le at a ca**fe**.
The **sun** is **shin**ing.
A **wait**er is bringing them **coff**ee.
A **man** is **play**ing **mus**ic.
A **wom**an is **sell**ing **flow**ers.

Reading
To introduce the reading, play the tape. Then do the questions together as a class.

Expansion Activity
Have students brainstorm different countries that they would like to visit. Then have them work individually to create a travel plan. Where would they go? What would they see? Why would they go there? Then ask the students to share their travel plans with the rest of the class.

▶**PRONUNCIATION TIPS**
Use the sentences under Ideas for Instruction for practice with intonation.

▶**ANSWERS**

Reading
1. She's in Paris.
2. She's having coffee with Pierre.
3. He's charming.
4. It's a beautiful day, the sun is shining, and she's feeling wonderful.
5. She's writing to Gloria Cole.
6. Her address is 1274 Pine Street, Wickam City, California, 95820, U.S.A.

CLASS ACTIVITY • *Talk about the picture. What's happening?*

Café La Palette

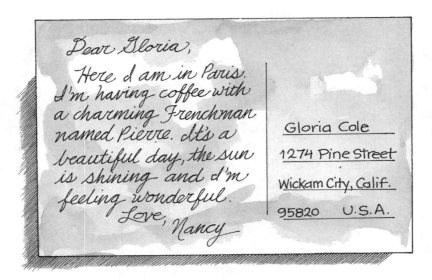

Dear Gloria,

Here I am in Paris. I'm having coffee with a charming Frenchman named Pierre. It's a beautiful day, the sun is shining and I'm feeling wonderful.

Love, Nancy

Gloria Cole
1274 Pine Street
Wickam City, Calif.
95820   U.S.A.

Answer the questions about the postcard.

1. What city is Nancy in?
2. Who is she having coffee with?
3. What is Pierre like?

4. Why is Nancy feeling so good?
5. Who is Nancy writing to?
6. What is Gloria's address?

PAIR WORK • *Work with a partner and write a similar postcard to a friend.*

PAIR WORK • *Ask and answer questions about the pictures.*

1. A: **What is the salesman showing Gloria?**
   B: **He's showing her some tennis shoes.**

2. A: **What is Mable serving her guests?**
   B: **She's serving them some cake.**

3. A: **What is Linda giving Fenwick?**
   B: **She's giving him a bone.**

4. What is Albert bringing Linda?

5. What is Mrs. Mango buying her son?

6. What is Dr. Pasto showing his friends?

7. What is Fenwick bringing Sam?

8. What is Mabel serving her guests?

9. What is Mr. Lassiter buying his daughter?

10. What is Mrs. Golo showing her students?

11. What is Marty giving Mrs. Golo?

12. What is Anne bringing Mr. Bascomb?

PAGE SUMMARY
PAIR WORK: Review of present continuous and direct object pronouns

▶**FUNCTIONS**
Describing actions

▶**NEW ELEMENTS**
tennis <u>shoes</u>
serve (v)
son
dau**gh**ter
guest
bone

▶**GRAMMAR**
Use of the present continuous tense
Use of indirect object pronouns before direct
  objects

  She's giving him a bone.
  He's showing her some tennis shoes.

▶**IDEAS FOR INSTRUCTION**

Pair Work
Talk about the pictures before assigning the Pair
Work exercise.
  Talk about family relationships: mother, father,
parents, son, daughter, brother, and sister.

Expansion Activities
1. Give each pair of students an object (a book, a
pencil, a notebook, a dictionary) and ask one
student to give it to another. Then they write two
sentences about it:

  Pat gave Rick the dictionary.
  Pat gave the dictionary to Rick.

2. Distribute pictures from your picture file that
show direct and indirect objects. Ask students to
tell what's happening in the pictures.

3. Have students make up questions about the
classroom using "what is/are . . . ?" Then have
them ask their classmates the questions. If you
want to make this more difficult, have students
close their eyes while answering.

▶**PRONUNCIATION TIPS**
Remind students that pronouns do not ordinarily
get the stress. If the indirect object is a noun, however, it will get secondary stress.

  Albert is bringing **Glor**ia some <u>**flow**</u>ers.
  Albert is **bring**ing her some <u>**flow**</u>ers.

▶**ANSWERS**

Pair Work
4. A: What is Albert bringing Linda?
   B: He's bringing her flowers.
5. A: What is Mrs. Mango buying her son?
   B: She's buying him a hat.
6. A: What is Dr. Pasto showing his friends?
   B: He's showing them his new painting.
7. A: What is Fenwick bringing Sam?
   B: He's bringing him a newspaper.
8. A: What is Mabel serving her guests?
   B: She's serving them coffee.

9. A: What is Mr. Lassiter buying his daughter?
   B: He's buying her some ice cream.
10. A: What is Mrs. Golo showing her students?
    B: She's showing them some butterflies.
11. A: What is Marty giving Mrs. Golo?
    B: He's giving her an apple.
12. A: What is Anne bringing Mr. Bascomb?
    B: She's bringing him a sandwich.

PAGE SUMMARY

CONVERSATION and **PRACTICE 1** and **2:** Naming personal items
PAIR WORK: Review of *to have*
FREE RESPONSE: Discussing a variety of conversation topics

▶FUNCTIONS

Indicating location of objects (inside something)

▶NEW ELEMENTS

a **lot** of	Can I **see**?
contents	**Sure.**
candy	
address **book**	
comb	
brush (n)	
name (v)	
change (n)	
food	
song	

▶GRAMMAR

Review of *to have*
Review of present continuous

▶IDEAS FOR INSTRUCTION

Conversation and **Practice 1**
Listen to the tape. Then practice the intonation of the items in Mrs. Golo's handbag.

Expansion Activity

Have a bag with different items in it. Make sure that there are as many items as there are students. Have each student put a hand in the bag and choose one item. Without pulling their hand from the bag, they should try to guess what the item is. If they want to, they can describe the item to the rest of the class. Then the rest of the class can help that student guess what the item is. After the student has guessed the item, have that student pull his or her hand out of the bag to see if the guess was correct. Remove the item that has been named. Then have each student do the same thing.

▶PRONUNCIATION TIPS

Practice the intonation of listing a series of things.

Mrs. **Go**lo has a **comb**/, some **mon**ey/, and an **add**ress **book**\.

▶ANSWERS

Pair Work
Answers will vary.

Free Response
Answers will vary.

Listen and practice.

 PRACTICE 1 • *Here are the contents of Mrs. Golo's handbag. Listen and repeat.*

1. candy   2. money   3. keys   4. pencil   5. address book

6. pen   7. stamps   8. comb   9. brush   10. mirror

PRACTICE 2 • *Close your book. Name three things Mrs. Golo has in her handbag.*

PAIR WORK • *Ask about the contents of your partner's handbag, wallet, or pocket.*

> A: **What do you have in your pocket?**
> B: **I have my keys, a comb, and some change.**
>   OR **I don't have anything.**

change

FREE RESPONSE

1. What are you wearing today? What are the students in your class wearing?
2. Are you a good talker? What do you talk about with your friends?
3. Do you have a camera? What kind is it?
4. Are you a music lover? Do you like rock music? jazz?
5. What is your favorite song? Who is your favorite singer?
6. Do you have a big family? How many brothers and sisters do you have?
7. Do you like American food? How is the food in your country?
8. Is there a market near your house? What street is it on? Is it open now?
9. What do you have in your refrigerator? Is there any ice cream?

1. This is Mr. Poole.

   _____ is a teacher.
   a. Him   c. He
   b. It   d. She

2. _____ book is interesting.
   a. These   c. Those
   b. There   d. This

3. _____ flowers are beautiful.
   a. Those   c. That
   b. There   d. This

4. The table is _____ the kitchen.
   a. on   c. to
   b. at   d. in

5. The umbrella is _____ the floor.
   a. at   c. in
   b. on   d. to

6. Nancy is _____ the airport.
   a. to   c. at
   b. on   d. with

7. Tino _____ thirsty.
   a. is   c. have
   b. has   d. are

8. Are _____ pretty girls?
   a. she   c. them
   b. they   d. her

9. The flowers _____ in the vase.
   a. are   c. be
   b. is   d. have

10. Tino isn't short.

    He's _____.
    a. poor   c. sad
    b. happy   d. tall

11. Those books aren't cheap.

    They're _____.
    a. old   c. small
    b. expensive d. rich

12. They _____ the bank.
    a. are going   c. are going to
    b. is going   d. going to

13. _____ is that? It's a coffee pot.
    a. Who   c. Where
    b. How   d. What

14. _____ He's at the garage.
    a. Where is he?
    b. What is he?
    c. Who is he?
    d. How is he?

15. _____ They're fine, thank you.
    a. Who are they?
    b. What are they?
    c. How are they?
    d. Where are they?

16. _____ is she going? To the market.
    a. What   c. Who
    b. Where   d. How

17. _____ is he? He's Dr. Pasto.
    a. Where   c. How
    b. What   d. Who

18. Wait _____ Anne.
    a. for   c. to
    b. at   d. from

19. Who is she looking _____?
    a. on   c. to
    b. at   d. from

20. He's listening _____ the radio.
    a. at   c. of
    b. in   d. to

PAGE SUMMARY
TEST

▶**FUNCTIONS**
Review and assessment of Chapters 1–8

▶**NEW ELEMENTS**
None

▶**GRAMMAR**
Review

▶**IDEAS FOR INSTRUCTION**
Have the students do this quiz as either an in-class assessment or a take-home practice quiz.

▶**ANSWERS**

1. c	6. c	11. b	16. b	21. a	26. c	31. d	36. c
2. d	7. a	12. c	17. d	22. c	27. d	32. a	37. d
3. a	8. b	13. d	18. a	23. b	28. d	33. c	38. b
4. d	9. a	14. a	19. b	24. c	29. b	34. a	39. c
5. b	10. d	15. c	20. d	25. a	30. a	35. b	40. a

21. Talk _____ them.

    a. to   c. on
    b. at   d. of

22. Put these glasses _____ the table.

    a. to   c. on
    b. in   d. at

23. They don't have _____ books.

    a. there   c. theirs
    b. their   d. them

24. This magazine is _____.

    a. to her   c. hers
    b. her   d. of her

25. That desk is _____.

    a. mine   c. me
    b. my   d. to me

26. Whose apartment is that?

    It's _____.

    a. to him   c. his
    b. Mr. Jones   d. him

27. Give the flowers _____.

    a. them   c. to they
    b. their   d. to them

28. That man is hungry.

    Give _____ some food.

    a. he   c. his
    b. her   d. him

29. Mrs. Jones is in Italy.

    Write _____ a letter.

    a. to her   c. hers
    b. her   d. him

30. Do they have a car?

    No, they _____.

    a. don't   c. aren't
    b. doesn't   d. have

31. _____ an apple in the kitchen.

    a. It has   c. It's
    b. There are   d. There's

32. Where are the cups?

    _____ on the shelf.

    a. They're   c. There is
    b. There are   d. Their

33. What are those?

    _____ dictionaries.

    a. There are   c. They're
    b. There's some   d. It's a

34. _____ milk in the bottle.

    a. There's some   c. It's a
    b. There's a   d. There are

35. _____ letters on the desk.

    a. There's   c. Their
    b. There are   d. They're

36. What time is it? _____

    a. It's hot.
    b. It's ten dollars.
    c. It's two o'clock.
    d. It's six years old.

37. How old is that watch? _____

    a. It's one o'clock.
    b. It's fifty dollars.
    c. It's expensive.
    d. It's six years old.

38. How much is that computer? _____

    a. It's in the office.
    b. It's five hundred dollars.
    c. It's six years old.
    d. It's very good.

39. Jimmy _____ ice cream.

    a. have   c. likes
    b. like   d. want

40. She's thirsty.

    She _____ a glass of water.

    a. wants   c. have
    b. want   d. likes

Preview

Teacher, see p. v

GRAMMAR
Can
Simple past
Future with "going to"

FUNCTIONS
Expressing ability/inability
Describing past actions
Expressing intention

PAGE SUMMARY
STRUCTURE and **PAIR WORK 1** and **2**: Discussing ability using modal *can*

► **FUNCTIONS**
Showing ability to do some action

► **NEW ELEMENTS**
can (modal verb, auxiliary verb)
can't (negative form)
checkers
chess
ski (v)
speak a language like English or French
swim (v)

► **GRAMMAR**
The modal *can* or its negative form *can't* are used before the simple form of the verb to show ability to do something.

► **IDEAS FOR INSTRUCTION**

Structure
Explain ability through the pictures at the top of the page. Ask the students some simple questions:

Can you speak English? (Yes, you can.)
Can someone play the guitar?
Can someone here speak Spanish? Italian? Chinese?

Expansion Activity
Play "Personal Bingo." By this time, the students in the class should know one another quite well. They should know what things people can and can't do. Make a grid for nine elements. Generate a list on the board of about fifteen things that people can do. Have the students choose nine abilities and write one ability in each square: play the guitar, bake a cake, swim, speak French, etc. Ask the students to find someone in the class who can do each of the things on their grid. They should ask, "Can you play the guitar?" If the person asked can play the guitar, then the student who was asked signs the square. The first person to have a full grid of signatures next to abilities wins.

► **PRONUNCIATION TIPS**
The modal *can* in a full sentence does not get stress. The negative *can't* always gets at least secondary stress. In a short answer, both *can* and *can't* get stress.

A: Can you **speak Eng**lish?/
B: **Yes,** I **can.**/
A: Can you **speak Jap**anese?/
B: **No,** I **can't.**/

► **ANSWERS**

Pair Work 1
3. A: Can Ed play the guitar?
    B: No, he can't.
4. A: Can Anne play the guitar?
    B: Yes, she can.
5. A: Can Nancy speak French?
    B: Yes, she can.
6. A: Can Fred speak French?
    B: No, he can't.
7. A: Can Johnnie swim?
    B: No, he can't.
8. A: Can Dr. Pasto swim?
    B: Yes, he can.
9. A: Can Gloria cook?
    B: Yes, she can.
10. A: Can Ula Hackey cook?
    B: No, she can't.
11. A: Can Nick repair cars?
    B: Yes, he can.
12. A: Can Mr. Bascomb repair cars?
    B: No, he can't.

Pair Work 2
Answers will vary.

Listen and read.

Barney **can** swim, but he **can't** ski.

Jenny and Marty **can** play checkers, but they **can't** play chess.

PAIR WORK 1 • *Ask and answer questions about the pictures.*

1. Bonita/sing?
2. Gladys/sing?
3. Ed/play the guitar?
4. Anne/play the guitar?

A: **Can Bonita sing?**
B: **Yes, she can.**

A: **Can Gladys sing?**
B: **No, she can't.**

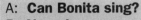

5. Nancy/speak French?
6. Fred/speak French?
7. Johnnie/swim?
8. Dr. Pasto/swim?

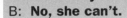

9. Gloria/cook?
10. Ula Hackey/cook?
11. Nick/repair cars?
12. Mr. Bascomb/repair cars?

PAIR WORK 2 • *Ask your partner the same questions.*

A: **Can you sing?**
B: **Yes, I can.** OR **No, I can't.**

Listen and read.

Yesterday Carlos **got up** at 7 o'clock.

He **took** a shower and **got** dressed.

Then he **had** breakfast.

At 8:30 he **left** the house and **went** to work.

PICTURE PRACTICE • *Answer the questions about Carlos.*

1. When did Carlos get up yesterday?
2. What did he do after he got up?
3. What did he do then?
4. What did Carlos have for breakfast?
5. When did he leave the house?
6. Where did he go?

PAIR WORK 1 • *Ask and answer the same questions about Suzi.*

> A: **When did Suzi get up yesterday?**
> B: **She got up at 6:30.**

PRACTICE • *Listen and practice.*

Did Suzi get up at 6:30?
Yes, she did.

Did she take a bath?
Yes, she did.

Did she have French fries for breakfast?
No, she didn't. (She had coffee and eggs.)

Did she leave the house at 8:30?
No, she didn't. (She left at 8 o'clock.)

PAIR WORK 2 • *Ask and answer questions about Carlos.*

1. Did Carlos get up at 7 o'clock?
2. Did he take a bath?
3. Did Carlos have orange juice and cereal?
4. Did he leave the house at 9 o'clock?

FREE RESPONSE • *Answer the teacher; then ask your partner these questions.*

1. When did you get up this morning?
2. Did you take a bath or a shower?
3. Did you have a big breakfast?
4. What did you have for breakfast?
5. When did you leave the house?
6. Did you go to the market?

PAGE SUMMARY

STRUCTURE, PICTURE PRACTICE, PAIR WORK 1 and 2, PRACTICE, and FREE RESPONSE:
Simple past

▶FUNCTIONS
Describing past actions

▶NEW ELEMENTS
get <u>up</u> → got <u>up</u>
get <u>dress</u>ed → <u>got dressed</u>
when
yesterday
take → took
have → had
go → went
do → did

▶GRAMMAR
The past tense forms presented here are all irregular. A past tense adverb, *yesterday*, is used to cue past action. The present tense is used for habitual or scheduled events.

▶IDEAS FOR INSTRUCTION

Structure
Distinguish between *every day* and *yesterday*. Note that it is not a good idea to talk about things that the students have done, are doing, or will do today, as these expressions will require past tense, present perfect tense, present continuous tense, or future tense.

Expansion Activity
Make a list of daily activities and ask students to write down their normal schedules. Then have pairs of students interview one another about what they did yesterday and when they did that activity.

Get up
Take a bath or a shower
Get dressed
Eat breakfast
Leave home
Go to school
Eat lunch
Go home
Do homework
Eat dinner
Go to sleep

▶ANSWERS

Picture Practice
1. He got up at seven o'clock.
2. He took a shower and got dressed.
3. He had breakfast.
4. He had cereal and orange juice.
5. He left the house at eight-thirty.
6. He went to work.

Pair Work 1
2. A: What did Suzi do after she got up?
   B: She took a bath and got dressed.
3. A: What did she do then?
   B: She had breakfast.
4. A: What did she have for breakfast?
   B: She had coffee and eggs.

5. A: When did Suzi leave the house?
   B: She left the house at eight o'clock.
6. A: Where did she go?
   B: I don't know. Perhaps she went to work or to class.

Pair Work 2
1. Yes, he did.
2. No, he didn't. He took a shower.
3. Yes, he did.
4. No, he didn't. He left the house at eight-thirty.

Free Response
Answers will vary.

PAGE SUMMARY

STRUCTURE: Past tense of regular and irregular verbs
PAIR WORK: Using adverbs of time to discuss activities in the past tense

---

▶FUNCTIONS

Talking about past actions

▶NEW ELEMENTS

ap**pen**dix	last **night**
buy → bought	this **morn**ing
ir**reg**ular	
regular	
see → saw	
study → studied	
play → played	
stay → stayed	
watch → watched	
read → read	

▶GRAMMAR

The regular past tense form is introduced:

study → studied
play → played
stay → stayed
watch → watched

Three more irregular verbs are also introduced: buy, see, and read. The pronunciation of the past tense of *read* is a short vowel.

▶IDEAS FOR INSTRUCTION

Structure

Note that there is a list of irregular verbs in the appendix.

Point out that *last night* and *this morning* are like *yesterday*. They are adverbs for the past tense.

Expansion Activity

Brainstorm a list of things that people can do to relax after school or work and write them on the board. This list will help the students do the Pair Work exercise.

▶PRONUNCIATION TIPS

Note that *play*, *study*, and *stay* all end with a voiced sound. The past tense ending, therefore, is the voiced *d*. *Watch* ends with a voiceless sound; therefore, the final sound on the past tense will be *t*. The past tense of *talk* and *work* are the same: they take the *t* sound as the final sound in the regular past tense.

▶ANSWERS

Pair Work
Answers will vary.

Listen and read.

Yesterday Suzi **went** to the market and **bought** some apples.

Last night Peter and Maria **went** to the Rex Theater and **saw** a movie.

Yesterday afternoon Linda **went** to the library and **studied.**

This morning Barbara and Tino **went** to the park and **played** tennis.

Last night Mr. and Mrs. Golo **stayed** home and **watched** TV.

Last Saturday Johnnie **stayed** home and **read** a book.

SIMPLE PAST Regular Verbs	
play – played	walk – walked
stay – stayed	watch – watched
talk – talked	work – worked

Regular verbs end in -ed.

SIMPLE PAST Irregular Verbs	
go – went	have – had
buy – bought	read – read
do – did	see – saw

For a list of irregular verbs, see the appendix.

PAIR WORK • *Ask and answer questions. Use past time expressions like **yesterday, yesterday afternoon, last night, this morning, last Saturday.***

A: **What did you do last night?**
B: **I went to the Rex Theater and saw a movie. What about you?**
A: **I stayed home and read a book.**
  OR **I didn't do anything.**

Listen and practice.

Barbara and Tino are going to play tennis.   Linda is going to see the Beach Bums.

PAIR WORK 1 • *Ask and answer questions about the pictures using* **going to.**

1. A: **What is Anne going to do?**
   B: **She's going to brush her teeth.**

2. A: **What are Carlos and Luisa going to do?**
   B: **They're going to eat dinner.**

1. Anne   2. Carlos and Luisa   3. Nancy

4. the boys   5. Barney   6. Peter and Maria

7. Suzi   8. Otis and Gloria   9. Dr. Pasto

PAIR WORK 2 • *Ask and answer three questions. Use* **going to** *with future time expressions such as* **tonight, tomorrow, Friday night, this weekend,** *and so on.*

A: **What are you going to do after class?**
B: **I'm going to study at the library.** OR **I'm going to see my friends.**

PAGE SUMMARY

STRUCTURE: Future with *going to*
PAIR WORK 1 and **2:** Discussing future plans using *going to*

▶ **FUNCTIONS**
Talking about future plans

▶ **NEW ELEMENTS**
be **go**ing to
future
beach
and **so** on

▶ **GRAMMAR**
The *be going to* structure works the same way as *can* in that it fits in before the root verb; however, it changes according to the subject.

▶ **IDEAS FOR INSTRUCTION**

Structure
Write these sentence beginnings on the board.

I am going to . . .
We are going to . . .

You are going to . . .
She is going to . . .
He is going to . . .
It is going to . . .
They are going to . . .

Fill in each of the blanks.

▶ **PRONUNCIATION TIPS**
The *be* verb will be contracted in natural speech.

I'm going to **leave** at <u>ten</u>.
We're going to **leave** at <u>ten</u>.
You're going to **leave** at <u>ten</u>.
She's going to **leave** at <u>ten</u>.
He's going to **leave** at <u>ten</u>.
It's going to **leave** at <u>ten</u>.
They're going to **leave** at <u>ten</u>.

▶ **ANSWERS**

Pair Work 1

3. A: What's Nancy going to do?
    B: She's going to watch television.
4. A: What are the boys going to do?
    B: They're going to play basketball.
5. A: What is Barney going to do?
    B: He's going to buy some flowers.
6. A: What are Peter and Maria going to do?
    B: They are going to dance.
7. A: What's Suzi going to do?
    B: She's going to take a bath.

8. A: What are Otis and Gloria going to do?
    B: They are going to see a movie.
9. A: What is Dr. Pasto going to do?
    B: He's going to play the piano.

Pair Work 2
Answers will vary.

VOCABULARY LIST

A

a 1
about 5
above 2
across 3
act out 8
address 3
address book 8
adjective 1
affirmative 1
afraid 4
afternoon 4
airplane 2
airport 1
all right 3
a lot of 8
already 7
also 6
am 2
American 2
an 1
and you? 1
animal 4
answer (v) 1, 4, (n) 2
antique shop 8
any 7
anything 4
anything else 4
apartment 4
apple 1
apple pie 4
are 2
aren't 2
art 8
artist 1
ask 1, 3
aspirin 4
at 1
athlete 7
avenue 2
average 6

B

bad 2
bag 7
bags (baggage) 8
balcony 7
ball 1
ballet dancer 2
banana 7
bank 1
banker 1
barber 3
baseball 5
basketball 5
bath 5

bathroom 5
bathtub 7
be 3
be in good hands 4
be left 8
be like 6, 7
beautiful 2
because 7
bed 3
bedroom 7
behind 1
bellboy 8
belong to 7
best 6
best friend 6
between 3
bicycle 2
big 2
bill 4
biography 8
bird 1
black 2
blackboard 3
blond 2
blouse 2
blue 2
bone 8
book 1
bookcase 1
boots 7
bottle 1
bowl 7
box 7
boxing 8
boy 2
Brazilian 2
bread 7
breakfast 5
bring 3
brother 5
brown 2
brush (v) 4, (n) 8
building 7
bum 4
bunch 7
bus 1
bus station 4
bus stop 1
business 2
businessman 1
busy 4
but 1, 2
butter 7
butterfly 7
buy 5
bye 1

C

cafe 3
cake 7
calendar 7
call 3
camera 6
can (n) 7, (v) 8
Can I help you? 8
Can I see? 8
candle 3
candy 8
can't PR
capital 2
car 1
card 1
carrot 7
carton 7
cartoon 2
cashier 5
cat 1
cereal 7
certainly 8
chair 1
change 1, (n) 8
chapter 1
charming 8
chapter 7
chase (v) 7
cheap 2
checkers PR
cheese 4
cherry, cherries 7
cherry soda 7
chess PR
chicken 1
children 6
Chinese 2
chocolate 8
choose 1, 7
church 3
city 2
city park 3
class 2, 3
classic 6
classical 8
clean (adj) 2, (v) 5
clock 1
close (v) 3
clothes 2
coat 1
coffee 2
coffee pot 7
coffeeshop 5
Coke 5
cold 2
collection 7

color 2
comb 8
come 3
comedy 8
comfortable 7
command 3
complete (v) 1
composition 8
computer 2
concert 8
concierge 8
contents 8
conversation 1
cook (v) 5
cookies 4
corn 7
corner 1
corn flakes 7
correct 1
couch 3
counter 5
country 3
country singer 2
country western 8
cowboy 7
cross (v) 8
cup 3
customers 7
cut (v) 5

D

dance (v) 5
dancer 2
dangerous 3
darts (n pl) 5
daughter 8
delicious 7
dental floss 4
dentist 4
department 3
department store 3
departure 4
describe 2, 6
desk 3
destination 4
dialogue 2
dictionary 2
did PR
different 8
dinner 3
dirty 2
dish 3
do 5
doctor 1
dog 1
dollar 2

don't (negative imperative)   3
door   5
doughnut   4
down   3
drama   8
draw   5
dress   2
dressed   PR
dresser   3
drink (v)   5, (n)   6
drugstore   3, 8
dry   3

E

each other   5
eat   3
egg   1
eight   2
eighteen   2
eighty   3
eleven   2
else   4
emergency   3
encyclopedia   5
England   2
English   2
enjoy   8
entertainment   8
envelope   1
evening   3
every   3
every day   3
everything   6, 7
excuse me   2
exercise   1
exhibition   8
expensive   2
expert   7
expression   8
eye   2

F

fact   2
family   5
far from   3
fast   4
fast food   4
fat   2
father   3
favorite   2
feel   8
fence   7
fifteen   2
fifty   3
film   8
Fine, thank you!   1
fire   3

fire department   3
firefighter   8
fireplace   7
first   8
fish   6
five   2
flag   7
flies (n pl)   8
floor   1
flower   1
food   4, 8
football   5
football game   5
for   5
forget   4
form (n)   4
for sale   8
forty   3
four   2
fourteen   2
free   3
French   2
french fries   7
Frenchman   8
Friday   8
friend   2
friendly   3
from   2
front   1
front desk   4
front yard   7

G

game   5
garage   1
garden   6
gas   1, 8
gas station   1
get   5
get dressed   PR
get up   PR
girl   2
girlfriend   2
give   3
glass   1
glasses   6
go   3
good   1
good-bye   1
good morning   1
got dressed   PR
got up   PR
grammar   1
grapes   8
grass   5
gray   2
green   2

group   1
guess   8
guitar   2

H

had   PR
hair   5
half   3
half past   3
ham   7
hamburger   4
hand   6
handbag   6
handsome   2
happen   5
happy   2
hat   1
have   1, 3, 6
Have a nice day!   3
have lunch (v)   5
he   1
hello   1
height   6
help (v)   5
her   3
here   3
here's   3
Here we are!   4
hi   1
hill   5
him   3
his   1
historical   8
home   5
homework   5
hospital   1
hot   2
hot dog   4
hours   3
house   3
how   1
How are you?   1
how long   8
how many   7, 8
How much does it cost?   2
hundred   3
hungry   2
husband   5

I

I   1
ice cream   4
idea   8
I'm fine   1
I'm not sure   4
imperative   3
important   3
in   1

include   8
incredible   3
in fact   2
information   4
in front of   1
intelligence   6
intelligent   2
interesting   8
interrogative   1
intonation   2
introduce   6
irregular   1, 2
is   1
Is it . . . ?   1
isn't   1
it   1
Italian   2
it's   1
It's good for . . .   4

J

Japanese   8
jar   7
jazz   8
jeans   5
job   1
juice   7

K

ketchup   7
key   8
kiss   5
kitchen   5
knife, knives   7

L

lamp   3
large   7
laugh   3
leave   3
(be) left   8
lemon   8
lemonade   2
letter   2
lettuce   7
library   1
life, lives   5
light (v)   3
like (v)   7
listen   1
little   3
living room   4
long   5
look at   1, 3
love   7
love story   8
lover   8
lucky   8
lunch   5

M

ma'am   3
mademoiselle   8
magazine   2
make   3, 5
man   2
manager   3
many   7, 8
market   7
married   2
matches   3
mayonnaise   7
me   3
me (as indirect object)   3
meat   8
mechanic   1
meeting   2
menu   5
midnight   3
milk   5
minute   7
mirror   6
modern   2
Mom   3
moment   7
money   7
month   7
more   4
morning   3
mother   5
mouth   4
mouthwash   4
move   4
movie star   1
movies   1
museum   1
mushroom   7
music   7
musical   8
mustard   7
my   1
My name's . . .   1
mystery   8

N

name (n)   1, (v)   8
nationality   2
near   3
need to   8
negative   1, 7
new   1, 4
newspaper   1
next (adj)   4
next to   1
next week   8
nice   6
Nice to meet you   1
night   5
nightgown   5

nine   2
nineteen   2
ninety   3
no   2
noon   3
not   1
nothing   5
noun   1
now   3
nurse   4

O

object   2
object pronoun   3
occupation   1, 4
o'clock   2
of   1
office   1
Oh, really?   6
old   2
olive   7
on   1
one   2
one (as pronoun)   3
one way   4
on fire   3
onion   7
open   3
opposite   2
or   2
orange   1
orange juice   4
oranges (n)   3
ordinary   8
original   6
other   2
our   6
outside   3
over there   4

P

page   1, 7
pain   4
paint (v)   5
painting (n)   8
pair   1
pajamas   5
pants   2
paper   6
park   5
parking lot   3
partner   8
party   6
passenger   8
past   3
(the) past   5
patient   4
pay (v)   4
peach   7

pear   2
pen   3
pencil   6
people   2, 6
personality   8
pepper   7
pet shop   8
phone   3, 6
phone number   3
piano   5
picnic   7
picture   1, 3
piece   6
pilot   1
pineapple   8
pizza   7
place (n)   1
plant (v)   6
plants (n)   7
plate   7
play (v)   5
plural   1
pocket   6
point to   3
police officer   1
poor   2
popular   7
postcard   2
post office   1
pot   2
potato, potatoes   7
practice (n)   1, (v)   1
predicate adjective   2
predicate noun   1
prefer   7
prepare   5
preposition   1, 5
president   6
price   3
professor   7
program   8
(the) public   8
put   3

Q

quarter to/past   3
question   1, 2, 3
quiet   3

R

rabbit   1
radish, radishes   7
raise (n)   7
rat   4
read   3
reading   2
ready   3
really   3
red   2

refrigerator   6
relax   5
repair   5
repeat   1, 3
replace   1, 2
reservation   8
response   3
rest (v)   5
restaurant   4, 5
review   1
rice   7
rich   2
right (adj)   6
right away   3
right now   6
roast beef   7
rock and roll   7
rock music   7
roof   8
room   3
rose   7
round trip   4

S

sad   2
sailboat   6
salad   7
sale   8
salesman   3
salespeople   3
salesperson   8
sandwich   4
Saturday   8
Saudi Arabia   2
say (v)   5
scene   8
school   7
science fiction   8
secretary   1
section   1
See you later   1
sentence   1
serve (v)   8
seven   2
seventeen   2
seventy   3
shape   8
she   1
shelf   3
She's a . . .   1
shine (v)   5
shirt   2
shoes   2
shop   3
short   1, 2
show   3
shower (n)   5
side (n)   6
sidewalk   7

similar 1
sing 5
singer 1
singular 1
sink (n) 7
sister 5
sit 3
six 2
sixteen 2
sixty 3
small 2
smile (v) 5
snack bar 5
snake 4
So are you 3
soccer 8
socks 3
soda 4
sofa 3
some (pron, adj) 7
someone 6
son 8
song 8
sorry 8
soup 7
spaghetti 7
speak PR
spider 4
sport 7
sports 8
stamp 6
stand (v) 3
star 8
statue 7
stay (v) 8
step 7
storekeeper 8
story 2
stove 7
strange 8
street 2
stress 2
string beans 7
strong 2
structure 1
student 1
sugar 4
summary 1
sun 5
Sunday 5
supermarket 3
sure 4, Sure! 8
sweater 2
sweet 5
swim PR

T
table 1
take 3

take a bath 5
take a shower 5
Take me to . . . 4
talk 3
talker 8
tall 2
taxi 1, 4
taxi driver 1
tea 5
teacher 1
team 7
teeth 4
telegram 5
telephone 4
television 5
tell 3
Tell her I'm busy 4
ten 2
tennis shoes 8
test 3
thank you 1
that 1
That's too bad! 8
the 1
theater 3
their 6
them 3
there is . . . 1
there's 3
these 1
they 1
they're 2
thin 2
thing 6
think 5
thirsty 2
thirteen 2
thirty (31) 3
this 1
this is . . . 1
   is this . . . ? 1
those 1
three 2
ticket 4
time 2
to 1
to + indirect object 3
today 5
toilet 7
tomato 7
tomato juice 7
tomorrow 8
tonight 8
too 1
too + adj 3
took PR

touch 3
tourist 2
traditional 7
trash 7
tree 1
truck 1
TV 5
TV program 8
TV star 8
twelve 2
twenty 2
twenty-one (29) 3
two 2
typewriter 7

U
ugly 2
umbrella 2
uncountable (n) 7
under 1
(the) United States 2
up 3
us 3
use 2, 4

V
vase 1
vegetables 6
vegetarian 8
verb 7
very 2
violin 2
visitor 7
vocabulary 1, 2

W
wait 2
waiter 2
waitress 7
walk (v) 5
wall 3
wallet 6
want 7
wash 3
wash basin 7
wastebasket 2
watch (n) 1, (v) 5
water (n) 5
weak 2
wear 5
weekend 8
went PR
we're 2
western 8
what 1
What kind of? 7
What time is it? 2
What's . . . for? 4
What's this/that? 1

What's your name? 1
when PR
Where are you from? 2
where's . . . ? 1
which 7
white 2
who 1
Who are you? 2
whose 6
why 7
wide 7
wife, wives 5
window 3
wire 7
with 1
with (to be with someone) 2
woman, women 2
wonderful 6
word order 1, 2
work (n) 1, (v) 5
worried 3
worry 3
write 3, write to 8
written 1

Y
yard 7
yellow 2
yes 1
Yes/No question with *is* 1
Yes/No question with
   you are 2
Yes, it is. 1
Yes, sir. 8
Yes, they are. 2
Yes, we are. 2
yesterday PR
you 1
young 2
your 1
yourself 6
you're 2
You're in good hands. 4
You're welcome! 8

ANSWERS TO WORKBOOK EXERCISES

CHAPTER 1

EXERCISE 1 (pp. 3–4)
1. It's Maria Miranda.
   She's a doctor.
2. It's Peter Smith.
   He's a businessman.
3. It's Anne Jones.
   She's a secretary.
4. It's Mr. Bascomb.
   He's a banker.
5. It's Mrs. Golo.
   She's a teacher.
6. It's Nick Vitakis.
   He's a mechanic.
7. It's Ula Hackey.
   She's a movie star.
8. It's Otis Jackson.
   He's an artist.
9. It's Nancy Paine.
   She's a pilot.

EXERCISE 2 (pp. 5–6)
1. Maria isn't a movie star.
   She's a doctor.
2. She isn't at home.
   She's at the hospital.
3. Peter isn't a mechanic.
   He's a businessman.
4. He isn't at the garage.
   He's at the office.
5. Anne isn't a student.
   She's a secretary.
6. She isn't at school.
   She's at the post office.
7. Tino isn't a banker.
   He's a waiter.
8. He isn't at the bank.
   He's at the restaurant.
9. Otis isn't a businessman.
   He's an artist.
10. He isn't at the office.
    He's at the museum.
11. Nancy isn't a secretary.
    She's a pilot.
12. She isn't at the office.
    She's at the airport.
13. Ula isn't a teacher.
    She's a movie star.
14. She isn't at school.
    She's at the movies.
15. Mr. Bascomb isn't an artist.
    He's a banker.
16. He isn't at home.
    He's at the bank.
17. Nick isn't a pilot.
    He's a mechanic.
18. He isn't at the airport.
    He's at the garage.

EXERCISE 3 (p. 7)
1. Is he at the garage?
2. Is she at the airport?
3. Is he at the bank?
4. Is he at home?
5. Is she at the university?
6. Is he at the office?
7. Is she at school?
8. Is he at the restaurant?
9. Is she at the office?
10. Is she at home?

EXERCISE 4 (p. 8)
1. The book is on the chair.
2. The flower is in the vase.
3. The magazine is next to the clock.
4. The dog is under the bed.
5. The cat is behind the bird.
6. Anne is at the post office.

EXERCISE 5 (p. 9)
1. This is a hat.
2. That is a glass.
3. This is a chicken.
4. That is a dog.
5. That is an apple.
6. This is a watch.
7. This is a pear.
8. That is a cat.
9. This is a bottle.
10. That is a chair.

EXERCISE 6 (p. 10)
1. These are flowers.
2. Those are apples.
3. Those are pears.
4. These are rabbits.
5. Those are dogs.
6. These are chickens.
7. These are cards.
8. Those are cats.
9. These are magazines.
10. Those are birds.

CHAPTER 2

EXERCISE 1 (p. 13)
1. I'm hot.
2. I'm cold.
3. I'm hungry.
4. I'm thirsty.
5. You're intelligent.
6. You're beautiful.
7. You're rich.
8. You're married.

EXERCISE 2 (p. 14)
1. We're tall.
2. We're short.
3. We're young.
4. We're old.
5. They're strong.
6. They're weak.
7. They're fat.
8. They're thin.

EXERCISE 3 (pp. 15–16)
1. No, he isn't. He's single.
2. Yes, he is.
3. Yes, he is.
4. No, he isn't. He's short.
5. No, he isn't. He's young.
6. Yes, he is.
7. No, she isn't. She's tall.
8. Yes, she is.
9. Yes, he is.
10. No, he isn't. He's old.
11. Yes, she is.
12. No, she isn't. She's fat.
13. No, he isn't. He's poor.
14. Yes, he is.
15. Yes, he is.
16. No, he isn't. He's weak.
17. Yes, it is.
18. No, it isn't. It's cold.

EXERCISE 4 (p. 17)
1. He's a mechanic.
2. We're at the garage.
3. It's on Maple Street.
4. They're at home.
5. She's a teacher.
6. He's a businessman.
7. They're at the art museum.
8. It's very interesting.
9. They're beautiful.

EXERCISE 5 (p. 17)
1. He's my friend.
2. I'm a businessman.
3. My name is Peter.
4. We're at the Martinoli Restaurant.
5. Barbara is here.
6. She's with Tino.
7. They're next to the window.
8. This is a beautiful restaurant.
9. The tables and chairs are very old.
10. They're from Italy.

EXERCISE 6 (p. 18)
1. She isn't a teacher.
2. They aren't at home.
3. We aren't on Main Street.
4. It isn't cold today.
5. I'm not hungry.
6. Barbara and Tino aren't at work.
7. She isn't ugly.
8. He isn't short.
9. They aren't married.

EXERCISE 7 (p. 18)
1. Are those men tourists?
2. Are they from Brazil?
3. Is that woman from Japan?
4. Is it a beautiful country?
5. Is Tokyo the capital?
6. Are you from Canada?
7. Is your home in Montreal?

EXERCISE 8 (p. 19)
1. Who's that man?
2. It's Roberto Cruz.
3. He's very tall. Is he a basketball player?
4. No, he isn't He's a pilot.
5. Is Roberto a Mexican?
6. Yes, he is.
7. Is he from Guadalajara?
8. No, he isn't.
9. What city is he from?
10. He's from Mexico City.
11. Is that the capital of Mexico?
12. Yes, it is.

EXERCISE 9 (p. 19)
1. They are mechanics.
2. She is at the post office.
3. You are a secretary.
4. I am a student.
5. That is a good clock.
6. We are at home.
7. They are at the movies.
8. He is a banker.
9. It is an old table.

EXERCISE 10 (p. 20)
1. These flowers are beautiful.
2. This vase is expensive.
3. That book is interesting.
4. Those men are strong.
5. These apples are good.
6. Those oranges are bad.
7. That television is old.
8. This hat is small.
9. That dog is ugly.

EXERCISE 11 (p. 20)
1. Those books are expensive.
2. These oranges are good.
3. Those are German cars.
4. Those clocks are old.
5. These are cheap coats.
6. Those are small tables.
7. These bottles are clean.
8. These are beautiful chairs.
9. Those are English newspapers.

EXERCISE 12 (p. 21)
1. It's ten o'clock.
2. It's seven o'clock.
3. It's five o'clock.

4. It's eight o'clock.
5. It's one o'clock.
6. It's six o'clock.
7. It's three o'clock.
8. It's twelve o'clock.
9. It's four o'clock.
10. It's eleven o'clock.
11. It's two o'clock.
12. It's nine o'clock.

CHAPTER 3

EXERCISE 1 (p. 25)
1. Pay the waiter.
2. Call the fire department.
3. Close the window.
4. Look at the cat.
5. Open the door.
6. Take the umbrella.
7. Read the book.
8. Eat the apple.
9. Play the guitar.
10. Light the candle.

EXERCISE 2 (p. 26)
1. Look at them.
2. Come and sit with us.
3. Wait for her.
4. Dance with him.
5. Please open it.
6. Wash them.

EXERCISE 3 (p. 27)
1. Call him.
2. Listen to them.
3. Take it.
4. Wait for us.
5. Talk to her.
6. Ask him.
7. Look at them.
8. Read it.
9. Dance with her.

10. Take her the table.
11. Bring us the magazines.
12. Take him that letter.
13. Give it a ball.
14. Bring her a cup of coffee.
15. Give them the oranges.
16. Bring us a sandwich.
17. Take him the newspaper.
18. Give them that picture.

EXERCISE 4 (p. 28)
1. Open the bottle.
2. Wash the glasses.
3. Close the door.
4. Eat the pear.
5. Call the police department.
6. Pay the bill.

7. Play the piano.
8. Look at the dog.
9. Read the newspaper.
10. Light the candle.

EXERCISE 5 (pp. 29–30)
1. It's forty years old.
   It's nine hundred and ninety-eight dollars.
2. It's seventy years old.
   It's one hundred and five dollars.
3. It's eighty-three years old.
   It's sixty-one dollars.
4. It's one hundred and twenty years old.
   It's two hundred and nineteen dollars.
5. It's one hundred and forty-seven years old.
   It's three hundred and thirteen dollars.
6. It's sixty-two years old.
   It's ninety-three dollars.
7. It's thirty-two years old.
   It's forty-four dollars.
8. It's fifty-seven years old.
   It's seventy-five dollars.
9. It's sixty years old.
   It's twenty-nine dollars.
10. It's ninety years old.
    It's four hundred and fourteen dollars.

EXERCISE 6 (p. 31)
1. Where are the women? They're in front of the men.
2. Where are the men? They're behind the women.
3. Where are the birds? They're in the tree.
4. Where are the girls? They're behind the tree.
5. Where are the cats? They're under the newspaper.
6. Where are the bicycles? They're next to the house.
7. Where are the cars? They're in the garage.

EXERCISE 7 (p. 32)

[s]	[z]	[iz]
lamps	beds	watches
students	tables	dishes
envelopes	chairs	oranges
pilots	magazines	exercises
mechanics	cars	buses
trucks	candles	dresses
hats	windows	glasses
books	apples	sandwiches

EXERCISE 8 (p. 32)

telephone	hospital	dangerous	newspaper
mechanic	magazine	interesting	guitar
garage	university	museum	restaurant
library	beautiful	secretary	umbrella
department	American	nationality	intelligent

CHAPTER 4

EXERCISE 1 (pp. 35–36)
1. Come in.
2. Go to her.
3. Give her the flowers.
4. Put the flowers in the vase.
5. Take her hand.
6. Sit down on the sofa.
7. Look into her eyes.
8. Don't laugh.
9. Take her in your arms.
10. Close your eyes.
11. Kiss her.
12. Now get up and leave.

EXERCISE 2 (p. 37)
1. Yes, they are.
2. No. He's tall and handsome.
3. No. She's young and beautiful.
4. They're Italian.
5. William Shakespeare.
6. It's a play.
7. Free response
8. Free response
9. He's English.

EXERCISE 3 (p. 37)
1. Where is he?
2. What is it?
3. Who is she?
4. Where are they?
5. What are they?
6. Who are they?
7. Where is she?
8. What is it?
9. Who is he?
10. What are they?
11. Where are they?
12. Who is she?

EXERCISE 4 (p. 38)
1. That man is weak.
2. That woman is sad.
3. That car is old.
4. That man is cold.
5. That cat is black.

EXERCISE 5 (p. 39)
1. Those men are poor.
2. Those women are thin.
3. Those windows are closed.
4. Those shoes are expensive.
5. Those women are young.

EXERCISE 6 (p. 40)
1. I'm not ready.
2. Don't take it.
3. Are they at school?
4. Who is he?
5. Take her these flowers.
6. We're thirsty.
7. Please wash them.
8. It's a beautiful day.
9. Listen to me.
10. Where is she?
11. Don't talk to us now.
12. Please give him this message.

EXERCISE 7 (p. 40)
1. man	men
2. wife	wives
3. city	cities
4. church	churches
5. flower	flowers
6. child	children
7. library	libraries
8. bus	buses
9. tree	trees
10. book	books
11. shelf	shelves
12. dictionary	dictionaries
13. watch	watches
14. day	days
15. life	lives
16. woman	women
17. secretary	secretaries
18. dress	dresses

EXERCISE 8 (pp. 41–42)
1. Who's that man? — He's Pierre Dupont.
   How old is he? — He's forty-five.
   Where's he from? — He's from France.
   What's his job? — He's a painter.
2. Who's that woman? — She's Hiroko Sato.
   How old is she? — She's twenty-two.
   Where's she from? — She's from Japan.
   What's her job? — She's a model.
3. Who's that woman? — She's Anna Pappas.
   How old is she? — She's thirty-nine.
   Where's she from? — She's from Greece.
   What's her job? — She's a taxi driver.
4. Who's that man? — He's Mario Fellini.
   How old is he? — He's thirty-four.
   Where's he from? — He's from Italy.
   What's his job? — He's a mechanic.
5. Who's that man? — He's Tarik Aziz.
   How old is he? — He's fifty-one.
   Where's he from? — He's from Egypt.
   What's his job? — He's an engineer.
6. Who's that woman? — She's Sonia Amado.
   How old is she? — She's twenty-six.
   Where's she from? — She's from Brazil.
   What's her job? — She's a dancer.
7. Who's that woman? — She's Natasha Romanov.

How old is she? She's forty-seven.
Where's she from? She's from Russia.
What's her job? She's a teacher.
8. Who's that man? He's Robert Blake.
How old is he? He's forty.
Where's he from? He's from England.
What's his job? He's a policeman.

EXERCISE 9 (p. 43)

1. Where is the boy?
   He's on the bicycle.
2. Where are the man and woman?
   They're under the bridge.
3. Where is the dog?
   It's behind the bridge.
4. Where is the motorcycle?
   It's next to the tree.
5. Where is the cow?
   It's in front of the car.
6. Where are the men?
   They're in the hot-air balloon.
7. Where is the cowgirl?
   She's between the cowboys.

EXERCISE 10 (p. 44)

1. It's twenty minutes to nine.
2. It's ten minutes past four.
3. It's five minutes to five.
4. It's fifteen minutes to two.
   (It's a quarter to two.)
5. It's twenty-five minutes past eleven.
6. It's nine o'clock.
7. It's eight thirty.
   (It's half past eight.)
8. It's ten minutes to three.
9. It's twenty-five minutes to seven.
10. It's twenty-five minutes to eleven.
11. It's twenty minutes past one.
12. It's fifteen minutes to twelve.
    (It's a quarter to twelve.)

CHAPTER 5

EXERCISE 1 (pp.47–48)

1. She's buying a motorcycle
2. They're going to the beach.
3. She's calling the fire department.
4. They're waiting for the bus.
5. He's eating a pear.
6. She's reading the newspaper.
7. She's writing a letter.
8. They're washing the dishes.
9. She's playing the guitar.
10. They're dancing.
11. He's opening the door.
12. He's closing the window.
13. He's paying the waiter.
14. He's walking to the park.

EXERCISE 2 (p. 49)

1. He isn't drinking tea.
2. I'm not writing a letter to Barbara.
3. You aren't listening to me.
4. We aren't waiting for the bus.
5. She isn't watching the children.
6. They aren't eating lunch.
7. He isn't cleaning the bathroom.
8. I'm not calling the library.
9. They aren't going to the museum.

EXERCISE 3 (p. 50)

1. Is he reading a magazine?
2. Are they waiting for Johnnie?
3. Is he talking to Mr. Bascomb?
4. Are they calling Otis?
5. Is he listening to Anne?
6. Is she playing the guitar?
7. Are Barbara and Tino sitting in the corner?
8. Are they singing a French song?
9. Is Mr. Bascomb going home?

EXERCISE 4 (pp. 51–52)

1. Yes, she is.
2. No, he isn't. He's watching television.
3. No, they aren't. They're waiting for the bus.
4. Yes, they are.
5. No, he isn't. He's eating a pear.
6. Yes, they are.
7. Yes, she is.
8. No, they aren't. They're going to the movies.
9. No, he isn't. He's buying a lamp.

EXERCISE 5 (p. 53)

1. Where's Mrs. Golo?
2. What's she looking at?
3. Who's she calling?
4. Who's Gloria with?
5. Where are they?
6. What are they buying?
7. Where's Albert standing?
8. Who's he talking to?
9. What are they waiting for?

EXERCISE 6 (p. 54)

1. He's taking her a letter.
2. He's giving them a bag of apples.
3. She's bringing us a cat.
4. He's giving him ten dollars.
5. He's taking her a vase.
6. She's bringing us a lamp.
7. She's taking them a record player.
8. He's buying her a hat.
9. She's bringing him a dictionary.

CHAPTER 6

EXERCISE 1 (pp. 57–58)
1. She has a handbag.
2. They have a refrigerator.
3. He has a lamp.
4. She has a motorcycle.
5. They have a bicycle.
6. He has a taxi.
7. They have a dog.
8. They have a cat.
9. He has a camera.
10. They have a record player.
11. They have a television.
12. He has a dictionary.
13. She has a computer.
14. She has a guitar.

EXERCISE 2 (p. 59)
1. But you don't have a hat.
2. But I don't have a desk.
3. But he doesn't have a Spanish dictionary.
4. But she doesn't have a piano.
5. But we don't have your vase.
6. But I don't have your address.
7. But he doesn't have a dog.
8. But she doesn't have a car.
9. But they don't have a telephone.

EXERCISE 3 (p. 60)
1. Do they have a stove?
2. Does she have a brown handbag?
3. Do I have your telephone number?
4. Does he have an Italian car?
5. Do we have a large vase?
6. Does she have a guitar?
7. Do they have a record player?
8. Do you have a dog?
9. Does he have an apple?

EXERCISE 4 (pp. 61–62)
1. Yes, the do.
2. No, they don't. They have a dog.
3. Yes, she does.
4. No, he doesn't. He has a pear.
5. No, he doesn't. He has a taxi.
6. Yes, the do.
7. No, he doesn't. He has a chicken.
8. Yes, he does.
9. No, they don't. They have a bicycle.

EXERCISE 5 (p. 63)
1. It's their camera.
2. It's his motorcycle.
3. It's your guitar.
4. It's her dictionary.
5. It's my clock.
6. It's our refrigerator.
7. It's his coat.
8. It's my lamp.

EXERCISE 6 (p. 63)
1. Her boyfriend is intelligent.
2. Their doctor is French.
3. Our television is new.
4. His umbrella is black.
5. My dog is hungry.
6. Their camera is Japanese.
7. Your garden is beautiful.
8. Her mother is young.

EXERCISE 7 (p. 64)
1. Whose newspaper is that?
   It's Mr. Bascomb's newspaper.
2. Whose magazines are these?
   They're the girls' magazines.
3. Whose pen is this?
   It's Lisa's pen.
4. Whose cats are those?
   They're the Golo's cats.
5. Whose envelopes are these?
   They're Anne's envelopes.
6. Whose car is that?
   It's Mr. Smith's car.
7. Whose chickens are those?
   They're Elmer's chickens.
8. Whose radio is this?
   It's the boys' radio.

CHAPTER 7

EXERCISE 1 (p. 67)
1. There's a table in front of the couch.
2. There's a telephone under the table.
3. There's a chair in front of the desk.
4. There's a typewriter on the desk.
5. There's a lamp next to the typewriter.
6. There's a television in the right corner.
7. There's a mirror on the wall.

EXERCISE 2 (p. 68)
1. There are some candles on the table.
2. There are some books on the chair.
3. There are some magazines on the floor.
4. There are some oranges on the table.
5. There are some glasses on the shelf.
6. There are some pots on the wall.
7. There are some flowers in the vase.
8. There are some dishes on the shelf.

EXERCISE 3 (p. 69)
1. There's some cereal in the box.
2. There's some ice cream in the carton.
3. There's some soup in the can.
4. There's some orange juice in the bottle.
5. There's some tea in the teapot.
6. There's some sugar in the bowl.

7. There's some honey in the jar.
8. There's some flour in the bag.

EXERCISE 4 (p. 70)
1. There's a dish on the table.
2. There's some ice cream in the dish.
3. There are some sandwiches on the table.
4. There's a bottle on the table.
5. There's some orange juice in the bottle.
6. There's a box under the table.
7. There are some apples in the box.

EXERCISE 5 (p. 71)
1. They like classical music.
2. He likes butterflies.
3. She likes flowers.
4. They like cats.
5. He likes bananas.
6. She likes chocolates.
7. He likes girls.
8. They like ice cream.

EXERCISE 6 (p. 72)
1. She wants a handbag.
2. They want a clock.
3. They want a camera.
4. He wants a sandwich.
5. He wants a dog.
6. They want a piano.
7. She wants a hat.
8. He wants a radio.

EXERCISE 7 (p. 73)
1. They need some socks.
2. He needs a secretary.
3. He needs an umbrella.
4. She needs some food.
5. She needs glasses.
6. He needs a lamp.
7. He needs a ride.
8. They need some money.
9. She needs some sugar.
10. He needs a coat.
11. She needs some shampoo.
12. They need some eggs.
13. He needs some ketchup.
14. She needs a stove.

EXERCISE 8 (p. 75)
1. One cent = A penny
2. Five cents = A nickel
3. Ten cents = A dime
4. Twenty-five cents = A quarter

EXERCISE 9 (p. 75)
1. One dollar
2. Five dollars
3. Ten dollars
4. Twenty dollars

EXERCISE 10 (p. 76)
1. One dollar and sixty-five cents
2. Three dollars and twenty cents
3. Four dollars and thirty-five cents
4. Two dollars and seventy cents

CHAPTER 8

EXERCISE 1 (p. 79)
1. There's a dog under the bed.
2. There's a shoe in front of the dog.
3. There's a lamp on the table.
4. There's a clock next to the lamp.
5. There's a coat in the closet.
6. There's a cat behind the door.
7. There's a picture on the wall.

EXERCISE 2 (p. 80)

ey		æ	
make	salesman	class	ask
table	dangerous	family	apple
paper	game	candle	taxi
name	station	happy	gas
take	airplane	camera	mechanic
radio	lemonade	handbag	nationality

ay		i	
fine	life	bring	office
behind	nice	big	window
price	write	city	single
bicycle	right	sister	dinner
drive	wife	capital	dish
tonight	light	give	kitchen

EXERCISE 3 (pp. 81–82)
1. Yes, they are.
2. No, he isn't. He's playing chess.
3. Yes, he is.
4. No, they aren't. They're sitting in a snack bar.
5. Yes, they are.
6. No, she isn't. She's calling the fire department.
7. No, they aren't. They're talking to Mr. Bascomb.
8. Yes, they are.
9. No, he isn't. He's closing the window.
10. Yes, they are.

EXERCISE 4 (p. 83)
1. How much are the bananas?
   They're twenty-nine cents a pound.
2. How much are the apples?
   They're seventy-nine cents a pound.
3. How much are the oranges?
   They're forty-nine cents a pound.
4. How much are the cherries?
   They're ninety-nine cents a pound.
5. How much are the peaches?
   They're sixty-nine cents a pound.

6. How much are the lemons?
   They're thirty-nine cents a pound.
7. How much are the grapes?
   They're eighty-nine cents a pound.
8. How much are the pineapples?
   They're fifty-nine cents a pound.

EXERCISE 5 (p. 84)
1. to/for/of
2. from
3. in
4. with
5. on/in
6. at/on
7. for
8. to/with
9. about

EXERCISE 6 (p. 84)
1. These are expensive pens.
2. Those are beautiful vases.
3. Those are interesting pictures.
4. These are good dictionaries.
5. Those are Japanese cameras.
6. These are new records.
7. These are large envelopes.
8. Those are interesting magazines.
9. These are old books.

EXERCISE 7 (p. 85)
1. Yes, he does.
2. No, she doesn't. She needs butter.
3. No, they don't. They need milk.

4. Yes, they do.
5. Yes, he does.
6. Yes, she does.
7. No, she doesn't. She needs cups.
8. No, they don't. They need stamps.
9. Yes, they do.
10. No, he doesn't. He needs gas.

EXERCISE 8 (p. 87)
Composition

EXERCISE 9 (p. 88)
1. Anne likes orange juice, but she doesn't want any right now.
2. I like Coca-Cola, but I don't want any right now.
3. Mr. Bascomb likes coffee, but he doesn't want any right now.
4. The Golos like tea, but they don't want any right now.
5. Maria likes apple juice, but she doesn't want any right now.
6. We like tomato soup, but we don't want any right now.
7. Peter likes French fries, but he doesn't want any right now.
8. Miss Hackey likes milk, but she doesn't want any right now.
9. Barbara and Tino like chocolates, but they don't want any right now.

EXERCISE 10 (p. 88)
Free response